D1187557

TRADITION AND CHANGE

A STUDY OF BANBURY

TRADITION AND CHANGE

A STUDY OF BANBURY

MARGARET STACEY

OXFORD UNIVERSITY PRESS

Oxford University Press, Ely House, London W. 1

GLASGOW NEW YORK TORONTO MELBOURNE WELLINGTON
CAPE TOWN SALISBURY IBADAN NAIROBI DAR ES SALAAM LUSAKA ADDIS ABABA
BOMBAY CALCUTTA MADRAS KARACHI LAHORE DACCA
KUALA LUMPUR SINGAPORE HONG KONG TOKYO

FIRST PUBLISHED 1960
REPRINTED LITHOGRAPHICALLY AT THE
UNIVERSITY PRESS, OXFORD
FROM SHEETS OF THE FIRST EDITION
1964, 1970

PRINTED IN GREAT BRITAIN

PREFACE

Tradition and Change is the outcome of three years' field-work and some six years spent analysing and sifting the data. The purpose of the research was to study the social structure and culture of Banbury with special reference to the introduction of large-scale industry. In studying the town an attempt was made to relate the parts to the whole.

As Lady Wootton has said, 'The various situations of family life, or the ingredients in social and political problems, are so much matters of everyday experience that we have long ceased to notice them. . . . It is, indeed, no accident that anthropology . . . never begins at home: remoter data are more easily seen in perspective.'[1] In Banbury the aim was to put these ingredients of everyday life in something like the perspective in which we view the Trobriands or the Nuer. That is to say the approach was similar to that which has been used for many years by social anthropologists in studying more primitive peoples and which, since the Lynds' *Middletown*, has been applied, particularly in America, to the study of more complex societies.[2]

Consequently, while the research was being done the members of the team made their homes in or near Banbury. Participation in the life of the town was a main method of the work. Each research worker took part in a different sphere.

But participation and discussion with people met in the daily round are by themselves inadequate for a town of the size of Banbury. Without the techniques developed by the statistician and the sociologist in their more specialized studies of complex societies, it would not be possible to apply the social anthropologists' methods to a place of this size. The work therefore follows in the tradition established by Booth, Rowntree, and Bowley.[3]

The published records about Banbury were analysed. A pilot questionnaire followed by a schedule inquiry into over 1,000 households was used to determine population composition, family and household composition, religious and political adherence. The inquiry, which is

[1] Barbara Wootton, *Testament for Social Science* (London, Allen & Unwin, 1950)

[2] R. S. and H. M. Lynd, *Middletown* (New York, 1929); W. Lloyd Warner, *i.a. Democracy in Jonesville* (New York, 1949). More recently in England, N. Dennis F. Henriques, C. Slaughter, *Coal is Our Life* (London, Eyre & Spottiswoode, 1956)

[3] e.g. C. Booth and others, *Life of the People in London* (Macmillan, 1902, 17 vols. B. Seebohm Rowntree, *A Study of Town Life* (Macmillan, 1901); A. L. Bowley and A. R. Burnett-Hurst, *Livelihood and Poverty* (G. Bell & Sons, 1915).

described in greater detail in Appendix 1, provided the statistical basis for the study.

As a main guide to the functioning of the social structure a study was made, by interview of the leading members and analysis of the records, of all the formal organizations of Banbury. The aim of this study was to show the composition of the leadership and membership of the organizations and to show in which cases their leaderships overlap and with what broader social groups the organizations are connected. The methods of this study are described in Chapter 5 and Appendix 4 and its results included in the chapters on Politics (Chap. 3), Religion (Chap. 4), and Voluntary Associations (Chap. 5).

Kinship was studied by interview of a number of selected families. The methods used are described in Chapter 7 and Appendix 6 and the results set out in the first part of Chapter 7. In Cyril Smith's study of neighbours, the focused interview was the main method used. This is more fully described in Appendix 5 and the results are given in the second part of Chapter 6. Information was obtained from key informants about the social structure of some neighbouring villages for purposes of comparison with the town.

Apart from the pilot questionnaire, the results of which were used only as a guide to the drafting of the schedule, and the village data, all unpublished material was collected either by personal interview or direct observation. Reports of observations and interviews were exchanged among the research workers who met frequently to discuss their findings and cross-check information.

The town was fully informed about the project from the beginning. A public meeting at which the Mayor presided was held in 1948 before the work began. Reports of any major events were published in the local press and occasionally short articles about the work.

The extent to which an area can be isolated for study in so closely integrated a country as Great Britain is limited. Reference has therefore been made wherever possible to statistical analyses and specialist studies which relate to the country as a whole and to comparable studies in other localities. For the same reasons of size and complexity it has not been possible in practice to deal exhaustively with every aspect of the life of the town: some selection of those topics most likely to be relevant to the main theme of the research had to be made.

Banbury was not chosen as being either typical or peculiar in its social characteristics. Its choice was in a sense fortuitous. I had lived in the town for a number of years and had been impressed by its suitability as a subject for research. Banbury is surprisingly isolated: there is no town of comparable size in a radius of more than 20 miles. It is small enough (just under 19,000) for all its leaders in whatever activity to be readily known. It has a long history and traditions of its own. It shows stresses and strains as a result of its sudden growth (in 1931 the population was under 14,000), and the relations of the long-established residents with the large number of 'foreigners' who came to man the large-scale modern factory in the 1930's presented an interesting social problem. It was on this problem that attention was focused, a focus which later shifted, as Chapter 9 describes, to the problem of tradition and change.

The initial opportunity to do the research was provided by the Banbury branch of the Workers' Educational Association who asked me to run a tutorial class connected with a social survey. Thanks to the personal support and encouragement of Professor Meyer Fortes, the project was started in the autumn of 1948.

In the early stages the King George V Jubilee Trust made a grant of £100. Later, in July 1950, the Nuffield Foundation made a grant of £2,000. Earlier that same summer Birmingham University had accepted academic responsibility for the project.

At that time I was employed jointly by the Oxford University Delegacy for Extra-Mural Studies and the Delegacy for Social Training. It was under the auspices of the Extra-Mural Delegacy that the three-year tutorial class in Banbury connected with the survey was held. The Delegacy for Social Training contributed to the work by releasing me from a number of teaching hours. Mr. Thomas Hodgkin, then Secretary of the Extra-Mural Delegacy, gave unfailing help and encouragement. Mr. Leonard Barnes, Secretary of the Social Training Delegacy, was also particularly helpful and encouraging.

From the time that Birmingham University took over academic supervision, Professor P. Sargant Florence and Professor Charles Madge spent much time criticizing and advising on the work in progress.

Special thanks are also due to Mr. E. J. Cleary of Swansea University College for his help in analysing the statistics and to the Nuffield Bureau of Health and Sickness Records who tabulated the statistics of the schedule inquiry.

I would particularly like to thank all the many hundreds of Banbury townspeople who so kindly helped with the work. The housewives who stopped the washing or *Mrs. Dale's Diary* to answer our knocks at their doors; the officials and members of associations of all kinds; civil servants and business men; councillors and officials of the rural districts and the county as well as of the Borough who talked to us and opened their records for us.

Members of the tutorial class played a valuable role in providing and checking information, in criticism of early analyses, and in giving freely of their time and loyalty.

Besides the tutorial class the team undertaking the work consisted for the first two years of myself and Charles Kimber. Students from Oxford and London joined us for short periods during the vacation. In the last ten months of the field-work, Cyril S. Smith joined the team as a research assistant. He collected, analysed, and wrote up the material on neighbouring in Chapter 6. Charles Kimber devised the studies of the extended family and formal associations and collected, analysed, and reported on the material. He was also responsible for the collection of most of the historical data. Furthermore, he was closely concerned with the drafting of the report through its many stages. His contribution to the study is therefore very considerable.

But the use which has finally been made of the material is my responsibility alone, since it is I who have put the report in the form in which it is presented here.

M. S.

Swansea, 1959

CONTENTS

LIST OF TABLES

TABLES TO APPENDIXES

LIST OF CHARTS

CHARTS IN APPENDIXES

NOTE

THE names given to various persons in the book are fictitious, and the characters do not exist in fact as they are described. The characters used are 'typical' in a social sense of people who do exist, but none of them may actually be found. The names of streets in which such characters are described as living are also fictitious.

1

A PORTRAIT OF THE TOWN

BANBURY lies in a country of regularly undulating hill and dale. The hills are level broad-backed ridges, so level that you may look across from one ridge to the next and see the trees on the one beyond that again. A fine day in late February is the time to see this country, for then the clutter and profusion of the last harvest have disappeared and the land has been cleared and tidied for the coming season. The trees stand naked in the newly layered hedgerows; the grass has shed its old growth but has not yet begun to put on new, so that the fields at the bottom of the slopes are like pale lawns about the winding streams; higher up, the ploughland glistens and thin sunlight draws out the mellow warmth of golden stone in the thatched villages which cling, tight-clustered, round the shoulders of the hills. It is a countryside of soft colours and firm but gentle contours, without dramatic feature. In this it matches the climate which, though fickle, is rarely violent; it may bring grumbles, but never mourning for catastrophe.

The hills, about 400 to 500 feet above sea-level, are a part of that chain which runs from west to east across England and which may be said to divide the Midlands from the south. In this neighbourhood they are about twenty miles across with Banbury lying in their midst. Some ten miles to the north of the town is an escarpment from whose crest you can see far out over the Midland plain as though into another country, while from points ten miles to the south of the town the land slopes gently away into the upper Thames valley. Through the hills, connecting the plain on the north with the one on the south, runs the small river Cherwell. Its valley forms a corridor which is now shared by railway and canal. Banbury lies in this corridor.

Lying thus between two plains this hill district, though far from being remote or inaccessible, is somewhat isolated in the sense that it does not clearly belong to any wider region. From its earliest times it has been undecided: it was on the border of Danelaw, the edge of a feudal bishopric, a besieged outpost of Royalist power; now it stands at the meeting of three counties (and of three packs of hounds); national organizations with regional committees put it now in the south, now in the Midlands, now in the west, and now in the east. Even nature is unsure, for within ten miles three rivers rise, each flowing in a different direction, a tributary of the Ouse into the North Sea, of the Cherwell into the Thames Estuary, and of the Avon into the Bristol Channel. And you may take your choice of two or three regional weather forecasts.

The district is a compact one and the frontiers fairly easily defined: escarpment to the north, slope to the south, and lift on to the 600-foot contour to the west, where hedgerow gives way to stone wall and brown to grey stone. All the main roads in this district, which is about twenty miles across, converge on Banbury in the centre like spokes on a hub. This geographic frontier is also the social frontier: it marks the limit of the local buses to Banbury, of the cricket and darts leagues, of the distribution of the Banbury papers. For people who live in this district Banbury is the centre for shopping, for the market, for the central, and some of the local, government offices, and for entertainment. It is the 'Banbury district' for purposes of this survey (see Chart I).

The district is well populated, for it is thickly sown with villages: within the radius of ten miles of the town there are more than seventy, none of which is more than a mile or two from its neighbours. Most are small: about sixty have a population of less than 500 while only half a dozen top the thousand. Two or three pubs, a post office which is often a small store, a church, some allotments, and a cricket and football field are features common to most. Many have a car-hire service, and the larger villages, besides having two or three general shops, a bakery, and a butcher's shop, may have a builder's yard and a small workshop as well.

Most of the houses in a typical village are little three- or four-roomed cottages built some two or three hundred years ago. A few rather larger houses, four to eight bedrooms and a fair-sized garden, a few council houses, half a dozen farm houses, with their clusters of old barns, cowsheds, and lean-to's, make up the rest. On the outskirts or in the country is the great house. Many of these are wonderful examples of the builder's art, reflecting the proud ambitions of noble families of every period from 150 to 700 years ago. They include a fourteenth-century moated castle, Tudor and Stuart manor houses, and some magnificent stone Georgian mansions set in broad tree-studded parks. Over half the villages have a house large enough to be marked and named on the one-inch Ordnance Survey map.

It must be clear from this description that, in such a countryside, history lies on the surface. The names of half the villages end with

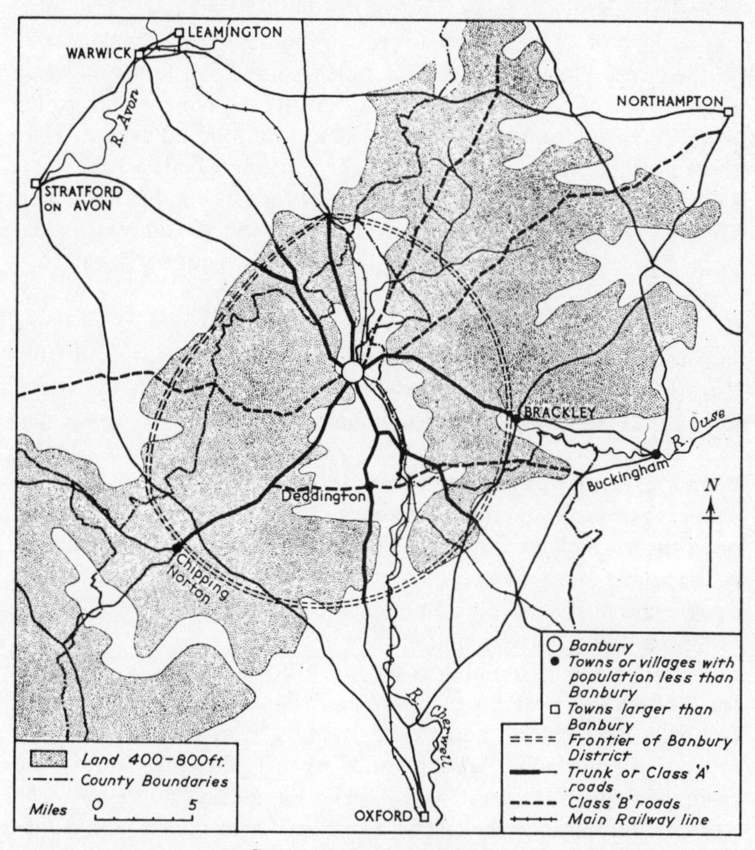

CHART I. Banbury District

the Anglo-Saxon suffix '-ton', so that their sites are not less than a thousand years old. Many must have been well established by the fourteenth century since there are many churches of that period. One of the fieldworkers has played cricket within the ruined vallum of a Norman castle, on the field of a civil war battle, in the park of an eighteenth-century mansion, on a field enclosed in the nineteenth century, and on a recreation field laid out in the twentieth century.

Every market day for the last 400 years the people of the district have gone into Banbury to buy and to sell and, not less important, to gossip.

The town itself, defined for purposes of this study by the Borough boundaries which include most of the built-up area and little else, lies in the hollow formed by a break in the ridge which runs parallel to the river. Along this ridge the north–south road looks down on the corridor of river, railway, and canal. At the old entrance to the town the road drops sharply and widens into a broad avenue. Here there is ample room on either side for stacking wood, as old prints show it, for tethering horses and carts, or for holding the horse fair, after which a part of the road is still named, and nowadays for a car park. Three country roads from the west, each formerly barred—from the south-west near the southern boundary, from due west at the Cross, and from north-west near the northern boundary—come into this thoroughfare; while to the east from the Cross and from the other side of the nearby parish church two streets run out which are narrow and serpentine as though worn by driven cattle and sauntering people. These two streets and the passages which connect them are, as they have always been, the congested and concentrated shopping centre of Banbury. In about 150 yards they converge at the open space which used to be called Cow Fair and this in turn narrows to the bridge over the river. Beyond the river the road forks again into open country, one road turning north-east and the other continuing eastwards (see Chart II).

The town has been a human settlement for some 2,000 years; and for the last 800, ever since a Norman bishop built a castle there, it has been both market and town.[1] It was fortunate not to become involved in medieval fighting, since by the sixteenth century the castle had fallen 'in great decay' while the market flourished. The town, rich from wool, had grown as a place for merchants and craftsmen working on their own account rather than under the patronage of a noble family. Its independence and importance at this time were recognized by the grant of a Royal Charter giving the burgesses rights of self-government: a borough council, a court, a regular market, and regular fairs.

Even the disasters of the Civil War, in which the renovated castle

[1] The account of the history of Banbury and district has been drawn largely from A. Beesley, *History of Banbury* (1840), and W. Potts, *Banbury Through One Hundred Years* (Banbury, 1942). I am also indebted to Mr. E. R. Brinkworth, a contemporary local historian, and to Miss Arkell, a local archivist

suffered a prolonged siege and a large part of the town was destroyed, proved only to be an interlude, for, the war once ended and the contestants withdrawn, the townspeople reasserted themselves: they razed the castle and used its stones to rebuild the houses which had been destroyed. During the eighteenth century Banbury seems to

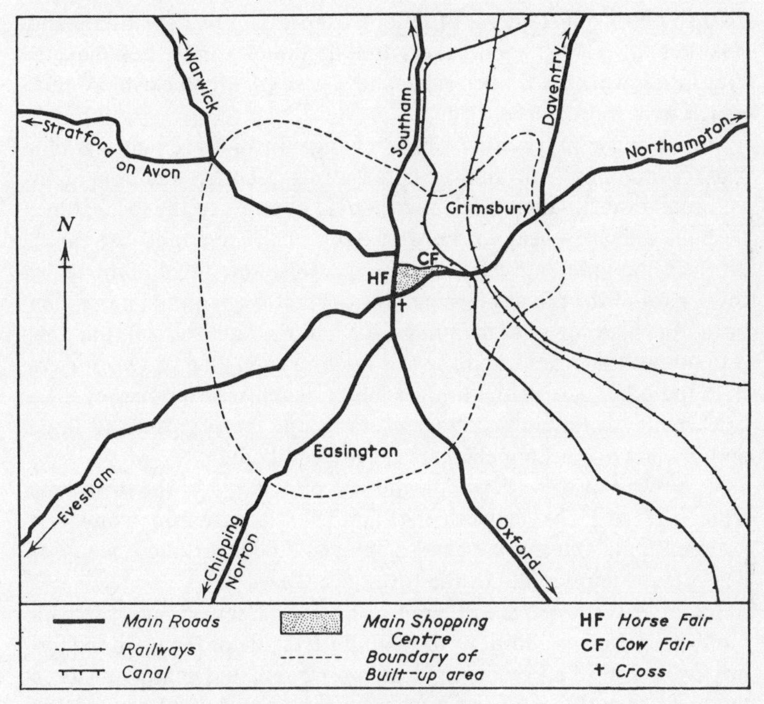

CHART II. Banbury

have regained its prosperity and its nineteenth-century historian is concerned mostly with the disputations of local priests and the fortunes of noble families living nearby.

In 1830 the population of what now constitutes the Borough (what was the Borough and two hamlets) was 6,400 and the town was about 460 yards across. It was shaped like a triangular pennant flying from a pole in a westerly breeze, the pennant representing the shopping centre and the pole the north–south road where the professional people lived. Out of this population 130 families were employed in agriculture and about 700 in 'trade, manufactures, and handicrafts'.

Of the manufactures, plush weaving and horse girths were the most important, but, since together they employed less than 200 of the inhabitants (more were employed at their homes in the villages), it is clear that the town's main wealth was in retailing, merchanting, and servicing. It was a town of inns and stable-yards; of blacksmiths shops, of harness-makers, and wheelwrights; of millers, corn-merchants, and wool-staplers; of tailors, drapers, milliners, hatters, and cobblers; of butchers and bakers and, no doubt, candlestick makers. A printing works, a timber-yard, and a brewery are in existence now which were in existence then.

But at mid-century came violent change. In 1848 the business of a local ironmonger who had invented a turnip cutter was bought by an immigrant. In alien brick and in vivid contrast to the local stone, he built a factory near to the west bank of the river and the canal. At the same time Banbury's communications were revolutionized by the arrival of the railways which, like the factory, required more men both for making and manning. Round the factory, on the low ground near the canal and the railway and spreading in two fingers over the other side of the bridge, long criss-crossed terraces of little brick-built 'workmen's' cottages sprang up; the first time so large and distinct a 'working-class area' had been built.

As a result of these developments the population of the town rose from 7,200 to 11,700 between 1841 and 1871. The foundry won international fame and markets and employed 2,000 workmen, many of whom were immigrants to the town (see Chart III).

But after this expansion there was a long pause and, apart from a number of smaller additions to the industrial life of the town including the arrival of a box factory and a flour-mill and enlargements to the local brewery, the period from 1870 to about 1930 was one of stagnation. The foundry ceased to expand and from the turn of the century slowly declined, finally to go out of business in 1933: the fashion for plush went out and with it died one of Banbury's most characteristic trades; the fliers, which used to come rumbling and trumpeting into the yards of the 'Coach and Horses', the 'Flying Horse', the 'Reindeer', and other inns at the end of a stage on their journey, had already been superseded by the railway. Now horse traffic as a whole, the carriers' carts, drays, wagons, haggle carts, gigs, traps, landaus, and a host of others, was replaced by motor traffic, buses, lorries, vans, tourers, and saloons. And with horse transport went all those trades and occupations, including girth weaving, which served horse transport and which had formed so large a part of the lives and skills of Banbury people. As the workshops and factories closed people left the town. The rapid rate of growth had slowed down after 1871 (see Chart III). In 1921 the population, which had been 13,000 in 1901, was a bare 400 more, an increase for the twenty years of only 3·3 per cent., while the increase for Great Britain was 16 per cent. in this period. By 1928 the population had fallen still further to within 200 of the 1901 figure.[1]

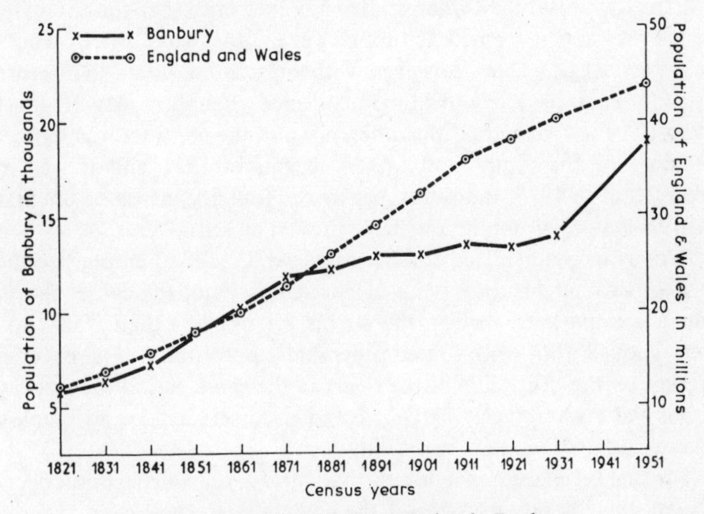

CHART III. Growth of Population in Banbury

It had, then, an ageing population; although its death-rate in 1931 was slightly lower than the national rate (11·90 deaths per 1,000 population as compared with 11·95), its birth-rate was considerably lower (13·21 live births per 1,000 population in 1931 compared with a national rate of 15·8 for the period 1930–2).[2]

Had these trends continued Banbury would have become a dying town with empty class-rooms and, like one of its neighbours, large hotels with fading signs advertising 'dinners and accommodation', but in fact fulfilling only the function of a local pub, and shops

[1] Census Reports (1821–1951) (London: H.M.S.O.); *Royal Commission on Population. Report*, Cmd. 7695 (London: H.M.S.O. 1949), p. 15. The actual increase of 16 per cent. in the national population between 1901 and 1921 is less than the natural increase (i.e. the excess of births over deaths): had it not been for emigration from the country, the increase would have been some 20 per cent. The increase of only 3·3 per cent. in Banbury therefore makes it clear that it had experienced a net emigration in those years.

[2] Banbury M.O.H. *Annual Report*, 1931 (Banbury, 1932).

clearly designed for a larger and more prosperous population. Indeed, it was at this time as if Banbury, wedded to the horse, looked on the new age of factories and mechanical transport with displeasure. For proposals to build a large railway-repair works and for a motor-car factory were turned down.

In 1929 an international company, wanting good communications, local labour, and a firm subsoil on which to build a rolling-mill to employ at least 2,000 people, made an offer for some land just outside the town. But the owner wanted a higher price than the company would pay and it seemed as though yet another large works would be turned away. Then, however, with only a few hours left before the offer expired, a few local men collected enough money amongst themselves to make good the difference and the contract was signed. Building of the aluminium factory began in 1931 and it was in production in 1933, the same year as the foundry, cause of the first rush of industrial immigrants to the town, closed.

A new age had started for Banbury. And, as if to emphasize the fact, other changes took place at about this time; the cattle, sheep, and horse markets, held in the streets for not less than 700 years, were moved (not without considerable opposition) to a covered market on the other side of the river; in the same period the railway goods yard was greatly extended and a corset factory, to employ several hundred women, was built.

The market place now has a tarmac surface on which ironmongers display their goods, patrons of the cinema park their cars, and the St. John ambulance stands ready. Where children used to play marbles at the Cross there are zebra crossings. Coaches, long-distance lorries, cattle-trucks, vans, private cars, and motor cycles stream past it along the north–south road on their way between London and the south and the conurbation of the Midlands. Many of the large stone houses flanking this road, where the professional people used to hold their tea-parties, have been converted into public buildings, offices, boarding houses, and an hotel. A modern cinema looks on to the Horsefair car park. The shops in the brightly lighted High Street have plate-glass windows and, though a few remain as family concerns, in this part of the town most are now branches of national concerns, run by managers: Woolworths has taken the place of the 'Red Lion', so that the farmers who used to do business at its bar have given place to young mothers with their prams; W. H. Smith stands in place of the 'Fox' where at fair times, and not only then, the fights were bloody and blasphemous: Montague Burton, the International, Dewhurst, Freeman, Hardy and Willis, and the Home and Colonial are all there, and many more besides. While, out of sight in the green fields beyond the town, surrounded by ten feet of barbed wire, immaculate flower-beds, orderly bicycle ranks, and lines of neatly parked cars, lies the aluminium factory.

The huge white and green-roofed hangar-like building, with its strange-shaped chimneys and tubes and its unpredictable noises, seems like something from a different world, alien to the town. Alien in the sense that all previous Banbury industry had in some way been associated with its role as a market, usually directly associated with the countryside (its nineteenth-century 'industrial revolution' was based on the manufacture of agricultural implements); alien also in the methods of production used—machines, techniques, and organization are unlike anything that had been before; and alien, too, in its administration and ownership, being part of a company with international connexions whose staff, while based on Banbury, may often be away in Canada or Switzerland, or London or Wales. Ownership being so remote, relations between management and men are alien to the Banburian used to a small workshop where the 'gaffer' is always about.

Moreover, the factory has a routine of its own. Outside there may not be a soul about, except the works policeman at the gate, yet inside are 700 to 800 men and women. At six in the morning, two in the afternoon, and ten at night, the shift changes and another 700 to 800 men and women take their place; bicycles and buses stream in and out, winding their way through the lanes to and from the villages. Working life is out of time with home life, with wives' cooking and shopping and sleeping, and with the children's school life, out of time too with the social life of other people.

Many of the two to three thousand workers at the aluminium factory, and many working elsewhere, are themselves strangers to the town, for hundreds of new workers and their families have moved in. The population, which was about 13,000 in 1931, rose to nearly 19,000 by 1951, an increase of 35 per cent. (a rate of increase much greater than that for the country as a whole).[1]

To meet the influx new housing was needed. The Council had already started estates to rehouse families from the older, overcrowded and dilapidated houses near the centre. Now, to house the

[1] Census Reports (1931 and 1951) (London: H.M.S.O.).

new-comers, the Easington estate of 500 mixed Council and private houses in the angle of the roads leading out of the town to the south and south-west was completed; another 500 were built on either side of the Warwick road to the north-west, Council houses on one side and private houses on the other. Since the war this Council estate has been more than doubled in size, and two further estates, one private, one Council, built beyond the nineteenth-century houses in Grimsbury on the east side of the river, have been greatly extended.

The town is now a mile across and every twenty minutes buses bring people from the new estates—the acres of new brick houses, of new concrete roads, and of gardens cut from turf—into the town centre, still the main focus for shopping, commerce, and entertainment.

The years around 1930 represent a divide. Life in Banbury before then would have been more easily recognizable to a man who had lived a hundred years earlier than to one living at the present day, only twenty years after. Speak to any born Banburian of middle age or older and he will recall a town and a way of life which seem very remote. He will tell of the scores of carriers' carts which came rattling and rumbling in from the villages; of steaming cattle tethered in the streets; of the shouting drovers and the muck on the pavements. He will tell of the dark ill-lit streets of tiny family shops; of the drunkenness and brawling at night, and of the constable waiting in the shadow outside at closing time with his truncheon ready to help laggards on their way with an admonitory whack on the backside. He will tell how the Fire Brigade was the town's most exclusive club reserved for leading citizens, who, having abandoned work for the day and fought the fire (with more or less enthusiasm according, it was hinted, to the popularity of the victim), would turn the affair into a social occasion with the help of their wives who would have followed with suitable refreshments. They will tell of the leisurely encounters in the street and of the gossip and the scandal (including the unrepeatable comments of other women at the sight of the first woman cyclist); of village women curtseying to the gentry; of hiring fairs, and of servants from the big house driving in a brake to church behind the carriage and pair of their master and mistress; of great house parties in the country mansions, and of how the King (Edward VII) used to visit in the neighbourhood, while the Prince of Wales used to come for the hunting. A woman will tell of the tea-parties, the tennis parties, and the Church working-parties. 'It was pure

Cranford', said one informant who had arrived soon after the First World War.

There had been changes, Banbury was not entirely out of step with the twentieth century: electricity, the motor-car, the typewriter, and the wireless had arrived. But, although they had accepted these innovations, Banburians could live as they had been brought up to live. Before the 1930's Banbury was a place 'where you knew where you were'. Time and time again the older Banburians describe the difference between those days and now in almost identical words: 'When I went into town I used to know everybody, now I hardly know anybody.' Partly, of course, they mean that the town has grown and that there are now very many more people whom they do not know by sight; but they also mean, for no one could 'know' all of 13,000 people, that in the old days they could 'place' anybody they did not literally 'know' in a well-developed social structure which had a recognized status system. This system they can describe; families of similar economic standing, respectability, and length of residence forming 'sets' who visited each other's houses and whose children were allowed to play together.

It was described, for example, by Mr. *X* whose family had been in the town for two generations and was numbered among the more prosperous tradesmen. The set his family moved in was made up of similar tradesmen and small manufacturers. They were on friendly terms with the doctors and the clergy, but these people were not in their set; they were 'professional' and a 'bit above' them. *X*'s set looked up, too, to the gentry and the nobility who lived in the countryside round about the town. They knew who they were, were honoured if they received custom from them, but had no relations with them except those connected with business or with charitable or public service. The inequality of status and manner of life between them was too great. His family also knew by name the owners of smaller shops, smaller master men, and some of the artisans. But they did not visit freely in their homes. 'And then there were the workmen', said *X*. They were mostly unknown by name except for those who had been somehow associated with his family or business. *X*, for example, did not know *Y*, a Liberal Free Church artisan, who worked on his own account two or three doors away from *X*'s shop. Passing him in the street *X* placed *Y* as a worker: but *Y* described sets within *X*'s undifferentiated 'workmen'. All the members of *X*'s set were Anglican in religion and Conservative in politics, as his own family was. They knew some 'highly respectable' tradesmen who were Free Churchmen and were on easy (equal) terms with them. But they did not belong to *X*'s set. For one thing, the Free Churchmen were teetotallers, while *X*'s friends met regularly for a drink. Furthermore, the Free Churchmen were nearly always Liberals and so there was a political division between them too. Nevertheless, *X*'s set considered that the 'best' people were Anglican and Conservative. In *X*'s own opinion, right up to the 1920's those who were 'getting on well' in business tended to change over from a Free Church to the Church of England, so that their social position could match their improved financial position. His set recognized the Roman Catholics; they knew who they were but had little to do with them. The 'R.C.s' moved in sets of their own. They were 'quite apart' in a way that Free Churchmen were not.

The places held by *X* and *Y* and others in Banbury in those days derived from their family's position. Family, together with place of origin and associations, such as religion and politics, was the test by which people 'recognized' or 'placed' each other. They asked 'Who is he?' in these terms rather than 'What does he do?' as an individual. So it was to a relatively small and close-knit town in which personal relations counted for much that the hundreds of immigrants of the 1930's, many of them from depressed areas, came.

According to the findings of the schedule inquiry,[1] immigrants now make up about half the adult population of the town, as Table 1 shows. True immigrants, those who were at least seven years old when they came to Banbury, outnumber born Banburians by nearly 4 per cent. But when these are reinforced by those born in the district and by those who came in early childhood, the local people outnumber the immigrants in the ratio 11:9.[2]

TABLE 1

Proportions of Banburians and Immigrants

	%
1. Born Banburians	41·4
2. Secondary Banburians	3·5
3. District born	10·0
4. True immigrants	45·1

[1] The schedule inquiry, into a sample of over 1,000 households, provided the greater part of the statistics for this study. See Appendix 1; p. 183 et seq.

[2] Further details of these definitions and how they were reached are given in Appendix 2, A, p. 186.

Many of the immigrants coming from great industrial cities, and particularly those who came from the north, found it difficult to adapt themselves to Banbury. Some found it unsociable. One Lancashire woman described how, in her first months in the town, she used to sit down and cry: 'I thought I'd never get to know anyone; they're so much more friendly at home.' Others found it self-centred and self-important: 'If they get a shower of rain in Banbury they think it's raining all over the world.' Many remarked on the slow tempo of life: 'I even found I was walking faster than anyone else.'

To the Banburians the immigrants seemed foreign. They still refer to them as 'Scots, Irish, and Welsh' with 'Those northerners' added as a concession to the possible Englishness of some.

TABLE 2

Places of Origin of True Immigrants—in Order of Numbers from Each (%)

Men		*Women*	
Industrial Midlands	13·7	10–25 mile radius	16·0
10–25 mile radius	13·3	Industrial Midlands	13·7
Lancs., Ches., and Yorks.	13·1	Greater London	11·9
Greater London	10·9	Lancs., Ches., and Yorks.	11·2
Home Counties	9·3	Home Counties	9·2
Wales and Mon.	8·2	South-west and South	8·7
South-west and South	8·2	Wales and Mon.	6·8
North-east	6·0	North-east	4·6
N. Ireland and Eire	4·8	N. Ireland and Eire	4·6
Scotland	3·2	Scotland	2·3
Other (inc. overseas)	9·3	Other (inc. overseas)	10·2

Total	
10–25 mile radius	14·7
Industrial Midlands	13·7
Lancs., Ches., and Yorks.	12·1
Greater London	11·6
Home Counties	9·2
South-west and South	8·4
Wales and Mon.	7·4
North-east	5·2
N. Ireland and Eire	4·7
Scotland	3·0
Other (inc. overseas)	9·8

Table 2 shows that this is a symbolic description, emphasizing that while the immigrants are not entirely alien, i.e. are British, nevertheless they *are* 'foreign'. Wales and Monmouthshire, Northern Ireland and Eire, and Scotland together provide only 15·1 per cent. of the total true-immigrant population, while 14·7 per cent. are drawn from an area between ten and twenty-five miles from Banbury, an area which contains no great industrial city and which is largely rural. 'Those northerners' is scarcely less marked in its emphasis on the foreignness of immigrants and no more well-founded. Midlanders and southerners together outnumber them by a ratio of more than two to one.[1] In sum, areas farthest away from Banbury have provided fewest immigrants.

Banburians consider the industrial immigrants 'foreign' because they came with values and customs greatly different from those of the town. Many of the men were used to working in large-scale industry for absentee owners; they had been brought up to take it for granted that a worker belonged to a trade union. One said that the Banbury workers were 'like sheep'; another, anxious to build his union, that they were 'pigs to organize'.

Professional people of a kind new to Banbury came too. Men who were graduates in metallurgy or engineering. Banbury could not place them: many of them were not 'Oxford or Cambridge', but came from provincial universities. They did not hold time-honoured positions as the priest and the doctor did.

As the town grew, and later the war came and the welfare state was further developed, new government offices were opened and old ones enlarged and rehoused, bringing with them more executive and clerical civil servants. The schools were extended and there were more posts for qualified teachers.

So, today, in Banbury and district there are traditionalists: those who are part of the traditional social structure and who live by the traditional values and customs of old Banbury. There are others, the non-traditionalists, who do not belong to the traditional social structure and do not accept its values and customs; they do not share any common social system or system of values and customs for they are composed of many different, and sometimes opposed, groups; they include those who have come in with quite other systems of values and customs and those who are developing new ways to meet the changed circumstances of their life and work.

The traditionalists still judge people by 'who they are', by reference to their total social status, their family and social background as well as their occupations. They are actively aware of fine status divisions. They accept their position and behave with the manners appropriate to it.

[1] This analysis is expanded in Appendix 2, B.

They all, for example, look up to Sir William, who comes of an old local family and who has lived in the same village, just outside Banbury, for the past thirty years. They acknowledge his public service and his work for charity. Sir William accepts his status. He is an active County councillor because he regards 'public service as a duty which a man in (his) position owes'. He feels, too, that he should 'set an example' and is, therefore, punctilious in his dress and manners. He is a member of the Church Council in the village and reads the lessons at Matins.

In the town itself, Mr. Shaw, a prosperous tradesman who owns a business, which has been in the family for three generations and in which his son also works, is an acknowledged leader. He, too, knows where he stands in the old-town society and accepts his position. Like Sir William, he considers that 'service to the community' is a duty. He has been Mayor of the town and gives freely to local charity. Mr. Grey, another of the leading trades-people, is very like him in his social position and in many of his attitudes. But Grey is a 'pillar of the Methodist Church' and a Liberal in politics, while Shaw is a sidesman at the parish church and a member of the Conservative Association.

George is an example of a traditional worker in Banbury. He has been employed at one of the old family businesses for twenty-five years. He accepts the leadership of Sir William and of the Shaws and the Greys in the town. For he feels that 'the ordinary working man hasn't got the education' and that 'it's better to leave things like that to people who know about them'. So he does not belong to a trade union and avoids political discussions. He votes Conservative and is 'Church', but his neighbour, a native like himself with a similar job, is a staunch Baptist and a Liberal.

Accepting time-honoured status divisions, traditionalists like these find associations in the town and district which cater for their 'own sort'. They join according to their interests, but it is by the social side of an association's activities that they judge it. They would feel uncomfortable in one which catered for a different 'class' from their own; the sociability of the association would suffer, the relations would be too formal.

Thus, Sir William rides with the hunt. Shaw and Grey play bowls with the Chestnuts, while George and his neighbour belong to the Borough Bowls. Shaw drinks at the 'White Lion' in the town centre, but George goes to the pub at the end of his street. Grey, like

George's neighbour, does not drink. George is a member of the British Legion (Sir William is its President).

These traditionalists, too, are all closely associated with the town and district. Men of the upper class, like Sir William, divide their associations between those which are local and those of their class which are national. Many of the traditionalists are natives as are the men in the examples. But by no means all of them are. Some are people who have come into the town from similar social backgrounds to follow traditional occupations, or who have accepted enough of Banbury's traditions to fit into it and to make their life in the locality with Banbury as their principal frame of reference. They, as much as the Banbury-born traditionalists, rely on the local papers as essential sources of information about the fortunes and misfortunes of local people and families and of the clubs and societies.

In all these respects, the life, the values, and attitudes of the traditionalists are similar to what was described for the town before 1930 by informants like *X*. But, in those days, traditionalists like these probably made up the greater part of the town. This they no longer do. Although they do not all know each other, it is possible to think of traditionalists as belonging to one social system. For traditional society is made up of a network of face-to-face groups, based on family, neighbours, occupations, associations, and status.

This is not true of the non-traditionalists who now make up a considerable and increasing part of the town. Non-traditionalists, as the name implies, have for the most part only negative characteristics in common: in one way or another they do not follow the traditional pattern of life. They are composed of two broad groups: those for whom the traditional structure has no place and those who reject that structure.

Many non-traditionalists do not apply 'Who is he?' as a test of a man's social acceptability. Their test is rather 'What does he do?', judging him on his merits as an individual both at work and at home, rather than on his family connexions and original social background. And on this basis they wish to be judged. Occupation is, therefore, more important for them than it is for the traditionalist. Furthermore, they do not belong to, or they do not accept, the status structure of Banbury. This is not to say that they do not recognize status. They do, and, in one way or another, are deeply concerned with it.

Sir William is matched, for example, by Lord A. who is chairman of a group of engineering companies. Lord A. owns a Hall in the district, but he is not often there because his work takes him to various parts of the country, to London, and to the United States. He has no roots in the locality and belongs rather to an international society, for he has face-to-face relations with people in and from all parts of the world. He does not belong to the traditional status system, for he derives his status, not from his family as Sir William does, but from his position in industry. He 'made his own way in the world' and, although he sent his son to a major public school, he expects him to make his own way too. His son had a post in Lord A.'s company, but he subsequently left.

Similarly, in the middle class, in the town itself, there are many who do not have a place in its traditional status system for there is no answer to the question 'Who is he?' in the way that Banbury understands it. Mr. Brown, for example, is a technologist on the staff of the aluminium factory. He is a graduate from a provincial university. Like Lord A. he did not inherit his position but has earned it on merit. He came to Banbury to work and, if he does not get promotion in the factory, he will apply for a better post elsewhere: his social aspirations are more closely linked to his job than to the status 'sets' of Banbury.

The second broad group are those who not only do 'not fit in' to Banbury society, but who actively reject its traditional standards. They follow a system of values and customs of an altogether different sort—in another place they might be traditionalists. George is matched today by people like Ted, who was brought up in an industrial city. He, like his father, has been a 'union man' ever since he started work. He is a Labour councillor. The class system for him is a matter of worker or not worker ('the boss class').[1] He accepts his status as a worker and is proud of it, but, unlike George, he will not receive patronage from his 'betters'. 'The workers look after their own', he says. He does not accept that he has 'betters' and rejects the leadership of people like Sir William, Shaw, and Grey. He supports the Labour Party. He wants to improve the lot and the chances of the workers as a class.

Many non-traditionalists had difficulty in finding associations to suit them in the town and district and have created or tried to create new ones. Some middle-class non-traditionalists have interests which

[1] Compare the 'two-valued power models' of Elizabeth Bott, 'The Concept of Class as a Reference Group', *Human Relations*, vii. 3 (1954), 259.

are more intellectual than those of old Banbury. Brown, for example, is an active member of the Banbury players, a new organization which is supported by immigrant non-traditionalists and which has also considerable support from the old-town society. But his friends who are interested in music and painting find it difficult to get people together for them.

The trade unionists found that there was no union in the aluminium factory and that, when they tried to form one, they had to meet in secret for fear of victimization. Indeed, they were not successful until the war and Ernest Bevin came and 'changed all that'. Now the factory has nearly 100 per cent. membership and relations with the management are said to be good. They found, too, that the Labour Party was weak. But their activities there were sufficiently successful for the Conservative majority to be reduced to less than 2,000 votes at the 1945 election.

Furthermore, non-traditionalists found that the associations which catered for their interests had values they did not appreciate. Many non-traditionalists are, for example, less interested in the social side of a sports club than in the standard of play. In one tennis club there was serious friction as a result of this between non-traditionalists who wanted a high standard of match play and traditionalists who wanted the social atmosphere preserved. As a result Brown, who was at one time a member, and others resigned.

Most non-traditionalists claim membership of one of the Christian denominations, but, in general, they are less active in the life of church or chapel than the traditionalists. Religious differences are not an important basis of grouping among them.

While many of the non-traditionalists are immigrants, by no means all of them are, any more than all traditionalists were born in the town. There are Banbury-born workers, for example, who have joined a trade union and vote for the Labour Party. Other Banburians have accepted the merit basis of judging people (perhaps because they do not wish to be tied to the position of their family). Others, again, are less concerned with church and chapel than they used to be. All these have, to a greater or lesser extent, joined the ranks of non-traditionalists. But perhaps the majority of non-traditionalists are immigrants, as emigrants from Banbury might also be found to be if enough of them could be traced.

The traditionalists themselves, although in many ways they still live by the customs and values of the period before 1930, have not been unchanged by the activities of the non-traditionalists and by the social and economic changes that have been going on around them. In the middle class, for example, people like Shaw and Grey, the tradesmen, are closer together than they used to be. They agree that 'private enterprise' means a business owned by an individual or a family. This agreement seems more important now that they are faced with international companies which run factories in their own town and with a growing number of 'company shops'; faced, also with a large and active trade-union movement, a Labour Party branch, and the Co-operative Society. They are united in their anti-socialism, which now seems more important than their disagreements about conservatism and liberalism. Indeed, Grey, although he is a Liberal, has appeared at recent general elections on the platform of the Conservative candidate. In their opposition to the Labour Party they are joined by the middle-class non-traditionalists (like Brown) who dislike socialism as much as they do. Furthermore, traditionalists belong to some of the newer organizations, like the Rotary Club, where they meet non-traditionalists.

In short, Banbury today is a mixture of old and new and all its inhabitants are influenced by the old and the new. Its established practices and customs, its institutions and the values associated with them are being modified by men who practise new techniques and new forms of organization. This division between old and new is not one between Banburian and immigrant so much as between traditionalist and non-traditionalist. The former cling, so far as they can, to the old values based on personal face-to-face relationships, preferring the small organization to the large. For the latter the old ways are irrelevant. Non-traditionalists judge people as individuals, are not afraid of large-scale organization and abstract ideas, and belong to groups (industrial hierarchies and nation-wide trade unions, for example) which extend beyond Banbury.

But a deeper division than this, for traditionalist and non-traditionalist alike, is the division into social classes. It is a division looked upon and operated differently by the two groups but which affects each as profoundly. A traditional worker like George accepts a total status system. He accords leadership to the gentry and to the business men on all counts, social, economic, political, and religious. Non-traditional 'trade-union-minded' workers like Ted concede the economic power of owners and managers, 'the boss class', but do not concede them a 'divine right' of social or political leadership. The middle-class non-traditionalist has a status in relation to his occupation of which Banbury is not the arbiter, for his status follows from the hierarchy of industry (be it aluminium processing or government department). He has also a status which he has made for himself in Banbury among neighbours and friends. But it is not a total status position as it is for the traditional middle class. For them many factors count towards one final social-status position: occupation, income, manner of life, reputation, and by no means least, family background, in the sense not only of the start their family gave them, but of lineage. Nevertheless, in terms of how and where they live and in their assumptions about the 'right' way to behave in everyday living, George, the traditional worker, and Ted, the non-traditional worker, have a great deal more in common than they have with middle-class traditionalists like Shaw and Grey or middle-class non-traditionalists like Brown.

Furthermore, social status, looked at broadly in terms of major social-class divisions, is allied to political divisions and cuts across the frontier between traditional and non-traditional. The alignment of Conservative and Liberal against Labour draws most of the non-traditional middle class together with traditionalists of all classes in opposition to the non-traditional (for Banbury) Labour working class. The widest gap, therefore, lies between the traditional middle class and the non-traditional working class.

It will be the purpose of the following chapters to develop these propositions, to show how these principal social groups relate to others, and to set out the evidence which has led to them.

2

EARNING A LIVING

BANBURY industries range from small, old-established concerns with personal and informal managements, much as they were a hundred or more years ago, to modern mass-production factories. Here is the contrast between old and new which is found in every Banbury institution. There is a contrast between those industries which are native to the town and those which have recently arrived. But the essence of the contrast lies in the organization of the industry. For the type of industry which is traditional to Banbury is the small, private-enterprise firm in which the owner takes a direct part. The factory or shop which is organized on a large scale with remote ownership and control is non-traditional to the town. Traditional industries, besides contrasting in scale and in management with non-traditional industries, are often also concerned with activities which have long been associated with the town. Some non-traditional industries are alien in the raw materials they use and in their technology. But this is by no means always the case.

Distribution in Banbury holds within itself the contrast between traditional and non-traditional. It is, of course, a traditional activity in Banbury in the historical sense and, as Table 3 shows, its second most important industry.[1] But in terms of organization it is in part non-traditional. Groceries that look like good-class family concerns (whatever may be their present ownership), where the smell of the coffee roaster is ever-present, keep company with 'chain' groceries that have the same names and layout that you may find in a hundred other English towns and with the self-service co-operative store. Facing shops like Woolworths with their wide plate-glass windows are shops housed in Tudor buildings or with their pargeting still preserved. The jeweller's shop which is part

[1] In evidence to the Royal Commission on Local Government Boundaries the Borough estimated that, although its citizens number less than 20,000, over 40,000 use the town for marketing, for commercial and public services, and for entertainment. Their point is a valid one. A similar ratio was found, for example, in Worcester where the 'market population' was double that of the city itself. J. Glaisyer, T. Brennan, W. Ritchie, &c., *County Town: Civic Survey for the Planning of Worcester* (John Murray, 1946).

of a nation-wide concern is opposed by a dark little jewellery and antique shop run by a local family. Meat may be bought from a local butcher and grazier or from branches of a firm to be found in London or Birmingham. Shoes may be taken for repair to any

TABLE 3

Banbury Industries

*Industry**	*Persons in sample*	%	*Men*	%	*Women*	%
Aluminium processing	350	23·9	301	28·6	49	12·0
Distribution	191	13·0	107	10·1	84	20·6
Transport	173	11·7	162	15·3	11	2·7
Clothing	95	6·5	24	2·3	71	17·4
Local government (inc. Education)	93	6·3	49	4·6	44	10·8
Building and contracting	86	5·9	86	8·1	0	0
Services (other than professional)	83	5·7	16	1·5	67	16·4
Professional and commercial services	64	4·4	35	3·3	29	7·2
Food and drink	54	3·8	41	3·9	13	3·2
Woodworking	39	2·7	34	3·2	5	1·2
Electrical machinery manufacture	36	2·4	33	3·1	3	0·7
Printing and periodicals	34	2·3	31	2·9	3	0·7
Agriculture	29	2·0	26	2·5	3	0·7
Gas, water, and electricity	23	1·6	19	1·8	4	1·0
All other	115	7·8	93	8·8	22	5·4
All industries	1,465	100·0	1,057	100·0	408	100·0

* Industries have been grouped on the basis of the Standard Industrial Classification which is used by all government departments. Only the main headings that are relevant to Banbury have been used here. Where only one part of a main S.I.C. heading is relevant, that part only of the heading has been used, e.g. 'metal manufacture' in Banbury is solely 'aluminium processing'. Only those industries have been classified which showed a total number of employees in the sample of 20 or more, i.e. have about a 100 in the town as a whole. The figures show everyone employed in an industrial group whatever their occupation except domestic servants who are included under 'other than professional services'.

of a number of nationwide shoe-shops or to the little cobblers whose small shops are half hidden among the bright displays of the new-comers. Clothes may be bought at standard 'reach-me-down' shops or made by the bespoke tailor or by the dressmakers whose small signs are likely to be overlooked except by those who know.

The thousand and more people who work in shops and in wholesale distribution are employed by over 350 different concerns.

Numerically, the small shops, the family concerns and the one-man businesses, are in the majority. But every year in Banbury there are fewer of these traditional shops. They are replaced by branches of large-scale organizations whose ownership and control comes from outside and which are still looked upon by many as alien. They are non-traditional and amount to about 20 per cent. of all shops, but they employ a much higher percentage than this of the workers in the distributive trades.

Among or near the shops, but tending to cluster towards the west end of the town centre, are the commercial services, the banks, the insurance offices, and some of the central government offices. Here, too, are the dentists and some of the doctors, the cinemas, and many of the sixty-odd pubs. All of these are historically traditional services provided by Banbury, part of its *raison d'être*, but, as with distribution, not all are now traditionally organized.

In the maze of small streets that lie behind the shops and between them and the canal and the railway (see Chart II, p. 5), muddled up with the nineteenth-century cottages in streets like Statham Terrace (see Chapter 6), is a miscellaneous collection of factories and workshops. Most of them are small, but two or three larger ones employ from 50 to 300 people. They include activities like flour milling and egg packing, constructional engineering, the manufacture of clothing, furniture, and packing. Also in this area are the wholesale distributors, the coal-yards, the oil depot, timber-yards, and builders' yards.

Many of these industries are of a kind long associated with the town, particularly, for example, those concerned with farm products. But not all may be called traditional.

Clothing, like distribution, is divided: dressmaking, tailoring, and cobbling are historically traditional industries still traditionally run; but the clothing industry is dominated by one large factory, employing several hundred workers, which is owned and controlled abroad. It is non-traditional in its technology and management.

Building and contracting, although the largest single employer is non-traditional, may as a whole be fairly described as traditional, for the majority of firms here (and taken together they form the major employer) are small-scale family businesses run on essentially traditional lines. This is also true of the food and drink industries (brewing, milling, &c.) and of printing and papers.

In contrast transport, the third largest industry, employing almost as many people as distribution, may be a traditional industry in Banbury in the historical sense, but it is now almost entirely run on non-traditional lines. The railway and part of road transport are nationalized; the buses are run by a large firm centred in one of the great Midland cities. The railway is a special case of an industry which has existed in the town for over a hundred years but which must still be classified as non-traditional. Indeed, it was non-traditional in our sense from its inception. It was something which happened to Banbury directed from outside the town. The fact that it was nationalized shortly before this study began merely served to underline its position.

The acme of non-traditionalism in Banbury is the aluminium factory. Lying right outside the town, it is also right outside the traditions of the town. Its raw materials come from overseas, it deals only with an intermediate stage of production, its techniques are modern, its ultimate ownership and ultimate policy-making authority are overseas. Cause of the new industrial revolution in Banbury and of the major influx of immigrants, it is the factory on which the present prosperity of the town is based. This one factory and its allied laboratories employ nearly one-quarter of the working population of the town. When shopkeepers and publicans complained that 'money was tight' it was generally not a reflection of the state of the national economy, but of production in the aluminium factory. When production was booming the workers' bonuses over and above their basic wages were high, trade was brisk, and the pubs full. When contracts were smaller or drawing to a close the bonuses fell and the tradesmen were aware of it within a fortnight. Throughout the period of the field-work these fluctuations were about a normally high level; there were some contractions at the aluminium factory, but no short time and no wholesale sackings. There was no doubt that the town prospered.

Banbury today concerns itself only slightly more with its market activities than with production: 47 per cent. of the employed population are in production and 53 per cent. in distribution and other services—a ratio little different from the national one of 46:54. The percentage of the employed population in distribution is, at 13 per cent., only slightly higher than the national one of 12·1 per cent. Banbury today is, at any rate numerically, no more a town of shopkeepers than England itself is a nation of shopkeepers.[1]

[1] *Classification of Occupations, 1950* (General Register Office) (London, H.M.S.O.).

Moreover, in terms of the numbers of male household heads they employ, the non-traditional industries now outweigh the traditional industries, as Table 4 shows. It shows also that they employ a higher proportion of younger people, both manual and non-manual.

TABLE 4

Traditional and Non-traditional Firms
Male Household Heads Employed
Numbers in sample

Occupational Status‡	*Total*	*Origin*		*Age*†	
		Banburian	*Immigrant*	*Under 50*	*Over 50*
		*Traditional**			
Non-manual . .	85	42	43	53	27
Manual . .	101	71	30	60	38
All traditional .	186	113	73	113	65
		*Non-traditional**			
Non-manual . .	64	18	46	48	15
Manual . .	322	156	166	213	95
All non-traditional	386	174	212	261	110

* Places of employment have been individually classified as traditional or non-traditional on the basis of the definition on p. 21.

† The ages of some household heads are unknown.

‡ Based on the Hall/Jones classification: classes 1–4 being counted as non-manual and 5–7 as manual. See Appendix 3 for application of the classification to Banbury. J. Hall and D. Caradog Jones, 'The Social Grading of Occupations', *Brit. J. Sociol.* i. 1 (1950).

Table 4 relates only to men who are heads of households. To this extent it is unrepresentative, particularly of women and of younger people. But the world of work in Banbury is principally a man's world: there are 10½ men employed to every 4 women (see Table 3, p. 22). For the most part the women work in the cleaner, lighter industries (distribution and clothing, for example, compared with aluminium processing and building) and, as Table 5 shows, in the less responsible posts. Clothing and distribution are both divided between traditional and non-traditional establishments, the major employers in each case being non-traditional. The evidence about the younger people is the same: more are found in non-traditional establishments. Table 4 is, therefore, more likely to under- than over-represent the personnel of the non-traditional undertakings.

TABLE 5

*Occupational Status in Banbury**

Hall/ Jones class	*Number employed (in sample)*						*% employed† (of those in the sample)*					
	All		*Male*		*Female*		*All*		*Male*		*Female*	
1	23	61	23	57	0	4	1·6	4·3	2·1	5·2	0	1·2
2	38		34		4		2·7		3·1		1·2	
3	132	271	88	182	45	91	9·2	18·9	8·0	16·6	13·3	26·9
4	139		94		46		9·7		8·6		13·6	
5	594		465		131		41·5		42·4		38·6	
6	352	1,099	281	857	71	244	24·6	76·8	25·6	78·1	20·9	71·9
7	153		111		42		10·7		10·1		12·4	
All classes	1,431		1,096		339		100·0		100·0		100·0	

* Based on the Hall/Jones scale. See Appendix 3, p. 190, for the application of the scale to Banbury.

† Percentages do not always add to 100 because of rounding.

Table 4 shows, furthermore, that the proportion of non-manual to manual workers is higher on the traditional side: this, by definition, one would expect, since local control means local managers and directors. Because of this and because the higher managements of the large-scale (non-traditional) industries are outside the town, Banbury may be called a 'middle-class town'. Table 6, which com-

TABLE 6

The Registrar-General's Classification of Occupations. Banbury and England and Wales Compared

Class	*Description of occupations*	*England and Wales** %	*Banbury†* %
I	Professional, &c.	3·3	1·6
II	Intermediate	15·0	14·0
III	Skilled	52·7	54·9
IV	Partly skilled	16·2	19·8
V	Unskilled	12·8	9·5

* Census, 1951, 1 per cent. sample.

† The Banbury schedule inquiry, 18·5 per cent. sample.

pares the Registrar-General's social status classification of occupations for England and Wales with the same classification applied to Banbury, shows that its main strength lies in the central occupational grades. Table 7 shows the income distribution, where the same concentration in the middle ranges is seen.[1]

TABLE 7

*Distribution of Incomes in Banbury**

Income groups (after tax)	*Replies*	
	No. in sample	%
Under £250	757	45·1
£250–£499	839	49·9
£500–£999	66	3·9
£1,000 and over . .	18	1·1

* No attempt has been made at a national comparison because (i) the official sources give no figure for the numbers earning under £250 per annum and (ii) married couples are here counted as two separate individuals, not one as is done officially.

Numerically Banbury may not be a town of shopkeepers, but shopkeepers and their like working in traditional industries form the backbone of its leadership. For the directors, owners, and managers of traditional industries are part and parcel of the close-knit traditional social structure of the town. They have in common a number of characteristics in contrast with those who are concerned with non-traditional industries.

In traditional industry the stress laid on social and personal values affects, and in some cases outweighs, purely economic or business values. It is remarkable, for instance, that traditionally minded owners do not open branch shops in the outlying districts of Banbury. There are a few shops in these districts: either they are individually owned 'corner' shops, unconnected with any in the town centre, or they are branches of the Co-op. The author believes that the traditionally minded proprietors have failed to open branches less from lack of capital than from lack of inclination. These businessmen fall among those who are concerned to have 'adequate' or 'reasonable' returns for their work rather than the maximum possible returns. They make enough for their needs, judged by the general standard of the town, out of one central shop. They do not consider

[1] A number of people who work in Banbury and who are in occupational class 1 and the higher income groups live outside the Borough boundaries and therefore did not appear in the schedule inquiry. It is unlikely that the addition of these people would bring the proportions of groups up to the national level. The relatively small numbers at the bottom of the scale result from the fact that Banbury industries rely on semi-skilled rather than unskilled labour for the bulk of their production workers.

that an increased income would be worth the added strain and effort of management on a larger scale that it would cost them. They are not familiar with administration through delegation, nor apparently are they anxious to learn. Furthermore, in delegation they would lose something of the personal relationship in their business which they value highly. The traditional relationship between 'gaffer and man', for example, would be more difficult to maintain. So would the personal relationship between shopkeeper and customer.

It is noticeable that manual workers in traditional industries are ill-organized from a trade-union point of view. The men, traditionally minded, accept the informal, personal relationship. How much this is the case was shown when the workers in one small firm applied to join the union only when this personal relationship had broken down: the boss, said to have been the worse for drink, had abused and sworn at them. This infringed tradition and so, at last, although they had been deaf to many previous overtures from the union, they too broke tradition and signed the union cards.

The emphasis upon the social and personal rather than the strictly economic and business values affects not only the relations of the traditional business man with his employees, but affects also who those employees are. For example, the owner of one business who is a leading Methodist has a remarkably high number of Methodists among his staff; similarly, the number of Roman Catholics in a Catholic-managed business is high. Another works, which is in the hands of a third generation of the same family, is remarkable for the number, not only of Banburians, but of particular Banburian families it employs. Indeed, there is a tendency throughout the industries which have been classified here as traditional to employ very significantly more Banburian than immigrant workers. Table 4 shows this for male household heads and Table 8, which refers to the total sample population, shows the same trend in the major industrial groups.

The total numbers of Banburians and immigrants recorded in the sample inquiry as being employed in the industrial groups classified in Table 8 is the same: 310 in each case. A direct comparison may therefore be made and the table shows that each of the six traditional industrial groups employ more Banburians than immigrants. Taken together the traditional industries employ more than twice as many Banburians as immigrants. Clothing (2), alone of the non-traditional industries, also shows a positive Banburian deviation. While it must be classified as non-traditional because of its type of ownership, nevertheless it possesses certain traditional characteristics: clothing manufacture is an historically traditional occupation; the attitude of the management is paternalistic; and there is no trade union. Furthermore it employs a high proportion of young women.

TABLE 8

Proportions of Banburians and Immigrants employed in Traditional and Non-Traditional Industrial Groups

Industry*	Numbers in sample				%			
	Born Banburians		*True Immigrants*		*Born Banburians*		*True Immigrants*	
Traditional								
Food and drink	23		17		7·4		5·5	
Woodworking	22		5		7·1		1·6	
Printing and Periodicals	15		8		4·8		2·6	
Building and Contracting	39		18		12·6		5·7	
Agriculture	10		4		3·2		1·3	
Clothing (1)†	16		7		5·2		2·3	
All Traditional		125		59		40·3		19·0
Non-Traditional								
Aluminium processing	107		165		34·5		53·2	
Clothing (2)†	22		17		7·1		5·5	
Transport	56		69		18·1		22·3	
All non-traditional		185		251		59·7		81·0
Total		310		310		100·0		100·0
All employed		524		525				

* Distribution, local government, professional, commercial, and other services have been excluded from this table.

† *Clothing* has been divided into two parts:
Clothing (1) is traditional and covers dress-making, tailoring, &c.
Clothing (2) is non-traditional and is mainly corset, &c., manufacture.

Owners and managers of traditional industries are by no means all Banburian born and bred, in fact only about half are. But even the immigrants tend to be 'Banburian by adoption' for, as a group, traditional local proprietors live in or near the town and play an active part in its life. They are men who have accepted the traditional way of life native to the town. There is a strong 'we-feeling' among them. The majority are firm believers in the merits of free competition: they are opposed to the large combine, which savours of monopoly; and to the Co-op. and the nationalized industries which savour of socialism. The traditional proprietors draw together and draw away from the new non-traditional industries. The owner of a traditional family chemist's shop is said to have declared that he would refuse to serve any of his customers who were seen entering a new branch of Boots' opened in the town. If you fail to find what you want in a traditional family shop and ask where you may be able to get it, you are directed to the shop's traditional competitor on the grounds that 'So and so's are an old Banbury firm.' 'So and so's' may not be the nearest or even necessarily the most likely shop for your needs, but these are not the criteria used. Furthermore, a lead given by the aluminium factory in support of an organization may be enough for that organization to fail to get the support of local proprietors. Again, for all their faith in free competition, they compete only in a controlled way among themselves. One shopkeeper, for example, let some premises to a firm new to the town. The competitors of this new firm, who had previously enjoyed a virtual monopoly in their field, now refused to speak to him because he had 'let competition into the town'.

Historically, new industries and new skills have generally been introduced by immigrants or taken over by them at an early stage. Banburians have tended to let their industries become outdated and to 'die on their hands'. Plush weaving is one example of this; coach builders who failed to change over their business to the motor-car are another example. In the villages the garage, electricity or radio shop takes the place once held by the smithy; but it is rarely the old blacksmith who takes over the new craft, more often it is an immigrant from the town or city. These histories appear to the observer as a reluctance on the part of the Banburian to turn over to something new; a resistance to change.

Banburians, furthermore, although many of them are in non-traditional industries, seem on the whole to prefer more traditional activities. It is possible that those Banburians who wish to turn to something new have left the town and sought work elsewhere. But in the town the proportion of Banburian manual workers in traditional industries is particularly high as Tables 4 and 8 show. Working with food products, with wood or stone, paper or cloth are activities which have long been established in Banbury. Flour millers, brewers, carpenters, masons, printers, and tailors appear in Banbury records over the centuries. Working with metal, electricity, internal combustion engines, and automatic machinery are new activities. Toolmakers, setters and fitters, electricians, motor-mechanics and engineers have only recently appeared in the town. A side result of a pilot questionnaire undertaken early in the field-work bears this out although the numbers are small. Of the people who replied sixteen Banburians and eleven immigrants were listed as 'miscellaneous manual'. They stated their occupations as follows:

Banburians

Road sweeper	Wood machinist
Labourer	Wheelwright
Stoker	Cabinet maker
Factory worker	Cooper
Builder's labourer	Carpenter
Flourmiller	House decorator
Watchmaker	Fitter
Printer	Maintenance

Immigrants

Gas fitter	Toolsetter
Fitter welder	Electrical engineer
Fitter mechanic	Radio engineer
Fitter	Stoker
Maintenance	Labourer
Bricklayer	

The almost complete absence of the older crafts and workmanship with the older materials in the immigrant list and their comparative importance in the Banburian list are striking.

The traditional business man in Banbury is, as has been shown, concerned less with making as much money as possible than he is with living comfortably and maintaining his social status and position. His place in the general social life of the town is as important to him as his strictly business position and, so long as this pays, he is not particularly ambitious. His is not the attitude of the experimentalist; he is not always on the look-out for new and better ways of working. This being so, it is possible that the traditional business man, lacking a questioning and scientific outlook, may fail to recognize in time the implications for his business of changing economic and social circumstances. Where this failure is complete his business will ultimately fail. Alternatively, and this has been the case in one or two small businesses and a number of shops, he may recognize the changes and their implications but may prefer to sell out to a non-traditionalist rather than take the risk of reorganizing his business himself. The risk involved would be much greater than he has been accustomed to taking and, furthermore, would affect his whole position in the town. If successful he would outclass his present social peers, and if unsuccessful he would lose his social position; in either case the results would be uncomfortable for a man closely integrated in the traditional social-status system of so small a town.

The many traditionally minded business men in Banbury who continue to run their businesses successfully and prosperously have, of course, made adaptations in their method of work to keep up with technical and social change. Furthermore, there are enough younger people left who actively believe in the values of the system to open new businesses on traditional lines. Every year small works are started on the old pattern and young couples take over family shops (mostly on the 'corners' or in the more outlying parts of the town). Some fail, some struggle on, some are notably successful: one cabinet-maker in particular may be mentioned who built up a prosperous small business virtually within the period of the field-work. Nevertheless, the general picture of the traditional economic system is of a stable system which is tending to contract. The traditionalists seem to cling to old methods, materials, and employees, and to change from pressure of circumstances rather than from inclination.[1]

The immigrant non-traditionalists provide a strong contrast to these men in their attitudes to work and their ways of working. They are not closely integrated with the traditional small-scale and tightly knit social system of the town; their frame of reference extends beyond it. It is more directly through their industrial efforts that they can achieve their social goals. They are involved in a hierarchy of management that may be on a national or even an international scale.

[1] There is much in this account of the traditional Banbury industry and the system of values associated with it which compares with the situation described among the older industries and in the 'local system' in south-west Wales. T. Brennan, E. Cooney, and H. Pollins, *Social Change in South-west Wales* (Watts, 1954), p. 51, point to the absence of local skills to man the immigrant industries; p. 55, the lack of native 'personnel with the ability and training to maintain a dynamic economic structure'; p. 110, the local social value system which accords more prestige to the man who gives local public service than to the one who 'gets on' economically. This comparison will be referred to again later and is more fully discussed in the final chapter of the present work.

They are, therefore, more concerned with the purely economic aims of greater production and greater earnings than the traditionalists.

Since one of their goals is to obtain maximum returns for their work, they seek more consciously and more thoroughly for new and better methods of production and organization; they are 'progressive' ('new-fangled' some traditionalists would say, while they consider many traditionalists are 'hidebound'). The aluminium factory, for example, employs men whose function it is to search for and test out new uses for aluminium alloys. The non-traditionalists, therefore, stress the experimental method. They are not afraid of change and, given the advice of experts, are prepared to 'try it out'.

Furthermore, they judge employees more strictly on merit than the traditionalists do. The majority of jobs in the aluminium factory were unknown in Banbury before the mid 1930's. Every man applying for a job there was 'on his own'. He had to show either special qualifications (gained outside Banbury) or an ability to learn on the job. Non-traditional industry, by virtue of its technology and the amount of training involved, must employ the man who has the right qualifications, regardless of his background. Because of the hierarchical nature of the firms involved and the strict occupational-status grading within each, individual performance on the job is important for those who seek promotion. And those who seek promotion are themselves men who accept non-traditional values, whose goal is maximum earnings rather than adequate earnings; who do not accept their starting-point on the social scale as their finishing-point and who, therefore, wish to be judged by their merits alone.

But it must be said that the aluminium factory is not entirely unaffected by traditional values. It includes among its annual intake a number of public school men, whose qualification is just that they are public school men. They have a 'social know-how' that the management consider valuable. Playing rugger may in some circumstances, it is said, help a candidate to a staff position, provided he has other necessary qualifications.

Relations within non-traditional industry are much less personal than they are in traditional industry. This is a result of the larger scale of non-traditional industry and of the stricter application of the merit basis of selection. The personal 'gaffer and man' is replaced by the impersonal 'two sides of industry'.

All occupations in these industries are ranked, but a particularly strict dividing line is drawn between manual and non-manual workers. In one non-traditional factory there is a physical wall which separates the two groups and a man promoted is said to have 'gone behind the wall'.

As a corollary to the concept of the 'two sides of industry', it is significant that the strength of the trade unions in Banbury lies almost wholly in the non-traditional industries, aluminium and transport. From among workers in these industries leaders have arisen to oppose the traditional leadership of the small business man in the town.

The merit basis of selection and the fact that many of the occupations are new to Banbury has had two effects on the type of people employed in non-traditional industry. The first is that there is a marked tendency for non-traditional industries to employ a larger proportion of immigrant than Banburian workers, although it is less striking than the opposite tendency for traditional industry to employ Banburian workers. Tables 4 (p. 25) and 8 (p. 29) show that non-traditional firms and industries employ about a third more immigrants than Banburians. The second effect is that the majority of the managements and staffs of non-traditional industries are immigrant; in at least one case all of them are. In the metallurgical laboratories, for example, of 30 department, division, and section heads, all are immigrant; of 48 investigators and technical assistants, the next most responsible grade, all of whom have special qualifications, 38 are immigrant; of 53 members of the clerical and administrative staffs, 42 are immigrants; while of 74 junior staff just over half are Banburian. The proportion of Banburians increases here as responsibility and amount of training decreases. The same is true of the staff of the aluminium factory itself: of 31 heads of departments, divisional, and section heads, 27 are immigrant; of 130 junior staff, 69 are Banburian. Of non-manual workers in all non-traditional industries over 70 per cent. are immigrant, compared with 50 per cent. in traditional industry.

Indeed, in the town as a whole there is a tendency for the more responsible and better-paid posts to be held by immigrants. Table 9 shows that the four higher (non-manual) classes have a higher proportion of immigrants than Banburians, the reverse being the case in the three manual classes (Hall/Jones scale). The deviations are particularly significant in classes 1, 2, 3, and 7, but the excess of immigrants in the higher classes is greater than of Banburians in the

TABLE 9

Occupational Status of Banburians and Immigrants Compared

Hall/Jones classes	Numbers in sample*		%	
	Born Banburian	True Immigrants	Born Banburian	True Immigrants
1	4	14	0·7	2·6
2	8	23	1·4	4·2
3	39	65	7·1	12·0
4	49	57	8·9	10·5
5	234	213	42·4	39·2
6	140	119	25·4	21·9
7	78	52	14·1	9·6
All classes	552	543	100·0	100·0

* i.e. numbers of respondents over twenty-one years who replied to this question and whose answers could be classified.

TABLE 10

Income Distribution among Banburians and Immigrants Compared

Income group	Sample population over 21 years			
	Numbers in sample*		%†	
	Born Banburian	True Immigrant	Born Banburian	True Immigrant
£1,000 and over .	5	8	0·9	1·3
£500–£999 . .	15	39	2·5	6·6
£250–£499 . .	327	331	54·6	54·7
Under £250 . .	252	227	42·1	37·5
All groups . .	599	605	100·0	100·0

* i.e. numbers of respondents over twenty-one years who replied to this question and whose answers could be classified.

† Percentages do not add to 100 because of rounding.

lowest. These facts are reflected in the distribution of incomes between Banburians and immigrants as Table 10 shows. Banburians do not form a labouring class, for they are found throughout all the seven classes, but immigrants certainly dominate the classes of highest status. This would probably be found to be the case in any town and particularly in small towns. These classes, by definition, require considerable amounts of higher education and/or training. They are relatively few in number. When a man's training is finished or he wants promotion, he must go where there is a vacancy. This applies to Banburians as well as to immigrants. The number of Banburians who are highly trained and who can find employment in Banbury of the sort they want at the time they want it must necessarily be small. The highly trained worker and adventurous worker alike go after employment and do not expect it to be brought to them. This may be, in part at least, the explanation of the shortage of Banburians in the higher occupation grades and in the newer skills. But also, in part, it may be that the atmosphere and values of traditional Banbury do not readily set men off on the road to economic advancement.

The immigrant non-traditional members of management rarely play any active part in the life of the town. Their frame of reference extends beyond Banbury. Those in junior grades frequently look upon the town merely as a temporary resting place until a better occupation appears elsewhere. (The youthfulness of non-manual workers in non-traditional industries is remarkable: only 24 per cent. are over fifty compared with 34 per cent. in traditional industry.) Those of higher occupational status are involved in relations, both personal and business, with people scattered all over the country and overseas. Neither group need become involved in the small-town society in which business and social interests closely overlap. Their attitude to their work and their outside interests (see especially Chapters 3, 4, 5, and 8) differ from those of the Banbury traditionalist.[1]

It is from the higher occupational status groups that the traditional leadership of the town is drawn. Since the more mobile non-traditional members of these status groups play little part in the town's affairs, this leadership is left to those with roots in the town; to people who, for the most part, are less widely travelled, less cosmopolitan, less highly educated and trained. A number of them are Banburians. The immigrants among them are those who have been prepared to adopt the town as their own, to accept its values and attitudes, and to play a part in its social and political life. They are traditionally minded immigrants.

[1] Brennan, Cooney, and Pollins (op. cit.) describe the changes taking place in south-west Wales in not dissimilar terms: (p. 58) owners who had a paternalistic relationship with their workers have been replaced by managers 'and a hierarchy of executives who lived either in the towns of the area or outside the Swansea Area altogether'; (p. 110) the acceptance of 'English standards' is replacing the local system of values with the result that 'the socially approved career is becoming more and more that of the man who "gets on" economically, and it happens that the organization of the community is such that he is debarred from playing his full part in social life, even if he wanted to'. It seems that in south-west Wales, as in Banbury, (p. 64) 'there is a conflict between the economically-minded leaders [cf. 'non-traditional'] and the traditional leaders'.

This traditional leadership is now being challenged by the leaders of the non-traditional workers through the trade-union and Labour movements. At the same time economic power is passing to non-traditional managements; the traditional sector is narrowing.

Traditional industry is part of the total social structure of the town while non-traditional industry is not. Non-traditional industry is related in particular ways to sections of the town and to sections of the nation and the world; the management, the workers, the industry, for example, are distinct and abstractly conceived groups. As non-traditionalism extends Banbury may less and less be thought of as a whole society, but rather as a place divided into sections, parts of larger wholes in a much wider society. In the traditional sector economic, social, religious, and political values and attitudes are closely linked and traditional industry closely related to the total social system. Non-traditional industry shows no such close linking of values. But, where stability is highly rated in traditional industry, in non-traditional industry the experimental and scientific attitude, involving willingness to change, is stressed. These are increasingly the keynotes of the economic life of Banbury.

3

POLITICS IN BANBURY

BANBURY is an ancient borough, proud of its rights, and independent in spirit, which received a charter over 400 years ago. It is not a county borough and therefore it has lost many of its powers to Oxfordshire County Council and to national bodies in the last twenty years. Banburians and traditionalists, conscious of local loyalties, dislike this loss of power and prestige. As a result the Borough has made official representations to be allowed to maintain its former rights. It failed in an attempt to keep its police force in the 1930's and its primary education in the 1940's. But it succeeded in obtaining the Lord Chancellor's permission to continue to hold Quarter Sessions in the town, although its population is under 20,000.

It is a local centre for many central government departments. All the social service ministries, for example, have offices in Banbury. These offices serve not only the town but a considerable rural area round about, thus increasing the importance of the town as a local centre.

The traditional party-political division in Banbury lay between the Conservatives and the Liberals. Although the Liberals have retained official local independence this traditional division has been overshadowed since the 1930's, and particularly since 1945, by the division between the Conservatives and the Liberals on the one hand and the Labour Party on the other. The town, which returned a Liberal member throughout the nineteenth century, has been consistently represented by a Conservative since the November election of 1922. It was in this election that the Labour Party, which had been formed in 1919, first put up an official candidate.

It is the Labour Party which represents the non-traditional element in the political life of the town. Its rise has so far altered the pattern of local party politics that only 8 per cent. of those interviewed in the schedule inquiry said they were Liberals.[1] Moreover, although the Banbury parliamentary division (which includes the town and the northern part of the county) was represented by a Conservative

[1] 1950.

member at the time of the survey, Labour voters (according to the schedule inquiry) outnumber Conservatives and almost match Conservative and Liberal voters combined, making it likely that the Conservative member owes his relatively safe seat to the rural voters in the constituency.

The traditional division into Conservative and Liberal was, and still is, associated with the religious division between the Anglicans

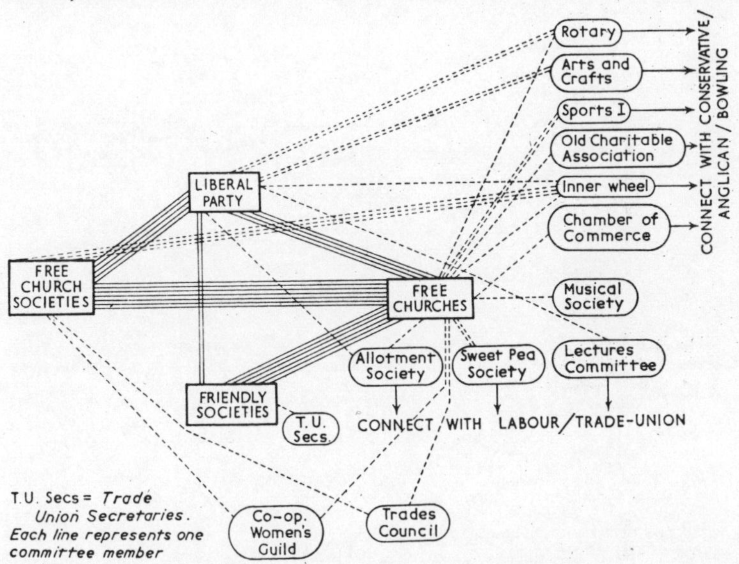

CHART IV. The Free Church/Liberal connexion

and the Free Churchmen, the connexion between liberalism and the Free Churches being most marked. Although the Liberal party is of less numerical importance today and religious differences of less profound significance, this connexion is still noticeable. Of the 138 Liberal voters recorded in the sample, 50 per cent. were Free Churchmen and 43 per cent. Anglicans. (Very few Roman Catholics are Liberals—only 6 out of 187 were recorded.) Chart IV shows the close connexion between the Free Churches and the Liberal party. One line is drawn between two committees for each person who sits on both.[1] Chart V shows that there is a similar, but less marked, connexion between the Conservative Association committees and committees of the Church of England; the connexion with bowls

[1] The method of recording and analysing data about formal associations is described in Appendix 4 and the analysis further developed in Chapter 5.

clubs is in fact rather stronger than the Church connexion. There are no direct connexions between Conservative committee men and the Free Churches. Of 720 Conservative voters, 77 per cent. were recorded as Anglican and only 11 per cent. as Free Churchmen.

By contrast, the point to remark about the Labour Party in Banbury is its lack of connexion with organized religion. Over 40 per cent. of those who said they were of no denomination, agnostic, or

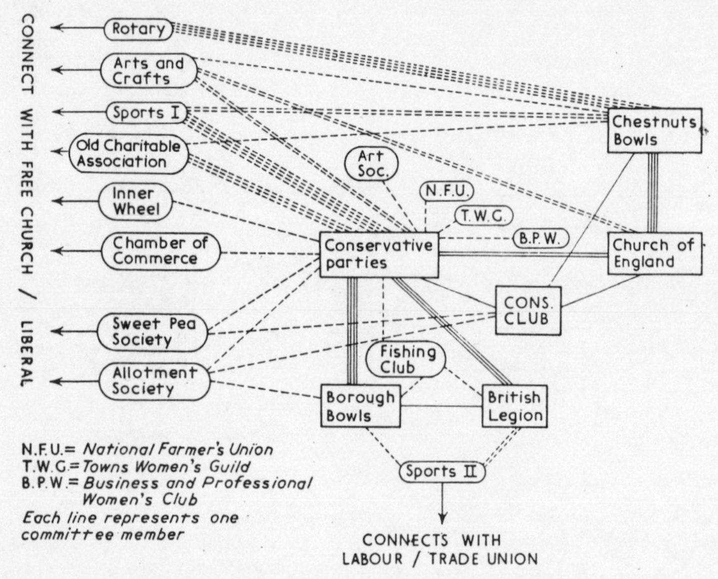

CHART V. The Conservative/Anglican/Bowling connexion

atheist, said they were Labour voters. Labour voters show a slightly greater bias towards the Free Churches than do the Conservatives: 17 per cent. of Labour voters are adherents of Free Churches, 70 per cent. of the Church of England, and 10 per cent. of the Roman Catholic Church. Chart VI shows only one connexion between Labour Party committees and a Free Church committee. This characteristic distinguishes the Labour Party in Banbury from local Labour parties in other parts of the country where close links with the chapels are found.[1]

Leading Conservatives and Liberals are frequently members of churches or chapels. Eleven of the sixteen Conservative Borough

[1] See, for example, Brennan, Cooney, and Pollins, op. cit.

councillors are church members: 8 of them are Anglicans, 2 are Roman Catholic, and 1 is a Baptist. Four members of the Liberal party committee (there are no Liberal Borough councillors) are on Free Church committees. Not so in the Labour Party: only one of the eight Labour councillors is a church member, a Methodist.

Compared with the Conservative, and particularly with the Liberal party, the Labour Party in Banbury might be called 'secular'. But this is not to say that it is anti-clerical or 'laïque' in its policy. It is not.

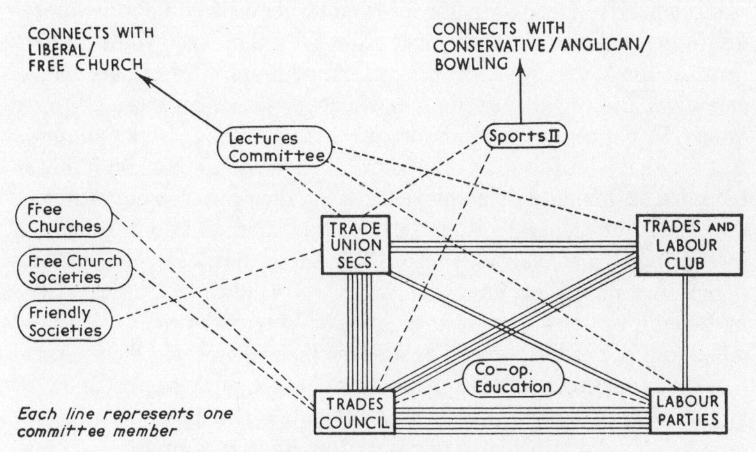

CHART VI. The Labour/Trade Union connexion

It is merely passive in religious matters, reflecting the majority of passive adherents described in the following chapter. It is noteworthy that it is supporters of the traditional parties who show most interest in organized religion, itself a traditional force as the following chapter suggests.

Despite the connexion between the Liberal and Conservative parties and religion and the lack of any such connexion in the Labour Party, it is remarkable, particularly when continental practice is remembered, that nothing is made of it in terms of politics and campaigns. The rule that religious difference remains unspoken is followed in the political as in other parts of the social life of the town.

The principal difference between supporters of the Labour and Conservative parties, who in Banbury, as elsewhere in the country, are the two main contestants for political power, lies along social class lines. Almost all members of the middle class are Conservative (or, if Liberal, at least anti-Labour) and almost all supporters of the

Labour Party are working class. This is indicated by Table 11, which shows the occupation[1] and income status and the source of income and education of party supporters. Over 60 per cent. of all non-manual occupational classes (Hall/Jones scale) are Conservative voters, while only 20 per cent. are Labour voters. In classes 1 and 2 the figures are even more marked: 70 per cent. are Conservative and only 10 per cent. Labour. Fifty-eight per cent. of all manual classes vote Labour, but the working-class nature of Labour Party support is most clearly indicated by the fact that 90 per cent. of Labour voters are in manual classes (Hall/Jones scale 5–7). Similarly, while 58 per cent. of those earning £500 per annum or more after tax are Conservative, and of those earning under £500, 48 per cent. are Labour voters, 97 per cent. of all Labour voters earn under £500 per annum. But the analysis of sources of income taken in conjunction with those recorded as 'managers', 'employers', or 'on their own account' (under the Registrar-General's Industrial Status Classification) is more interesting. This analysis suggests that it is not only those with higher income and occupational status who tend to be Conservative or Liberal, but also those whose interests in terms of their work are allied to those of the owners, or who see their interests in these terms (i.e. the proprietors or near proprietors).[2] Some of these people have a relatively low income or occupational status. The data on source of income shows that 36 per cent. of Conservative supporters, compared with only 5 per cent. of Labour supporters, receive their income as profits and fees or salaries; 69 per cent. of those receiving profits and fees vote Conservative against less than 12 per cent. who vote Labour. The data about managers and proprietors shows that of 44 voters recorded in the sample as 'managers' only 5 were Labour, 38 being Conservative, one Liberal, and one 'floater'. Of 76 people recorded as 'employers' or 'working on their own account', 58 were Conservative or Liberal and only 10 Labour (3 'floated' and 4 were non-voters). So far as education is concerned, 55 per cent. of those with secondary education and 63 per cent. with higher education vote Conservative, 26 per cent. and less than 5 per cent. respectively vote Labour. Of Labour voters, 89 per cent. have only an elementary education.

These economic and social biases shown by party supporters

[1] Cf. M. Benney and P. Geiss, 'Social Class and Politics in Greenwich', *Brit. J. Sociol.* i. 4 (1950), especially Table VI, p. 316.

[2] Cf. John Bonham, 'The Middle Class Elector', *Brit. J. Sociol.* iii. 3 (1950), pp. 225 and 229, who suggests a special connexion between proprietors and Conservative voting.

TABLE 11

*Characteristics of Voters**

<table>
<tr><th>Sex</th><th>Conservative</th><th>Labour</th><th>Liberal</th><th>Floaters and others†</th><th>None‡</th><th>Total</th></tr>
<tr><td>Male</td><td>331</td><td>475</td><td>55</td><td>33</td><td>51</td><td>945</td></tr>
<tr><td>Female</td><td>419</td><td>395</td><td>95</td><td>24</td><td>96</td><td>1,029</td></tr>
<tr><td>Total</td><td>750</td><td>870</td><td>150</td><td>57</td><td>147</td><td>1,974</td></tr>
<tr><td colspan="7">Age</td></tr>
<tr><td>Under 50</td><td>395</td><td>615</td><td>64</td><td colspan="2">124</td><td>1,198</td></tr>
<tr><td>Over 50</td><td>326</td><td>212</td><td>75</td><td colspan="2">77</td><td>690</td></tr>
<tr><td>Total</td><td>721</td><td>827</td><td>139</td><td colspan="2">201</td><td>1,888</td></tr>
<tr><td colspan="7">Occupational Status (Hall/Jones)</td></tr>
<tr><td>1 and 2</td><td>35</td><td>5</td><td>3</td><td>4</td><td>3</td><td>50</td></tr>
<tr><td>3 and 4</td><td>137</td><td>50</td><td>27</td><td>5</td><td>11</td><td>230</td></tr>
<tr><td>5</td><td>144</td><td>217</td><td>30</td><td>14</td><td>22</td><td>427</td></tr>
<tr><td>6</td><td>67</td><td>173</td><td>7</td><td>6</td><td>14</td><td>267</td></tr>
<tr><td>7</td><td>21</td><td>81</td><td>6</td><td>3</td><td>8</td><td>119</td></tr>
<tr><td>Total</td><td>404</td><td>526</td><td>73</td><td>32</td><td>58</td><td>1,093</td></tr>
<tr><td colspan="7">Income (after tax)</td></tr>
<tr><td>£500+</td><td>40</td><td>15</td><td>6</td><td colspan="2">8</td><td>69</td></tr>
<tr><td>£250–499</td><td>221</td><td>364</td><td>41</td><td colspan="2">54</td><td>680</td></tr>
<tr><td>Under £250</td><td>205</td><td>190</td><td>49</td><td colspan="2">58</td><td>502</td></tr>
<tr><td>Total</td><td>466</td><td>569</td><td>96</td><td colspan="2">120</td><td>1,251</td></tr>
<tr><td colspan="7">Source of Income §</td></tr>
<tr><td>Profits and fees</td><td>71</td><td>11</td><td>9</td><td colspan="2">12</td><td>103</td></tr>
<tr><td>Salary</td><td>70</td><td>16</td><td>16</td><td colspan="2">11</td><td>113</td></tr>
<tr><td>Wages</td><td>255</td><td>480</td><td>45</td><td colspan="2">68</td><td>848</td></tr>
<tr><td>Total</td><td>396</td><td>507</td><td>70</td><td colspan="2">91</td><td>1,064</td></tr>
<tr><td colspan="7">Education</td></tr>
<tr><td>Private, &c.</td><td>62</td><td>22</td><td>6</td><td colspan="2">8</td><td>98</td></tr>
<tr><td>Higher</td><td>22</td><td>2</td><td>4</td><td colspan="2">7</td><td>35</td></tr>
<tr><td>Secondary</td><td>121</td><td>57</td><td>24</td><td colspan="2">18</td><td>220</td></tr>
<tr><td>Elementary</td><td>482</td><td>715</td><td>101</td><td colspan="2">161</td><td>1,459</td></tr>
<tr><td>Total</td><td>687</td><td>796</td><td>135</td><td colspan="2">194</td><td>1,812</td></tr>
</table>

* Totals vary because of varying rates of refusal and 'don't know'.

† 'Floaters' are 'Labour/Liberal', 'Conservative/Liberal', &c., 'others' are Communists, Socialist Party of Great Britain, &c.

‡ 'None' refers to those who replied 'none' or 'do not vote'; some may be disguised refusals.

§ Independent means, pensions, &c., are excluded in this table. Employees paid monthly are defined as salary earners and those paid weekly as wage-earners.

TABLE 12

Characteristics of Party Committee Members and Borough Councillors

	Party committee members			*Borough councillors**		
	Cons.	*Lab.*	*Lib.*		*Cons.*	*Lab.*
Sex						
Male . . .	12	9	16		12	7
Female . . .	0	2	8		4	1
Total . . .	12	11	24		16	8
Average age	44	44	50		49	50
Occupational status classes (Hall/Jones)				*Classes*		
Range . . .	2–4	3–6	1–5	1 and 2	10	0
				3 and 4	5	3
Average . . .	2·65	4·30	2·77	5	1	3
				6	0	2
				7	0	0
Source of income†						
Profits and Fees .	8	0	15		9	2
Salary . . .	4	4	6		6	1
Wages . . .	0	7	1		1	5

* There are no Liberal Borough councillors.
† Details are not available for two Liberals.

appear even more markedly in members of party committees and councillors, as Table 12 shows. The committee of the Conservative Association is composed of 12 people whose occupation status on the Hall/Jones scale ranges from 2 to 4 with an average of 2·65. All are non-manual workers, 8 are employers or working on their own account: 3 in professions, 2 in distribution, and 3 in production. The remaining 4 have office jobs of one sort or another. There are also two district groups of Conservatives: one in Grimsbury and the other in Easington. One member from each of these is also on the central Banbury committee. Easington committee has 5 members and Grimsbury 10. The Grimsbury committee shows a wider occupation range (2–5) and averages 3·57: 5 are employed workers (2 are in offices and 3 do manual work); one is an employer in productive industry, and the remainder are proprietors in distribution. Easington shows the same range as the central committee (2–4), but has a lower average (3·25), none is in a profession, nor are any manual workers. The leadership of the Conservative Association is thus largely in the hands of those in the higher occupational status groups. However, there is a noticeable absence of anybody from class 1, i.e. the higher professional, managerial, and administrative classes. The majority of these people are Conservative supporters, but do not concern themselves (officially at least, and often not at all) with the actual running of the local Conservative Association in the town. (In the parliamentary division some people of this class, residents in the district, do play an active role, but not in the town itself.)

In the Liberal party the 24 members of the committee range more widely, from class 1 to class 5, with an average of 2·77. But in general, in terms of their occupations, the Liberal leaders are much the same sort of people as the Conservative leaders: 15 are employers or self-employed (6 in professions, 4 in distribution, 5 in production), 6 are office workers, and one a manual worker.

Not so in the Labour Party: of 11 committee members all are employed workers, with an occupational status range of from 3 to 6 and an average of 4·3. Four work in offices and 7 are manual workers. The occupational status of Labour Party leaders is, therefore, higher than that of its supporters in general, but noticeably lower than that of Conservative or Liberal leaders.[1]

The occupational status of Borough councillors tells the same story. Fifteen of the 16 Conservative councillors are non-manual workers, and ten of them are in classes 1 and 2 (some higher in status therefore than members of the Association committee). Nine are in the professions or proprietors in trade receiving their incomes from profits and fees, 6 are salaried workers, and only one is a wage-earner. By contrast, 5 of the 8 Labour councillors are wage-earning manual workers, one is a full-time trade-union official, and two are proprietors in trade receiving their incomes from profits.

These social and economic factors, in which there is so marked a variation between the two opposing groups, are all ones which contribute to, but do not add up to, social class. They are indications of the truth of the assertion that almost all the middle class are Conservative or Liberal and almost all Labour supporters are working class.

The statement must be made this way round because, while a member of the middle class is usually a Conservative, or perhaps a

[1] None of the parties has any committee members of occupational status 7.

Liberal, no such assumption may be made about the working class in relation to the Labour Party. It is true that almost all Labour supporters are working class, but it is not true that all the working class are Labour. (Obviously, or a Conservative candidate would never be returned.) Twenty-nine per cent. of the manual classes (Hall/Jones scale) vote Conservative and 58 per cent. of Conservative voters are manual workers. In the author's opinion the main reason for this is traditionalism. The traditionalist in the working class is not a Labour supporter.

TABLE 13

Party Supporters in Traditional and Non-traditional Firms Compared

	Male household heads of known politics			
	Traditional firms		*Non-traditional firms*	
	Cons. or Lib.	*Labour*	*Cons. or Lib.*	*Labour*
Non-manual	72	13	36	18
Manual	47	54	89	233

An analysis of the political bias of personnel in different industries shows that all the groups with a Conservative bias are those which were classified as traditional in Chapter 2. While in traditional industries the proportion of managerial to employed people tends to be higher than in non-traditional industries, the traditional industries do seem to have a relatively high proportion of manual Conservatives, as Table 13 shows. Nearly half the manual workers in traditional firms are Conservative or Liberal compared with less than one-quarter in non-traditional firms. Furthermore, since only male household heads are included in these figures, the effect of uneven distribution of female labour (and women have a greater bias to conservatism than men) is avoided. These are the industries, as was pointed out in Chapter 2, in which the tradition of 'gaffer and man' still applies and in which the amount of trade-union organization is small. By contrast, all those industries classified as non-traditional show a bias to Labour and are those industries in which trade-union organization is highly advanced.[1] Manual workers in traditional industries have

[1] Distribution shows a bias to conservatism. It is partly traditional and partly non-traditional. In this case the bias probably results from the fact that the proportion of owners and managers to total manpower is high. It is also likely that in distribution, which is split into so many small units, promotion from the floor to managerial ranks is still more customary than in other industries. In that case more people might see their interests as allied with those of the proprietors.

apparently been less open to Labour influences than those in non-traditional industry.

It is a logical conclusion of the traditional attitude for the working man to vote Conservative (or Liberal if he is a Free Churchman). For the essence of the traditional attitude is an acceptance of the traditional social class system. This means that a man accepts his position in it, although he may improve his lot by thrift and individual effort, and accepts also the right of those in higher classes to lead. The lead the middle classes give is towards conservatism.

The non-traditionalist in the working class, on the other hand, does not accept the rightness of the traditional class system or the status of the working class as unalterable. He recognizes the existence of class, seeks to modify the system by reducing the distinctions between classes, and to better the position of his class and thus his own position. The trade union in industry and the Labour Party in politics are the expressions of this attitude. In their aims they replace individual upward mobility by group (class) upward mobility.

It is, in the main, the older workers who vote Conservative or Liberal. Conservative voters are on the average older than Labour voters: 47 per cent. of the over fifties vote Conservative compared with 31 per cent. who vote Labour; 45 per cent. of Conservative voters are over fifty compared with 26 per cent. Labour voters. The average age of manual Conservative and Liberal voters (male household heads only) is also high: 46 per cent. in this group are over fifty compared with 32 per cent. in the sample analysed (549 male heads of households) and 26 per cent. among Labour manual voters. Furthermore, of retired manual workers half as many again vote Conservative or Liberal as vote Labour (35 Conservative or Liberal, 23 Labour).

Women tend more often to be Conservative than do men: 41 per cent. are Conservative compared with 38 per cent. Labour. Furthermore, 56 per cent. of Conservative voters are women compared with 45 per cent. of Labour voters. The tendency for women to be traditionally minded is one which recurs and which is discussed in Chapter 7, p. 136. The close connexion between the trade union and the Labour Party adds to its male bias for the world of the trade union in Banbury is a man's world.[1]

[1] There was a belief current at the time of the schedule inquiry that the Labour Party had lost the support of numbers of housewives because of continued rationing and a rising cost of living

But while a traditional social attitude leads its holders in all classes to a Conservative political attitude, it does not follow that non-traditionalism leads to socialism. This is only true in the working class. Both traditionalists and non-traditionalists in the middle class, in common with traditional workers, look upon individual effort as the means to a change of status. Both groups oppose the socialist policies of the Labour Party. For the most part they are Conservative. This is particularly true of the non-traditionalists. It is among the traditionalists that the division, so closely connected with religion, into Conservative and Liberal is found. The disparity of attitude and interest, for example, between the small-scale traditional proprietor and the large-scale, non-traditional manager, which was demonstrated in the previous chapter, is obscured by a common opposition to the Labour Party and its policies. But the differences between them are reflected in their attitudes to conservatism. For the traditionalist the expression of individualism and enterprise implies small-scale informal economic organization and maximum freedom from State interference. The non-traditionalist, himself accustomed to and probably involved in large-scale organization, is prepared to accept some forms of State intervention, so long as they are in his economic and personal interests, and is prepared to accept and deal with trade unions to an extent that the traditionalist is not. But, in terms of their party allegiance, the common social and economic interests and values of the owner and manager are paramount.

Nevertheless, as the previous chapter indicated, the immigrant non-traditionalist, whose horizon extends beyond Banbury, plays little part in the general social life of the town. Politics are no exception to this rule. The middle-class non-traditionalists, and particularly those of the highest occupational status, support conservatism, but they rarely seek office in the town Association or on the Council.

By no means all traditionalists are Banburians, but there is some correlation here. Both Conservative and Labour votes reflect the proportions of Banburians and immigrants found in the total population. But it is interesting that eight of the twelve members of the Conservative Association committee are Banburian. Half of the Conservative councillors are Banburian. This proportion reflects the distribution of Banburians and immigrants in the town as a whole, but is higher than the proportion of Banburians in the middle class, the class from which the Conservative councillors are drawn.

The Labour Party is not only non-traditional to the town, but most of its active members are immigrants: nine out of eleven Labour Party committee members and six out of eight Labour councillors are immigrant.

Banbury is, therefore, divided into two evenly balanced political camps: Conservative and Liberal on one side, composed of middle- and working-class traditionalists[1] and middle-class non-traditionalists; on the other side, the Labour Party composed of working-class non-traditionalists. From a right-wing point of view the division is seen as the struggle between the socialists, represented by the Labour Party, and the 'anti-socialists', represented by the Conservatives and Liberals. From a left-wing point of view, it is between Labour and Tory—'they (non-Labour voters) are all Tory really'. This biased use of language ('Tory' and 'socialist' are both used as terms of abuse) is interesting as an indication of the emotions involved. Labour speakers nearly always refer to the Conservative Association—and often the Liberal party as well—as the 'Tory party' and the Conservatives to the Labour Party as the 'Socialist party'. The issues between the two groups are serious and the rift deep.

The issues do not touch the method of government, they are those found elsewhere in the country: issues of economic management, who shall run the country and in whose interest, whether and how markets, prices, and wages shall be controlled. They are the issues that lie between sectional interests, between employer and employee, richer and poorer. But not only these: they are also issues between the traditionalist and the reformer, between an individualist and a collectivist or statist attitude.

The effects in voluntary activities of the differences between these last two sets of attitudes may be seen in Charts VII and VIII which show the activities of Conservative, Liberal, and Labour leaders in the town. Leaders are here defined as those who are members of political party committees. In the charts one line is drawn between a party committee and another committee for each person who serves on both committees. While Conservatives and Liberals engage in social services run by voluntary associations, Labour leaders are only found on officially sponsored social services agencies: the advisory committees attached to the social service Ministries, the County

[1] The position of the Liberal working class is less clear than that of the Liberal middle class. The latter are almost wholly 'anti-socialist'. The former in some cases incline to the Labour Party: the Labour Party owes part of its slight chapel connexions to some ex-Liberals. The Liberal tradition in the working class has elements in common with the non-traditional Labour Party not possessed by middle-class liberalism.

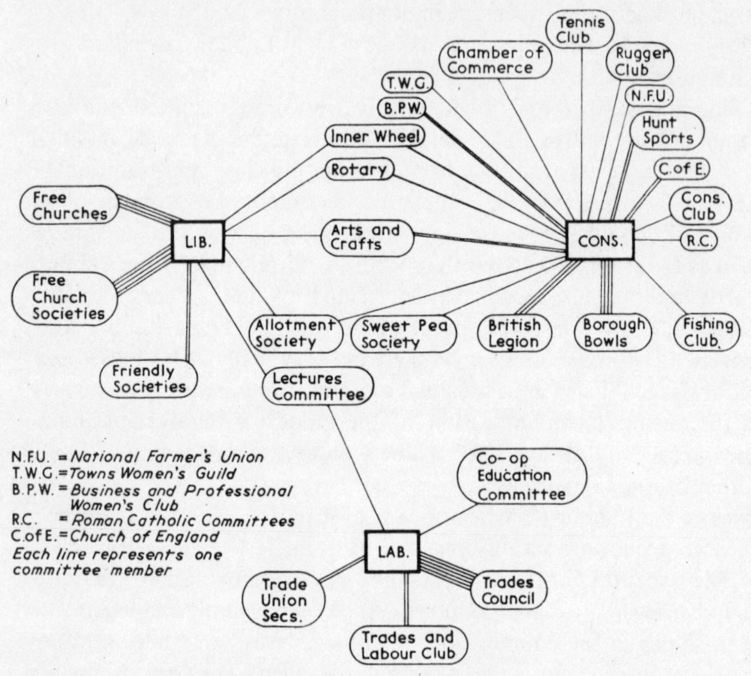

CHART VII. The Social Isolation of Labour. Connexions between Political Party Committees and other Committees

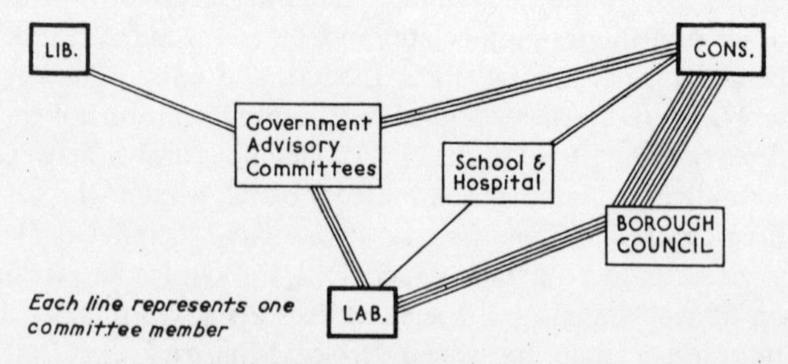

CHART VIII. The Political Isolation of the Liberals. Connexions between Party Committees and Government, Administrative, and Advisory Committees

Council sponsored Youth committee, and so on. They are not on committees like those of Rotary social service and the Old Charitable Association. It is part of the individualistic attitude, which is associated in politics with conservatism, that people have a responsibility to help their 'less fortunate brethren' and should perform individually or in groups acts of service for or charity to others. (See section on charity in Chapter 4, pp. 67–68.) Labour supporters do not accept this attitude. They object to the traditional class system and the charity and patronage traditionally associated with it. They are not willing to see their fellow men suffer and are willing to do voluntary work to prevent or overcome such suffering. But they do this voluntary work in the Labour Party or trade union with the aim of modifying the traditional social structure, improving the lot of the working class, or of the workers in a particular firm or industry. Where immediate ameliorative action is needed for someone in distress, they prefer to take this action either among themselves or through official social service agencies. They do it among themselves through mutual-aid organizations or less formally through, for example, the factory 'whip round'. No worker would have the resources to help the distressed man single-handed, but by collective action the workers prevent 'their own' falling under patronage. It is for this same reason that they prefer the official agencies which, in their opinion, do not savour of 'charity' as they feel the voluntary bodies do.

While Banbury reflects the national issues between the two great parties, in the relatively small scale of a country town the depth, and indeed the bitterness, of its effects upon personal relations is sharply seen. There is a hatred of the 'boss class' on the side of the Labour supporters which was born of their experience of short time, low pay, unemployment and the dole, and of the indignities of their economic and social status. These hard feelings are found in many parts of the country. In Banbury it is the immigrant industrial workers who express them most strongly. One tells that his father was blacklisted by the employers for trade-union activity: he was therefore unable to get work. He died of T.B. Our informant attributes his father's early death to the years of unemployment he suffered. Another immigrant worker told how his family had been broken up and the children put into foster homes because he had been unemployed and houseless for years in the depressed area from which he had come. In Banbury itself the trade union members in the aluminium factory in the 1930's had to hold their meetings in secret for fear of victimization by the management. (During the 1939–45 war the trade union was recognized and relations between it and the management are now good.)

The 'anti-socialists' also (and here one speaks of the more well-to-do) are suspicious and, rather than being resentful of the past, are afraid for their future. This becomes an extreme antagonism in the case of the gentry who feel that they are living at the end of an era. They can no longer pass on inherited wealth to their children in sufficient amount to maintain the status and privilege previously enjoyed by their class. They see their estates broken up and their homes demolished or sold. They blame the Labour Party for this state of affairs.

In the town itself the Conservative and Liberal leaders and their associates received a profound shock when a Labour Government was returned in 1945 and not long after their Borough Council almost became Labour-controlled. (Aldermen and councillors were equally divided between the parties.) Two wars and a certain amount of social reform legislation had already reduced the once secure position of the middle class. The 'socialists' as persons were for the most part quite unknown to them, they thought of them as 'upstarts' and 'foreigners'. In 1945 the 'socialists' had taken political power and were taking economic power from its traditional holders. They increased the power of the State and reduced the economic power of the individual. The 'anti-socialists' saw the traditional assumptions, upon which they had always lived, successfully challenged and foresaw their whole way of life crumbling around them.

This was emphasized by the attitude taken up to this survey and the form that resistance took. A 'social' survey was thought somehow to be 'socialist' and to be connected with the (then) socialist government. Not only this: the survey was known to have some connexion with the Workers' Educational Association in the town. Because this association is prefixed 'Workers', many believe (quite mistakenly) that it has a formal connexion with the Labour Party. The protestations of the field-workers that their survey was quite independent of any political connexion, left wing or other, went unheeded. This form of resistance is perhaps analogous to the accusations made against social anthropologists in primitive societies when they are accused of 'eating up the land'. Land in these societies is the means of life. So the proprietors in Banbury expressed their resistance to the survey by identifying it with socialism, the threat to their livelihood just as much as loss of land threatens the livelihood of the tribesman.[1]

The nature of the rift between the two political sides is illustrated by the way in which representatives who do not know each other personally, and they rarely do, speak of each other: 'Just look at old Smith, he's about 80 and he's only got a small bakery. What does he know about running the town or what the ordinary people need? Only wants to line his own pocket, he does.' So said a Labour Party man of a Conservative alderman, a Banburian who was in fact only sixty or so, and not remarkable for his wealth. 'Who is this Bob Jones, anyway? Is he the man that's caused all this trouble with the unions? Nothing more than an upstart and an ignoramus, coming here from Coventry and telling us how to run the town.' (A middle-class Conservative woman speaking of a Labour Party official who had been on the Council long enough to be scheduled as the next Mayor.)

Although Labour supporters, unlike middle-class Conservative supporters, overtly look upon the division between the parties as a 'class' issue, they expect a number of manual workers to be Conservative. Nevertheless, they despise and distrust them, particularly if they are not in a trade union or if their loyalty to their union in a crisis is doubted. One union official reckoned these people do not know 'which side their bread is buttered', and he was bitter because he thought they might 'black leg' in a strike. Conservatives, on the other hand, are less overt about the class issue, they object to the Labour Party 'always bringing class into it'. But they do not expect men in positions of responsibility in the professions, trade, industry, or commerce, and particularly proprietors, to be Labour supporters. Their expectations are usually justified. Nationally, 'middle-class socialists' are found particularly among the 'intellectuals'. There is marked absence of this group in Banbury. When the middle class do come across a member who is a Labour supporter they are surprised and shocked. They avoid social relations with the recalcitrant. When they cannot, as with one who is both a near relative and a business associate, considerable embarrassment is caused. The author was

[1] The defensiveness which resulted from this resistance sometimes led to absurd positions, as in the case of the man who refused to tell an interviewer his politics although he had recently stood as an official party candidate. Even more absurd was the refusal on the part of some organizations to give information about their members for fear that the Communists might come to power—there were two Communist party members of Parliament before 1950 and none thereafter—get hold of the lists, and persecute the members.

present in a house on the eve of a poll when such a man, a Labour supporter, was visiting his relatives. It was impossible to keep politics out of the discussion altogether, it was in the front of everybody's mind, and the awkwardness of the situation was only got round by a good deal of joking and backslapping.

Indeed, our observation was that whenever political opponents happen to meet socially, if politics is mentioned the only possible technique is the joking one: no serious or 'ordinary' discussion is possible. Feelings run too high. In general, politics are little discussed 'across the line'. 'No religion, no politics, good comrades all'—so runs one Banbury club motto.[1]

But, generally speaking, cross-party encounters only occur within the working class, for middle-class Conservatives rarely meet (working-class) Labour supporters except in some formal, usually economic, relationship: they do not spend their leisure time together for their interests and the pattern of their lives are different (see Chapters 5, 6, and 8). They meet only in certain formal circumstances, for example round the table at one of the officially sponsored committees, and here numbers are carefully balanced: an equal number of employers' and workers' representatives and a few independent members. Numbers must be carefully balanced because of the amount of suspicion each side feels for the other. They are willing to work together in these carefully controlled circumstances.

Representatives of the two sides also come together in the Council chamber and on Council committees, where they sit as democratically elected representatives of the town. Both sides are prepared to accept this situation for both, despite their disagreements, believe in the principles and practices of parliamentary democracy. They would unite against any serious threat to it as they did in the Second World War.

This common agreement, the well-known electoral techniques of democracy, and the taboo on discussing political questions outside the political arena, make it possible for two such opposed groups to

[1] This observation is in direct opposition to one made by Mogey at Oxford (J. M. Mogey, *Family and Neighbourhood* (O.U.P. 1956)). He found, as we did, that religion was avoided as a subject for discussion, but reports in contrast (p. 147) that groups in the Snookers Rest enjoyed talking politics, although he points out (p. 149) that the subject is generally avoided at home. In our observation the taboo may be lifted among intimates who enjoy a high degree of social ease. It is possible that the groups he observed enjoying talking politics would come under this heading. But they do appear to have different party allegiances, even though they have the same (working-class) social background.

live and work together without violence. To these are added other social and political techniques. For example, parliamentary election campaigns appear to perform a most vital function of the 'safety-valve' variety. They provide a licence to say in public about a political opponent or his policies what it is otherwise taboo to say. In local elections the taboo still holds: it is still not permissible to say what one really thinks of one's political opponent (after all, one may have to work with or for him tomorrow). 'Blowing off steam' at local elections only occurs when politics at national level are introduced into the campaign. In this case there is licence as in parliamentary campaigns.

Furthermore, the operation of the democratic system itself tends to soften the acute differences between the parties. When political opponents find themselves together as councillors, particularly when doing hard and complicated work on committees, they are often surprised that the man on the 'other side' is, after all, human, quite capable, and even tolerable. Not that they become personal friends nor that they pull their punches at the next election, but there is a marked softening of attitude on both sides.

Outside the Council chamber the differences between the parties locally appear to be greater and more bitter and both parties to express themselves more extremely than they do at Westminster. The centrifugal effect upon the parties of sitting in the House is well known and comparable to the effects observed in Banbury of sitting on the Council. But the local party supporters do not sit at Westminster, they do not have to carry out policies at national level, nor to make workable face-to-face relationships with members of the opposition as do members of Parliament and national party leaders. They are personally involved only indirectly. There are no forces to modify the extremeness of their views about national policies. Looking at national politics through the eyes of Banbury, therefore, almost certainly gives the impression that there is more difference, and particularly more bitterness, between the two great parties than appears at national level.

Locally, beneath the taboos, the issues remain profound. They are the views of two groups of people who rarely meet on the social level. They contain the differences of economic interest between management and worker, the differences in attitude between the individualist and the collectivist or statist, the traditionalist and the non-traditionalist, and, to a lesser extent, the active and the passive Christian.

These are differences about which values are the important ones to emphasize in social organization and behaviour. They are closely connected with the acceptance or rejection of the traditional class structure. To a marked extent, therefore, the political divisions in Banbury are drawn from and underline differences of economic and social status and differences of social class. That the political division is not a pure class division is largely due to the influence of traditionalism.

4

RELIGION IN BANBURY

CHRISTIANITY is undisputed in Banbury in the sense that there is no organized opposition to its doctrines and no organized non-Christian religion. There is, for example, no noticeable Jewish community and there is no Synagogue. There is no branch of the Rationalist Society nor other 'free thinking' organization. Furthermore, in replies to a question about religion in the sample inquiry, only 3 per cent. said they did not belong to any Christian denomination. Of these only one in five (0·6 per cent. of the total) professed themselves agnostic or atheist. The remainder merely said 'no denomination'. This may in some cases imply a positive religious belief, but disagreement with attending a special place of worship, or it may be a cover for agnosticism.

Furthermore, so complete is the assumption of the rightness of Christianity that people who do not attend church[1] (with the exception of the convinced agnostic or atheist) feel that they 'have left undone what they ought to have done'. When, in an attempt to measure the respective numbers of active and passive believers, interviewers asked a respondent whether he attended a place of worship, they were faced with the problem of deciding whether he was telling the truth. Even allowing for the fact that a man who went to church at Christmas or Easter only was classed as an attender, it is certain that interviewers gave too many respondents the benefit of the doubt.[2]

But although almost everyone counts himself Christian, religious matters are rarely discussed (apart from teaching and preaching in church and school). It is taboo (except among the very few disbelievers) to question the validity of Christian doctrine. On a few occasions the field-worker succeeded in discussing the subject with people in Banbury and district. In every case it was the field-worker who opened the subject and who kept it going. He found that if he

[1] 'Church' is used to cover all places of worship.

[2] Six of the ten interviewers made 'attenders' outnumber non-attenders by about 2:1, three made attenders and non-attenders about equal, and one made non-attenders outnumber attenders by 3:2. No such wide variations were found in replies to other questions. Mogey, op. cit., p. 147 and footnote, doubts the veracity of his Oxford informants on this subject.

questioned a central theme of Christian belief—that Jesus Christ was the incarnation of God and that His teachings therefore have divine authority—he was reminded that the Bible is now known to be historically accurate (in other words that Jesus was a real and not a mythical character); or he was asked 'But don't you believe in God?'; an alternative response, which also avoided the question, was: 'But surely you believe in a future life?'

It is equally 'not done' to question the strength of a person's belief. When the field-worker persisted in asking 'Are you a Christian?' respondents were embarrassed and suspicious, and frequently demanded: 'Do you mean you are not a Christian?'. For in Banbury even those who 'don't bother' with religion (i.e. who do not go to church) regard it as an accusation if it is said of them that they are not Christians.

The taboo on religious discussion is, furthermore, a social technique to avoid friction and to aid the accepted principle of tolerance among divergent religious beliefs. There are no less than 13 differently named religious groups and two of these, the Baptists and the Christian Brethren (Plymouth Brothers), are divided among themselves. Altogether, therefore, there are fifteen kinds of Christian belief and forms of worship represented by Christian denominations and sects in the town. Each has its own interpretation of the meaning of Christianity. Such differences remain unspoken. It is 'not done' to discuss belief with a member of another denomination. On the rare occasions when spontaneous discussions on religious matters were heard among Banbury people, they were confined to members of one denomination. For example, the field-workers have heard Anglicans discussing the 'popery' of High Churchmen. Except among intimates and those of common persuasion, religion and politics, both sources of profound disagreement, are taboo subjects. As the club motto (p. 54) had it, 'No religion, no politics, good comrades all.'

Table 14 shows how people in the town are divided among the denominations. Six main denominations were distinguished: Church of England, Roman Catholic, Methodist, Baptist, Salvation Army, Congregationalist. Other denominations and sects were grouped together because of smallness of numbers; they include Presbyterians (who have no Church of their own in Banbury and usually attend the Congregationalist Church), Unitarians, Society of Friends (Quakers), Christian Brethren (Plymouth Brothers), Four Square Gospellers, Jehovah's Witnesses, and Christian Scientists. Those who returned

TABLE 14*

Distribution of Denominational Adherents and Church Members in Banbury; Comparison with England and Wales

	Banbury						England and Wales†	
	Adherents		Members					
	1	2	3	4	5	6	7	8
Denomination	Nos. in sample	Col. 1 as % of sample population	Church members	Denominational % of church members	Church members as % of adult population	Church members as % of denominational adherents	Denominational % of church members	Church members as % of adult population 1950
Church of England	1,544	67·6	1,040	45·6	9·6	13·5	43·9	10·0
Methodist	270	12·0	448	19·7	4·1	33·2	10·4	2·4
Roman Catholic	230	10·0	560§	24·6	5·2	48·7	28·2	6·4
Baptist	53	2·3	90	3·9	0·8	34·0	4·3‖	1·0‖
Salvation Army	37	1·6	72	3·2	0·7	38·9	..	..
Congregational	15	0·7	68¶	3·0¶	0·6¶	..**	3·2	0·7
Total, excluding other denominations	2,149	94·2	2,278	100·0	21·0	20·7††	..	..
Other denominations‡	66	2·9	Not available		..	..	9·9	0·8
Total denominational adherents	2,215	97·1	..	..	..	..	100·0	22·9
No denomination	52	2·3	..	..	..	..	..	..
Agnostic and atheist	13	0·6	..	..	..	..	..	..
Total in sample	2,280	100·0	..	..	..	..	..	..

* Percentages do not always total 100·0 because of rounding.
† This part of the table is taken from John Highet, 'Scottish Religious Adherence', *Brit. J. Sociol.* iv. 2, 146, table II.
‡ 'Other denominations' include Presbyterians, Unitarians, Quakers, Christian Brethren, Four Square Gospellers, Jehovah's Witnesses, and Christian Scientists.
§ This is an estimate of adult members from a return of 285 households within the Borough boundaries.
‖ The Salvation Army is here included with other denominations.
¶ Presbyterians attend the Congregational Church and are included in the list of church members.
** Since Presbyterians were not counted with Congregationalists in the sample but are included as church members, this figure cannot be calculated.
†† Excluding Congregationalists.

'no denomination' are here listed separately from those who returned 'agnostic' or 'atheist'. Col. 1 in Table 14 shows the number of respondents recorded in the sample as adherents of each of the groups. Col. 2 shows these figures as percentages of the total sample population.

'Adherents' is used here to include both active and passive members of a denomination. Wide variation is found in the closeness of adherence. At one extreme are those who only enter a church for baptism or dedication, marriage, and funeral, and some less often than that. At the other end are those who attend at least weekly and play an active personal role in church affairs. Between are ranged those who attend more or less often than at the great festivals of the Christian year. (Congregations are particularly larger than average at Christmas and Easter.)

Church membership has, therefore, been taken as the only practicable index of the active as opposed to the passive adherent (since some were not honest about their degree of activity). The meanings and implications of church membership and the methods of compiling the lists vary from one denomination to another. But there are, in all denominations, a number of people who are regarded as members of a particular church within a denomination. One may, for example, have been confirmed into the Church of England but not be a member of a particular parish church, or have been baptized in the Baptist Church but not be a member of any chapel. Lists of church members were obtained from parish electoral rolls, or from priests, ministers, or clerks. They form what each church or chapel understood to be its membership. The numbers of such members of each of the six main denominations are shown in col. 3 of Table 14, and col. 4 shows their distribution on a percentage basis. Cols. 7 and 8 show comparable figures for England and Wales.

The Church of England, the established Church, has by far the largest number of adherents and also the largest number of church members; but while two-thirds of all adherents are Anglican, less than one-half of all church members are, a figure similar to that for England and Wales.[1] Among active adherents, therefore, the predominance of the Church of England is less marked than among adherents in general. Part of the explanation of this is almost certainly that, for reasons of social convenience, some who in effect belong to the small number (3 per cent.) who admit they have no denomination say 'C. of E.' in answer to any question about religious adherence.

[1] John Highet, op. cit.

Adherents of the Free Churches amount to less than 20 per cent. of the total, but they have 30 per cent. of the total of church members—a similar figure to that for England and Wales. However, in Banbury Methodist members more heavily outnumber the other Free Churches than in England and Wales. 19·7 per cent. of church members in Banbury are Methodist compared with 10·4 per cent. in England and Wales.[1] But since in terms of their social interaction it is Free Church adherents as a group who are important, no particular weight has been attached to this difference: that is to say, the differences between the Free Churches and the Church of England and between them and the Roman Catholic Church are marked; in contrast the differences among the Free Churches are slight. There is, for example, fairly close interaction between the Baptists and the Methodists.

The Roman Catholic Church is the third largest in terms of the number of its adherents, with 10 per cent., but in terms of church members it comes second; nearly one-quarter of all church members are Roman Catholics, a total slightly lower than the national estimate of 28 per cent.[2]

The Salvation Army is large enough in Banbury to be listed separately. It has almost as many members as the Baptist Church. The 'Army' was active among unemployed workers in the depression of the 1930's and was directly responsible for bringing several groups of unemployed people to Banbury when the aluminium factory opened. It retains a proportionately large number of adherents in the town as a result.

The proportionate sizes of the denominations listed in Table 14 do not reflect the proportionate sizes of the congregations seen in the town churches. Some of the Churches draw their congregations from the Borough or from a part of it, while others draw from a wide area round about as well. This is particularly true of the Roman Catholic Church, whose congregation is so large as apparently to belie the figures, but in fact its parish includes a wide area outside the town.

The separateness of the Christian denominations in Banbury is reflected in the lack of contact or co-operation among them. There is a 'Clergy and Ministers' Fraternal' which is composed of Anglican

[1] John Highet, op. cit.

[2] The Roman Catholic figures are an estimate from a return of 285 households, for the Roman Catholic Church does not count its members in terms of individuals. Highet (op. cit.) has had to estimate the national figures in a similar manner.

priests and Free Church ministers. In practice it is rare for an Anglican to attend, so that the 'Fraternal' is nearly confined to the Free Churches. One Free Church minister was of the opinion that the Anglicans did not want to co-operate; another concurred with this view when he said: 'The non-conformist churches (i.e. the Free Churches) work very harmoniously together; they feel very much the present Anglican vicar's attitude who won't have anything to do with us.' However, the minister first mentioned said that 'there is little co-operation here compared with other places' and included co-operation among the Free Churches in this when he said: 'There's no Free Church Federal Council in Banbury.' There is no united service in the town—even of Protestant denominations, quite apart from Roman Catholics—on Armistice Day nor on any other national or religious occasion. Attempts, for instance, to bring all or most of the Protestant Churches together for the carol service round the tree in the Market Place at Christmas time did not in fact succeed in combining all the denominations.

Any co-operation among the denominations does not include the Roman Catholics. The priests do not belong to the 'Fraternal'. A typical reaction of Protestant priests and ministers when asked about co-operation with Roman Catholics was to say 'of course' it was impossible; one Free Churchman said: 'Oh, the Catholics, I don't include them.'

That co-operation should not be sought, or when sought should prove difficult, is perhaps not surprising, for the denominations diverge widely both in tenet and in organization. They are ranged according to belief about the directness of the relation of man to God and about the role of the clergy.

The difference is marked between the Free Churches, where it is considered that a man must interpret the scriptures for himself, and the Church of England, and to an even greater extent the Roman Catholic Church, where the clergy interpret the scriptures. This difference of emphasis about the role of the lay member is reflected both in the church service and in church organization. Those denominations which stress the importance of individual interpretation tend to be democratic and those in which interpretation is left to the clergy to be hierarchical. In the case of the Roman Catholics and the Anglicans, where priests are appointed to local churches by a higher authority, the appointment may not be to the liking of the local congregation. Banbury, which traditionally has many low churchmen, lies in a diocese whose Bishop (at the time of the survey) was a strong high churchman. He appointed high churchmen to all the Banbury churches. This led to a certain amount of ill-feeling: a number of people said they would not attend church 'while the present vicar is there', because they disapproved of the ritual: 'I can't stand all that bobbing up and down.' The Free Churches are more democratic. In some, including the Methodists, Baptists, Congregationalists, and Unitarians, the minister or pastor is elected by the congregation or appointed for a limited number of years. In others, including the Society of Friends, Christian Brethren, and a number of smaller sects, there is no clergyman.

In the services held in the more hierarchical denominations, in the Church of England and more particularly the Roman Catholic Church, the forms of service and prayers are set in a prayer book and the ritual uses fully charged symbols of sight, sound, and movement. The more democratic denominations, on the other hand, reject ritual of this sort; vestments and symbols are little used and prayers are often 'free' (not set in a prayer book). This follows from the emphasis placed upon a personal relationship with a personal God: 'Proclamation of the gospel and a personal response to it seem more important than institutional religion. They (Free Churchmen) stand for a high doctrine of the church as the company of believing men and women knit by the Holy Scriptures.'[1] The extent to which vestments and symbols are rejected by the Free Churches and to which the service is informal ranges fairly widely. The most complete rejection is found among groups like the Christian Brethren.

The amount of congregational participation in the service also varies with the degree of emphasis upon the individual; least apparent attention to and participation in the service was observed in the Roman Catholic Church (which had one of the highest attendance ratios in relation to the number of adherents and absolutely the largest congregations). More was seen in the chapels than in the Anglican Churches: 'You don't get the congregation singing out in church like you do in chapel.'

It must be pointed out that the intensity of participation increases as the size of the congregation decreases and that inattention would be more noticeable in a small group than in a large. But this mechanical explanation, while contributory, seems inadequate to cover the differences observed. Those denominations which emphasize the importance

[1] Introduction, *Who's Who in the Free Churches*, 1951.

of the personal element in religion apparently rely on an intense personal-congregational participation in the service as compared with the apparently less intense and less thinking, more routine, response to the more highly ritualized form of service.

The differences in organization and tenet between the Church of England and the Free Churches are associated with differences in the social background and social attitudes of their adherents. The Church of England draws members from the upper classes to an extent that the Free Churches do not.

In the Banbury district the gentry and aristocracy are usually Anglican; those who are not are Roman Catholic. The field-workers learned of none who is a member of the Free Churches. No members of the upper classes live within the Borough boundaries, but 21 per cent. of Church of England members are in occupational classes 1 and 2 (Hall/Jones scale) compared with 14 per cent. of Free Church members.

The differences of social status between members of the Church of England and the Free Churches can clearly be seen in their lay organization at national level. The monarch is the temporal head of the Church of England. Its governing body is closely associated with the aristocracy and the gentry. The 1954 edition of *The Official Year Book of the Church of England* shows that of 346 members of the House of Laity (one of the three houses of the National Assembly of the Church of England, elected from the Diocesan Conferences in 1950 in proportion to the numbers of persons on the roll) 39 were titled persons and 37 held the rank of Major or above (where persons held titles and service ranks they have been counted as titled). Together these two groups represent 23 per cent. of the House. In contrast to this the *Methodist Directory 1950* lists 820 lay members of committees appointed by the Methodist Conference of whom only 17 were titled and 6 held the rank of Major or above—3 per cent. of the total.

In the Introduction to *Who's Who in the Free Churches* (1951) the author, speaking of the Wesley brothers and of Whitefield, says: 'they were on fire for Christ and before long had kindled the flames of an enthusiastic personal religion in the hearts of thousands of their fellow countrymen, *particularly those of the lower orders*, though not solely among these . . . an organization centred in local fellowship'. (My italics.)

Historically the Anglican Church in Banbury has accepted and reflected the traditional class system. The main church in the town, St. Mary's, which is large enough to hold 2,000 and has an electoral roll of 730, was built at the end of the eighteenth century on the site of an earlier church dating from the twelfth century. It stands on the main north–south road dominating the old town, and up to the middle of the nineteenth century it served the whole town. At that date, soon after the opening of the iron foundry and the railway, the parish was divided. A new church, Christ Church, was built in South Banbury to serve the (then) new houses on the low ground between the north–south road and the canal and across the canal. This church was a bare three hundred yards from the old, but a new kind of social distance was developing and becoming more important than geographic distance: 'the pew rents were too high at St. Mary's', said an informant connected with Christ Church. At the same time a chapel of ease was built some 500 yards away in the opposite direction 'for the spiritual good of the poor of Neithrop', as the church record says.

As the town expanded two other churches were built. In 1891 the amount of building in Grimsbury on the east side of the river was thought to justify another chapel of ease, this time included in the parish of Christ Church (in 1921 Grimsbury became a separate parish). In 1933 the housing estate being built at Easington to the south-west of the town was provided with a church hall used for religious services on Sundays and for social functions on weekdays.

These latter two churches are three-quarters of a mile from St. Mary's and are in clearly defined and named districts of the town. Unlike the two mid-nineteenth-century churches they were built for geographic districts rather than for social classes. Nevertheless, the evidence of the electoral rolls (i.e. church members) suggests that virtually all those in the three highest occupational-status classes, who attend an Anglican church, ignore parish boundaries and attend St. Mary's regardless of where they live. The effect of this is not to segregate the classes altogether. The congregation of St. Mary's is not confined to the three highest occupational-status groups, since others attend there. But the effect is to confine the congregations of the other churches to the lower status groups. 'Our congregation', said one informant from Christ Church, 'is entirely artisan; they would never dream of going to the parish church' (i.e. St. Mary's). Checking this statement it was found that about thirty residents of the parish of Christ Church had their names on the electoral roll, not of Christ Church, their parish church, but of St.

Mary's. Twelve of the thirty were managers of ten or more men. The electoral roll of Christ Church itself contains no such names and has no one of higher occupational status than the owners of one- or two-man shops.

The Anglican acceptance of the traditional class system is further reflected in the tradition, still maintained in village churches in the Banbury district, that the owner of the great house should read the lesson at Matins. It is reflected also in the seating arrangements whereby the gentry sit in front and the working class behind. It is seen, too, in the assumption that members of higher social status have the right and, indeed, the duty to lead in the lay organizations of the Church, assumptions with which both leaders and led concur. This is particularly noticeable in the women's church organizations.

The Free Churches are also involved in the social class structure of the town. Among the Methodists, for example, there was, until twenty years ago, a division between Wesleyans and Primitive Methodists. This involved religious differences and also, it appears, social differences. 'The Prims', said one informant who was herself previously a Primitive Methodist, 'were the poor people and the Wesleyans were the middle class, the tradespeople; they [the Prims] were the less educated—more evangelical.' But in 1932 there was a union: in Banbury the Primitive Methodist chapel was sold and since that date there has been no division within the Methodist denomination. The four Methodist Church buildings are widely scattered and correspond to the distribution of the Anglican churches except that, unlike the Anglicans, the Methodists have only one church in the town centre. The numbers in the congregations are a good deal smaller than in the Anglican churches, but even in the smaller numbers there is the same tendency for people of higher occupational status to attend the central church and to disregard nearness. A member of the Grimsbury chapel recognized this status question: 'We're a mixed up lot', he said, 'no rich people, mostly artisans, not what you'd call working class; the factory workers [he meant workers at the aluminium factory] aren't touched by churches; we've got three or four teachers and shop assistants, not many of the professional classes, we've got the in-betweens.'

Furthermore, in Banbury the leaders of the Free Church lay organizations are often the same sort of people in terms of their social status as are the Church of England leaders. But their attitude to class is different. They consciously bear in mind that they are all members of one 'fellowship'. Those of higher social status may accept their duty to lead, but assume less a right to leadership: they recognize and act upon, but attempt to overlook, the status differences among them.

Details about the social background of members of the Roman Catholic Church in Banbury are not available to the author. However, it is known, that, unlike the Free Churches, they include members of the aristocracy. In the town the most significant fact about them is the large number of adherents in the lower occupational grades: over 90 per cent. of Roman Catholic adherents in the town are wage-earners (the figure for the town as a whole is 80 per cent.). It is, indeed, the only one of the large denominations in which there are proportionately more manual than non-manual workers. Non-Catholic informants describing the relationship between religious adherence and the social structure of the town tend to ignore Roman Catholics. When questioned they say that Roman Catholics are 'apart' or 'separate'. This is true in so far as Catholics tend to marry among themselves and to send their children to Catholic schools. It is also true that at the informal level they tend to have more friends of their own Church than of others. But Roman Catholics do play a part in the general life of the town. The point seems to be that as a group they are not related in any particular way to the traditional social structure. They have, for example, no particular connexion with any political party. Very few are Liberals, as the last chapter remarked, but the division of Catholic adherents between the two main parties follows social class lines and shows no religious bias at all. Nor are they particularly connected with any network of associations. This is partly because, as with the schools, organizations associated with the Church cater for a wide range of social activities.

Anglicans and Free Churchmen tend to stress different Christian principles for the conduct of everyday life. This is undoubtedly associated with history, with the differences of tenet and organization between them, and with the social status of their members.

The Anglicans value charity highly. By this is meant doing good to other people and especially to people in misfortune; it includes the giving and collecting of alms, social service, and voluntary public work. And Anglicans in Banbury are active in these respects. Chart V, p. 40, shows the connexions between voluntary social service and charitable associations and the Conservative Association committees and Church of England committees. While direct lines between the Church and other committees are not many, it is known that the majority of the people involved in that chart are members of the Church of England.

Free Churchmen also value and practise charity in this sense, but they emphasize rather more heavily the principle of brotherhood or fellowship. Connected with this is a network of values supporting the ideal of independence and self-improvement: thrift and self-denial, temperance and a strict attitude to sex relations; education as a means to self-enlightenment and social mobility; mutual aid developed in friendly societies such as the Rechabites in which the insurance principle is preferred to charity, thus avoiding a dependent status. Chart IV, p. 39, shows the connexion between the Free Churches and Mutual Aid Societies. Chart XI, p. 84, shows the connexion with cultural organizations.

These are not the only Free Church connexions. Free Churchmen share the charitable works with the Anglicans, but Free Churchmen of a higher social status.

All those committees on the extreme right of Chart IV, with the exception of the Lectures Committee, have an average occupational status of class 1 or 2 (Hall/Jones scale). That committee is mixed and all the remainder have a status of class 4 or 5. Members of the Liberal/Free-Church connexion of higher status join with members of the Anglican/Conservative connexion in 'good works' committees. Those of lower status are associated with the mutual-aid committees. That is to say the more well-to-do Free Churchmen lean further towards charitable works and in politics towards conservatism. This is what one would expect, since as resources increase so do security of independence and the ability to dispense charity.

Today Liberalism has declined and the work of the friendly societies has been taken over by the Ministry of National Insurance, but the secular lives of Anglicans and Free Churchmen still show marked differences, particularly among the middle classes, where the majority of active church-goers are found. The leisure-time lives of Free Churchmen and Anglicans overlap little as Chart XIII, p. 85, shows: Free Churchmen are more concerned with 'culture' and Anglicans with sport. Anglicans prefer clubs to have bars, Free Churchmen do not drink and in consequence 'club' less. Although made less overt, it seems that clubs like Rotary are as careful to balance Anglican and Free-Church groups as are government agencies to balance the 'two sides of industry'.

But the traditional division between Anglican/Conservative and

Free-Church/Liberal has been overshadowed by the political division between anti-Labour and Labour and between traditionalists and non-traditionalists. Organized religion in Banbury is part of the traditional social structure. It is not surprising therefore to find that the groupings into traditional and non-traditional and into Conservative and Labour are associated not so much with members of different denominations as with active and passive Christians.

Three-quarters of the population must be defined as more or less passive since, while 94 per cent. returned themselves as adherents of one of the six main denominations, only 21 per cent. are members of any church or chapel. A comparison of the characteristics of active and passive Christians (based on an analysis of church membership and the returns of the sample) showed that all groups from which active adherents (i.e. by definition church members) are drawn are groups which also show other traditional tendencies; and that the passive adherents are associated with groups which show non-traditional tendencies. Among active adherents the elderly outnumber the young; women outnumber men; natives outnumber immigrants; and non-manual workers outnumber manual workers.

Non-manual workers tend in Banbury as elsewhere to belong to associations more often than manual workers.[1] Religion is no exception to this. In the total population over 76 per cent. are manual workers while among church members analysed only 45 per cent. are. Manual workers, furthermore, more often admitted non-attendance at church to interviewers.

In Banbury tradition there are two kinds of connexion between the workers and organized religion: one is that of the Conservative working man who accepts both the Church and the traditional class system; the other, found not lower than the artisans, is of the Free-Church Liberal who accepts the class system in modified form and believes in a personal religion and the value of independence.

But the working class as a whole is much less involved in religious activity than the middle class. It is noteworthy that the campaign for Sunday cinemas, which was successfully conducted before the field-work began, was publicly supported by the trade unions in the town. Many in the working class have rejected the old order and are non-traditional. They reject the traditional class system with which

[1] See, for instance, T. Cauter and J. S. Downham for England (*The Communication of Ideas*, pts. i. iii, Chatto & Windus, 1954), and Lloyd Warner for America (*Democracy in Jonesville*).

organized religion is closely involved. The secularity of the Labour Party was remarked in the previous chapter.

An analysis by politics as well as by occupation shows that Conservative and Liberal voters of all occupational grades returned fewer non-church-goers than Labour voters. 36 per cent. of non-manual Conservatives and 43 per cent. of manual Conservatives said they did not attend church compared with 45 per cent. and 54 per cent. of non-manual and manual Labour voters respectively. Within the non-manual group those working in traditional industry admit to non-attendance at church less often (36 per cent.) than those in non-traditional industry (39 per cent.), and the same is true of the manual group (46 per cent. in traditional industry and 52 per cent. in non-traditional industry). Table 15 sets out this data.

TABLE 15

Non-Traditionalism and Non-Church-going

	Male household heads only			
	Conservative and Liberal supporters		*Labour supporters*	
	*Non-manual**	*Manual†*	*Non-manual**	*Manual†*
Non-church-goers	42	58	14	155
Church-goers‡	*76*	*78*	*17*	*132*
Total	*118*	*136*	*31*	*287*
% non-church-goers	36%	43%	45%	54%
	Traditional industry		*Non-traditional industry*	
	*Non-manual**	*Manual†*	*Non-manual**	*Manual†*
Non-church-goers	31	46	25	167
Church-goers‡	*54*	*55*	*39*	*155*
Total	*85*	*101*	*64*	*322*
% non-church-goers	36%	46%	39%	52%

* Hall/Jones 1–4. † Hall/Jones 5–7.
‡ Those who claimed to interviewers that they attended church.

The figures may be in part the result of the different attitudes engendered by traditional and non-traditional industry (see Chapter 2) and, as far as manual workers are concerned, may be associated with the greater hold that Labour has in non-traditional industry. They are also almost certainly associated with the fact that the proportion of Banburians in non-traditional industry is lower than that in traditional industry.

Fewer immigrants, it seems, go to church than Banburians. The immigrant, simply by moving away from the place in which he was brought up, has made one break with the ways of his childhood. He is, therefore, peculiarly liable to break with ways which are associated with a particular locality and a particular set of people, his parents among them. The habit of church-going seems to be of this order.

Many remarks were made during the course of the survey in support of this view. A typical example was the immigrant who said: 'I haven't been inside a church since I came to Banbury. I always used to go when I was at home and still always do when I go home on a visit.' Even more striking was the case of the woman who used to be an active Sunday school teacher and church committee member in her home town and who also confessed she had not been inside a church since she came to Banbury: 'I know I ought to go, but I don't seem to find the time somehow.'

Religious observance has a social as well as a personal importance. In an area where you are known as a church-goer you have, so to speak, a reputation to maintain and friends to meet at church. In a strange place there is no social reason to attend. It will not bring you into touch with a group of people to whom you feel you belong as it does in your home town. If, as in Banbury today, church-going is no longer a *sine qua non* of social acceptance, an immigrant's decision to attend church follows from religious conviction rather than from social habit or convenience.

The Banburian who remains active in his church or chapel is not only following a general English religious tradition, but a particular local tradition in which church and chapel and the people in them are bound together in the local traditional social structure; a social structure which embraces work, play, and politics as well as religion and in which an individual's withdrawal from one part would affect his relations in the other parts. It is a structure, moreover, into which the immigrant may, but need not, be drawn.

Furthermore, it is a tradition which appears to be shrinking in the religious as well as in the economic field. For the evidence is that the Churches are not recruiting active adherents from among the young people in very large numbers.[1]

[1] B. Seebohm Rowntree and G. R. Lavers, *English Life and Leisure: A Social Study* (Longmans Green & Co. 1951), chap. xiii, found this to be true of High Wycombe and York.

The ages of church members are not available, so that the characteristics of active adherents must be deduced from the evidence of the sample. Those who returned themselves as non-attenders have been taken as an indication of the minimum number of non-church-goers, i.e. passive adherents. They have been assumed to characterize non-church-goers as a group. The sample shows that significantly more people under fifty fail to attend church than would be expected from the age structure of the population as a whole. Active adherents have, therefore, been assumed to have a higher than average age.

In all cases where the sex of church members is known women outnumber men. The preponderance of women is most marked in the Methodist Church and least in the Church of England; the largest Anglican Church has a male: female ratio not widely different from that of the town as a whole. (The Roman Catholic Church cannot be analysed in this way—see footnote, p. 61.)

It was remarked in Chapter 3 that women have a tendency to traditionalism in politics and this tendency appears again in their greater attachment to religion. The reasons for this tendency will be discussed in Chapter 7. It is particularly noteworthy that women should be more active than men in the churches and chapels since women have a low status in church life. It would be fair to assume that those women who nevertheless are active accept the traditionally lower status of women as compared with men.

Organized religion holds its place in the official life of Banbury as it does elsewhere in the country. Banbury listens to religious broadcasts, teaches Christianity to its children in school, holds its annual Mayor's Sunday when the Mayor and Corporation attend divine service at the church of his choice. But its hold upon the daily and, indeed, the Sunday lives of the people is declining, although most people still call upon the Church at the domestic crises of birth, marriage, and death. There is certainly no religious revival as has been described for the United States by Norman Birnbaum.[1]

Banbury is not un-Christian; its people were careful to avoid any such title and felt guilty about their lack of religious activity. But they feel that religious and secular life should be kept apart. An illustration of this point comes from the case of the priest who, in trying to overcome the charge of unworldliness, visited and drank in public houses, behaving there as laymen behave. Some church-goers and some non-church-goers condemned his behaviour, the churchmen

[1] *The Listener*, 24 May 1956, p. 677, 'Religion in America'.

holding it unseemly that the Church should be represented in such places and the non-churchmen seeming to resent his presence as an intrusion into mundane affairs.

Banbury people are Christians who own to the denomination their parents gave them. But it would be difficult to obtain a clear account from many of the passive adherents of the main points of difference between the denominations. Their beliefs are frequently confused and vague. Many show some doubts about the miraculous features in Christian doctrine although they may incorporate selected items from it. Most usual, however, is the attitude 'I don't bother with it' or 'I don't see that it matters much anyway'.

On the other hand, many who expressed serious doubts about Christian beliefs, and even some who rejected them, said that they believed in Christian principles. There is little doubt that most people think of Christianity as the authority for morals. Many of these so-called Christian principles are not specifically Christian; they are shared by adherents of other religions and by humanists. That they should be called Christian is a measure of the extent to which Christianity is regarded as the source of morality.

In the trade-union movement, for instance, the principle of brotherhood is highly valued; in many unions the formal method of address between members is 'Brother'. While some trade-union leaders are devout church-goers, others are among the small number of avowed non-Christians whose values are based on rationalist and humanist grounds. Both sets of men act from a sense of dedication.

Organized religion remains strongest among those who are most closely associated with the traditional social structure of the town which supports and is supported by the churches and chapels. It is weakest among the less stable sections of the population: among those who have been geographically mobile and those who have adopted or are open to non-traditional ideas, supporters of the Labour Party and workers in non-traditional industry for instance.

Yet although active adherents lament what they feel to be the decline of religion, they do little to draw into their number members of these groups. The Churches have ancillary organizations connected with missions to overseas territories, but there are no 'missions to Banbury' (although some denominations are more evangelistic than others). In this respect active adherents are in a sense passive. The taboo on religious discussion, is, of course, a bar to home missionary activity. Belief and disbelief among the majority of the population is no less passive—it is merely a matter of 'not bothering'.

The frontiers of the traditional social structure and of religion within it are narrowing. Organizations based on non-traditional attitudes are increasing and so is a passive attitude to religion. If, as Norman Birnbaum has suggested,[1] England is due for a religious revival associated with an increased material standard of life (achieved by non-traditional techniques, one must add) there are no signs yet of its arrival in Banbury.

[1] Op. cit., p. 678.

5

VOLUNTARY ASSOCIATIONS

ONE hundred and ten formal associations were recorded in Banbury: 39 of these were connected with religious and political institutions and have been discussed in the two previous chapters; the remaining 71 voluntary associations are the matter of this chapter. They range from a sweet pea society to a rugger club, from university lectures to tropical fish keeping, from charitable organizations to trade unions.

For the purposes of this study voluntary associations have been defined as groups which have the following five characteristics:

(i) They are formal associations having some kind of constitution by which the affairs of the group are ordered;
(ii) membership is voluntary;
(iii) the qualifications for membership are determined by the members themselves;
(iv) the group has some continuity and is not convened merely for a special purpose or occasion;
(v) the group has some formal name by which it is known.

By definition, therefore, *ad hoc* bodies, sets, cliques, and other informal associations are excluded from consideration here.[1] Among the excluded groups are: the committee raised specially to get money for repairs to the church; the groups of men and women meeting regularly for 'elevenses'; the 'regulars' who 'belong' to the sixty-odd pubs and form a nucleus for their darts teams and thrift clubs and who justify abundantly the licensees' dictum that 'the pub's the club'; the band of collectors whom the representatives of the national charity organizations can call on to help with a house-to-house collection.

The 71 associations which are considered here have been divided for purposes of analysis into eight categories:

1. *Sport*. This covers bowls, cricket, football, tennis, cycling, golf, sailing, squash rackets, and table tennis.
2. *Hobbies*. These cover a wide range, from pigeon racing and

[1] Informal groups based on the neighbourhood are dealt with in Chapter 6.

coarse fishing, through the allotment, fanciers, and sweet pea societies to old-time dancing, chess, and tropical fish keeping.

3. *Cultural.* These include art and musical societies, adult education, amateur dramatics, and non-party political organizations such as the United Nations Association.
4. *Social.* In this category are some clubs with their own premises and facilities for billiards, table tennis, darts, and cards; and societies without premises whose main function is to provide a regular meeting for their members. The Townswomen's Guild is an example of the last type.
5. *Social Service.* A prime function of associations in this category is that members are called upon to fulfil some activity for the benefit of non-members. Rotary, Toc H, and St. John Ambulance are included.
6. *Charity.* These associations raise money for the benefit of non-members. Save the Children Fund and Wireless for the Bed-ridden are examples.
7. *Mutual Aid.* In these associations members band together to insure themselves against personal misfortune.
8. *Occupational Associations.* These include professional and staff associations and trade unions.

These eight categories are not rigid and in practice merge into each other.

In the analysis which follows there are inevitably some omissions. In the first place, although the list of associations is as complete as it could be made, it is probable that even more voluntary associations exist than are recorded. There is no register of voluntary associations in Banbury, so that a new-comer, wishing, for example, to join a racing pigeon club, must keep a look-out in the local paper, inquire of his neighbours whether there is such a club, and, if so, who is the secretary. He may even have to write to the national centre to which such a club might be affiliated to find out if it exists locally.

The associations recorded here include all those that were mentioned in reports, announcements, or advertisements in the local papers over a period of two years and include also a number that were not mentioned. But inevitably some associations have been overlooked, because their members, meeting for their own enjoyment and recruiting members from their own acquaintances, sought no publicity. These omissions are unlikely to be serious, for such associations are likely to have the character of the 'set' or 'clique' rather than that of the voluntary association.

Some omissions are more serious, much the most serious of which relate to the trade unions. Some unions are not allowed by their rules to divulge the names of members. This rule affects some of the most important unions in Banbury, such as the National Union of Railwaymen and the Transport and General Workers' Union. It was decided, therefore, not to include the results of analysing any separate union but to list the secretaries of all the unions as one association. Fortunately this shortcoming is considerably offset by the full information supplied about the Trades Council, a large body consisting of a number of delegates from most of the unions.

A second omission is that of the Freemasons, which is a secret society to which many of the leading citizens of Banbury belong. It is not included in the list which is analysed statistically, but a good deal is known about it and reference will be made to it later. Lastly, Group 6—Charity—represents only a small amount of the charitable work done in the town, since collecting is done on an *ad hoc* basis and therefore excluded by definition.

A study of voluntary associations shows chosen interests and chosen relationships: the type of interest for which people choose to associate and the social characteristics of those with whom they choose to associate. In other words, a man may choose to join a cricket club rather than a musical society because that is what he is interested in; and he may choose to join one cricket club rather than another because, he says, 'the members [of the second club] are not my sort' or because the club 'has not got a good atmosphere'. In short, he is looking, not only for an outlet for his interests, but also for the social comfort of mixing with those with whom he has most in common.

Voluntary associations have two characteristics which make them especially valuable as a guide to social structure and social behaviour. The first is that they are voluntary: a man joins freely and on his own initiative so that his choice expresses an active interest. This point was implicit in the discussion of active 'members' and passive 'adherents' of a denomination. The second characteristic is that in the main the associations are small and as a result they may be studied in some detail. This is valuable, since most of these associations are to some extent aligned with one or other of the religious/political groups which have been analysed in the two previous chapters. The greater detail obtained from the voluntary associations throws more light on these larger groups. In particular it helps to show the relationship between attitudes and values characteristic of political parties and religious denominations and those found in other spheres.

The first conclusion to be drawn from the analysis of the 71 associations is that membership has certain special characteristics: it is predominantly male,[1] middle-aged, and above-average occupational status.[2]

Men play by far the largest part in running the associations: 39 of the 71 are run by men only against 6 by women only; on the mixed committees men are in a majority on all except one, outnumbering women by nearly 3½ to 1. Table 16 shows the sex composition of the different types of committee.

TABLE 16

Men and Women on Committees

Type of assoc.	Men only committees: No. of committees	Men only committees: No. of members	Mixed committees: No. of committees	Mixed committees: No. of members M.	Mixed committees: No. of members F.	Women only committees: No. of committees	Women only committees: No. of members	Total committees	Total members
Sports	15	143	5	57	13	0	0	20	213
Hobbies	7	61	2	16	2	0	0	9	79
Cultural	1	4	8	57	20	0	0	9	81
Social	5	56	2	20	9	3	26	10	111
Social Service	4	42	2	14	3	2	19	8	78
Charity	1	13	2	12	9	0	0	3	34
Mutual Aid	3	27	2	19	9	1	11	6	66
Occupational	3	33	3	70	8	0	0	6	111
Total	39	379	26	265	73	6	56	71	773
Religious	5	26	16	118	79	6	30	27	253

It will be seen that sports, hobbies, and occupational associations are overwhelmingly male; that all categories have mixed committees but that on these mixed committees men are everywhere in the majority, the charitable group being the one in which women most

[1] W. Lloyd Warner and Paul S. Lunt, *The Social Life of a Modern Community* (Yankee City Series) (New Haven, Yale University Press, 1941), point out (pp. 305, 337) that while male adult associations are most numerous, in the three higher classes they define there are more women members, while in the three lower classes there were more men than women members. In no class in Banbury do women exceed men members.

[2] This has been noticed elsewhere, both here and in the U.S.A.: Cauter and Downham (op. cit., pts. i, iii); Yankee City, vol. 1, p. 329; *Jonesville*, op. cit., p. 117.

nearly approach parity; and that the 'women only' associations are centred in the social and social service groups. The figures for the religious associations have been put below the totals to show the very much higher proportion of women in them compared with the other voluntary associations. At the same time they serve to emphasize the concentration of women in social associations, since the fellowships, sisterhoods, and mothers' unions which make up the womens' religious associations are closely akin to a women's social association.

This strong bias towards masculine management and the width of masculine compared with feminine interests outside the home show again that the saying 'a woman's place is in the home' is also practised custom in Banbury. Chapter 2 showed how few married women work and Chapter 7 will show that women who work tend to follow occupations which are an extension of their home activities. So in their spare-time activities women tend to concentrate on those which involve meeting when the housework is finished and before the men get back from work. Only one of the 'women only' associations meets in the evening: it is the Business and Professional Women's Club, which in conception, as its name suggests, opposes the traditional attitude; not surprisingly the majority of its members are immigrant. Very few women go out in the evening or at the week-end on their own, whereas it is expected that men will do so. It is common to hear a man say that he has been out a good deal lately and that it is time he took his wife out for the evening: the assumption being that she is dependent on him for such outings. Management of the home is woman's work; outside interest and management of public affairs is men's.[1]

A word of caution should be added to these generalizations. Obviously there are many exceptions; and, moreover, attitudes change with age and status groups. Active participants in voluntary associations are predominantly middle-aged, so that the generalizations apply particularly to this group. Again there is little doubt that in the higher income-groups women are considerably more independent and may therefore take a more active part in affairs; with a car, a telephone, and perhaps some domestic help, they are less housebound.

[1] Here again the contrast with Yankee City is seen (Warner and Lunt, op. cit., p. 337): 'A few well-placed women at the top (of the social scale) who belong to an interlocking set of associations exercise great power in a community like Yankee City.' If women in Banbury wield power it is not through voluntary associations.

The second characteristic of voluntary associations was that their members are predominantly middle-aged. This is particularly true of committee members as Table 17 shows. Table 17 sets out the average age of committee members in each category of association. The great majority of associations are served by committees whose average age is forty to sixty; and indeed, apart from six sports clubs, only one association has a committee whose average age is less than forty.

TABLE 17

Age of Committee Members

No. in each type of Association	*Average age of committee members*								
	–29	30–34	35–39	40–44	45–49	50–54	55–59	60–64	65–69
Sports .	0	3	3	4	5	2	2	1	0
Hobbies .	0	0	0	1	3	4	1	0	0
Cultural .	0	0	0	3	4	2	0	0	0
Social . .	0	1	0	2	1	3	3	0	0
Social Service	0	0	0	1	3	4	0	0	0
Charity .	0	0	0	0	0	2	0	1	0
Mutual Aid .	0	0	0	0	0	1	3	2	0
Occupational	0	0	0	0	2	2	2	0	0
Total	0	4	3	11	18	20	11	4	0

In some societies this might suggest rivalry between the age groups showing itself in institutionalized segregation. In Banbury, however, it is the field-workers' experience that there is a widespread desire for more young members and that when they are found they are generally welcome. But even among the sports clubs, whose activities call for physical fitness, the age, often of the players themselves, is far beyond that at which people are at their physical peak. The explanation lies in the facts mentioned in Chapter 7 on the family. The great emphasis laid on the individual family and the importance of home-making means that in the early years of marriage and while the children are dependent, men and women find it more difficult to play a regular part in the kind of association which is discussed here. Nevertheless, while there may be no explicit rivalry, there are traditional influences at work to explain what is undeniable: that younger people rarely play much part in voluntary associations. Such of these as there are for adolescents are run by the middle-aged as a form of social service, often with an explicitly religious basis; there are no associations for adolescents run by and for themselves.[1] A field-worker was present when a group of eighteen-year-old girls in a day continuation class were discussing the absence of any girls' clubs in Banbury. All deplored the situation, yet when the field-worker suggested they should form one themselves the idea was laughed off as utterly fanciful; it was not for young people to form organizations and run them.

TABLE 18

Occupational Status of Committee Members (Hall/Jones Scale)

	Median status class of committee members							
Type of Association	1	2	3	4	5	6	7	*Total*
Sports	2	8	1	4	5	0	0	20
Hobbies	0	3	1	1	4	0	0	9
Cultural	0	7	1	1	0	0	0	9
Social	0	1	4	0	5	0	0	10
Social Service	0	5	1	1	1	0	0	8
Charity	0	0	2	1	0	0	0	3
Mutual Aid	0	0	0	5	1	0	0	6
Occupational	1	2	1	0	2	0	0	6
Total	3	26	11	13	18	0	0	71

The third special characteristic of voluntary associations is the relatively high social status of their members. Furthermore, the committee tend to have a higher social status than the membership. Table 18 shows the median occupational-status class of committees in the different categories. The largest single group of associations by a considerable margin is that with a median class of 2. This points to the fact that the higher occupational-status classes concern themselves with voluntary associations to an extent out of all proportion to their numbers. By contrast those in classes 6 and 7 are hardly ever found on committees: only 7 per cent. of all committee members are in these classes, against 35 per cent. of the employed population. Three points need to be made here. If each trade union had been counted separately the number of associations with a median of 5 would have been increased considerably; secondly, a large number of people in classes 6 and 7 participate in informal groups such as darts teams and thrift clubs which to some extent replace the formal association in lower-status classes; thirdly, people in these occupation

[1] Lloyd Warner reports for Yankee City (op. cit., p. 304) that although there is a variety of 'sub-adult' associations they are usually run by adults from related associations.

classes are present in larger numbers among the membership than on the committees. Despite these riders these groups are under-represented in both the leadership and the rank and file of formal associations in Banbury.

The relationship of the voluntary associations to each other and to the religious and political institutions was determined by mapping the links between them. Initially all known voluntary associations, the Borough Council, and government advisory committees were plotted on one map.[1] This revealed six groups of associations. Within

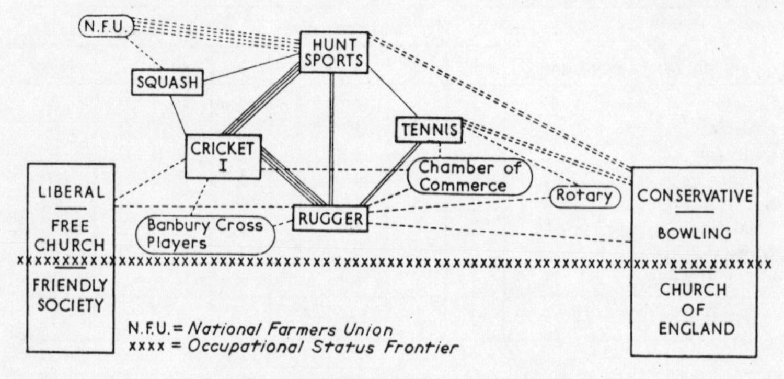

CHART IX. Sports I and its connexions

each group associations were closely connected with each other in the sense that they had committee members in common. Each of these groups of associations is reproduced as a separate chart (Charts IV to VI and IX to XI and the connexions between them are shown in Chart XIII).

Three of these groupings are major: the Conservative/Anglican/Bowling connexion (Chart V, p. 40), the Liberal/Free-Church/Friendly Society connexion (Chart IV, p. 39), and the Labour/Trade Union connexion (Chart VI, p. 41). Each of these connexions has a 'territory' of its own and a shared 'frontier' with one or both of the others. Sports I (Chart IX, above) and Sports II (Chart X, opposite) are important sub-groupings closely associated with the Conservative/Anglican/Bowling connexion: indeed they largely fall within its territory. The cultural connexion (Chart XI, p. 84) lies in a neutral zone between the other territories and is, with one exception, the Arts and Crafts Festival, much weaker than the number of lines involved

[1] See Appendix 4 for a fuller description of method.

would lead one to suppose. Chart XII shows the women's organizations, which fall within the Conservative and Liberal territories. (The Co-op. Women's Guild falls by our test into the Liberal/Free Church territory and not, as one might reasonably have expected, in the Labour territory.)

The absence of connexion between the Labour Party and religious or voluntary bodies was pointed out in Chapters 3 and 4, an isolation in part compensated for by official connexions as Chart VIII, p. 50,

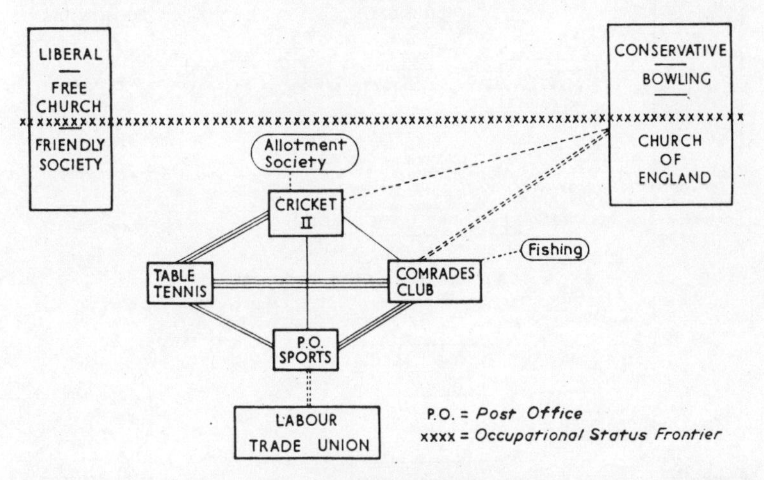

CHART X. Sports II and its connexions

showed. The isolation of the entire Labour/Trade Union territory is even greater than is shown on Chart VI: as the closely interlocking relationships within the territory suggest, active committee members are few in number and are found on two and often three of the component committees. For example, the three lines stretching out to the University Extension Lectures committee represent one man who is a trade-union secretary and a committee member of both the Labour Party and the Trades and Labour Club. Incidentally he rarely, if ever, attends the Lectures committee. Similarly one man is responsible for the two lines reaching to the sports club and one other for the two to the Co-op. Education committee.

The Labour/Trade Union connexion has two other characteristics besides its isolation. The first is that it is an immigrant group: Banburians are outnumbered 2:1. The second is that, as voluntary associations go, it is of low occupational status. Moreover, it has a narrow range of status: the median of the Labour Party committees is 4 and of each of the other three associations in the connexion, 5: the occupational-status class of an overwhelming number of individuals on all four committees is 5. These two facts, that it is an immi-

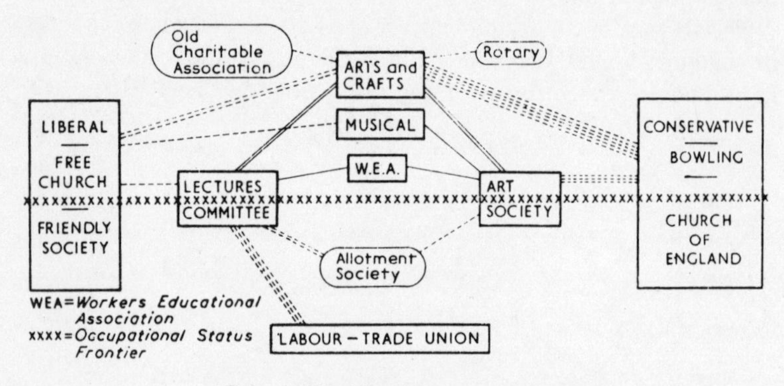

CHART XI. The Cultural connexion

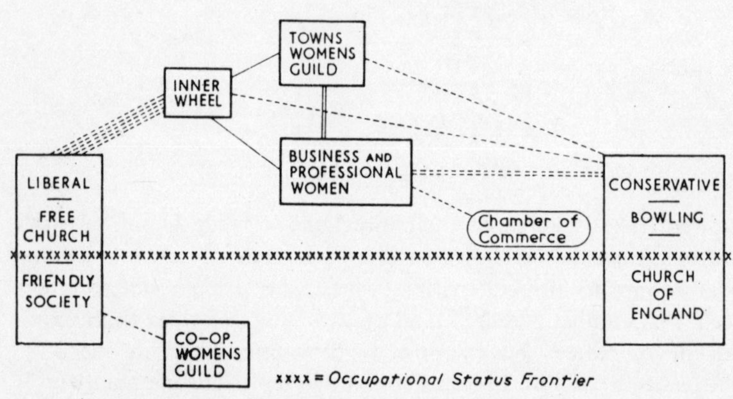

CHART XII. The Women's Clubs and their connexions

grant group and a working-class group, do not cause but do assist its isolation.

It is important to remember that isolation in this context does not mean that Labour Party supporters are not found in voluntary associations. It does mean, however, that, unlike Conservative and Liberal leaders, Labour leaders confine themselves to political activities. It is remarkable, for example, that in the wide field of sport, in which interest is almost universal and from which politics are reasonably easily excluded, only one man from Labour territory should be found. From the research workers' point of view it is satisfying to find that this man is a Banburian rather than an immigrant.[1]

It may perhaps be thought that the method adopted of regarding trade-union secretaries as one association gives a false impression,

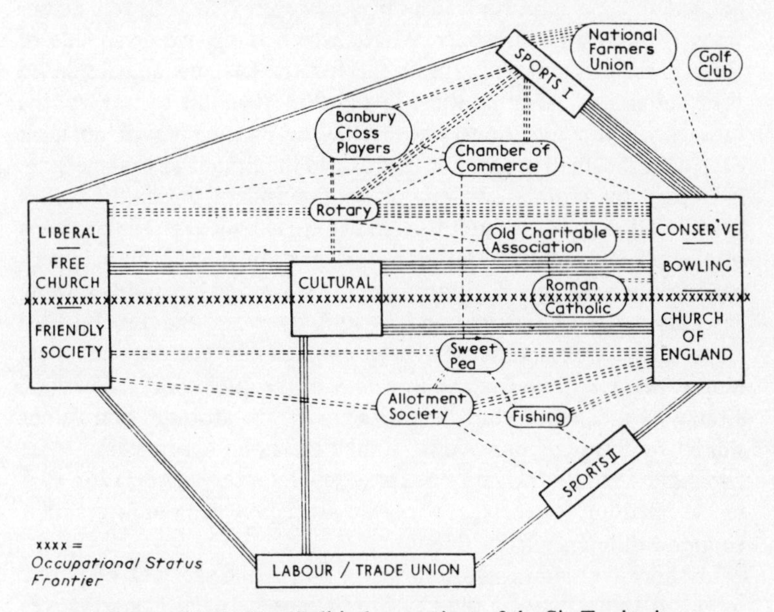

CHART XIII. Non-Political connexions of the Six Territories

that it selects only those trade-union representatives whose time is most occupied with trade-union matters and who are most dedicated to that sort of work. The field-worker concerned, however, does not believe this to be the case both from his knowledge of the individuals found on the various committees and also from the composition of the Trades Council, which is a large body widely representative of trade unions in the town.

The Liberal/Free Church connexion is also clearly defined and closely interlocked as Chart IV, p. 39, showed. The Liberals have no club of their own and little or no connexion with sport, those with cricket and rugger, i.e. the two connexions with Sports I, are provided by one man. Liberals consequently rely for 'the social side' on the

[1] Many Labour supporters, of course, follow the local works' football team.

women's fellowships and sisterhoods and the men's brotherhoods attached to the Free Churches.

Unlike the Labour/Trade Union connexion (whose points of contact with the Conservative/Anglican/Bowling connexion are in the State structure), the Liberal/Free Church connexion shares a long frontier among the voluntary associations with the Conservative connexion. It is important to notice, however, that with two exceptions (Rotary and the Inner Wheel, which is the women's side of Rotary) associations which lie on this frontier have no 'social side' to their activities. The committees involved meet simply to transact the business of the associations, whose rank-and-file members do not meet except for the small proportion who attend the annual general meeting.

Rotary, therefore, occupies a place of considerable significance, as Chart XIII suggests, even if its significance is limited to the relations of the higher occupational classes in the town. The club is self-conscious about this position, operating a taboo on politics while carefully balancing power in the club between the Liberal/Free Church and Conservative/Anglican connexions. The club takes its motto 'Service' seriously and is jealous of the quality of 'fellowship' among its members. Thus members emphasize attitudes and values shared by the two connexions. Unlike the Labour connexion these two hold that the private enterprise of voluntary association is a proper medium for social service—an attitude which reinforces their common difference from Labour.

In short, voluntary associations in which the element of public service is important are the key to relations between Conservatives and Liberals and occupy the frontier between these two 'territories'. When social activities are an important function of associations they tend to be either Conservative or Free Church. A not unimportant factor in this situation, as the previous chapter showed, is the Free Church emphasis on temperance: for a man who does not drink is liable to find himself 'out of things' in many associations which stress 'the social side'.

The Conservative connexion, despite its common frontier with the Liberal/Free-Church connexion, represents an extraordinary contrast both with it and with the Labour/Trade Union connexion. For it shows a diversity of interest and a range of status which the others do not approach: all categories of voluntary associations are touched.

The Conservative/Anglican/Bowling connexion itself is divided into two parts (Chart V, p. 40): the upper associated with the Chestnuts

Bowling Club and 'the parish church' (i.e. St. Mary's), and the lower with the Borough Bowls, the Conservative Club, and the British Legion. The upper group, which is composed of men prominent in the life of the town, is even more closely knit than appears in this chart. The chart shows no line connecting the Chestnuts with the Conservative Association. Nevertheless, the members of the Chestnuts are at least 90 per cent. Conservative and the committee contains three past Conservative Mayors and two Conservative Borough councillors. This is the part of the Conservative connexion which is closely associated with Rotary. In this group, too, come the Freemasons, who are not shown on the chart.

The second, lower, part of the Conservative connexion is not only closely interconnected, but also has strong links with three hobbies associations. All the associations in this part of the connexion have a lower occupational-status median than those in the upper part. Some wage-earners are found in these associations, but more frequently assistant managers of shops, some clerical workers, and owner-managers of small shops and businesses. It has no self-employed professional men or bank managers.

This division at the heart of the Conservative connexion is repeated in the two important sub-groups Sports I and Sports II.

Sports I (Chart IX, p. 82) is made up of the rugger, cricket, tennis, and hunting group. It is a distinctive group with close interconnexions. It has two features of importance. The first is the high proportion of committee members who live outside the Borough: for these are the associations through which neighbouring farmers are brought into contact with the formal social life of the town. The second feature of the group is its high occupational status. The farmers concerned have farms of above-average size, while many of the Borough residents who are on these committees are in business on their own account or are professional men. Here, again, the Freemasons are found. The group has more connexions within itself than it has with associations outside. The chart does not show close contacts with the Conservative connexion; those that exist are with the upper group. The chapter on politics noted that those of higher occupational status do not play an active part in local politics. But the overwhelming majority of committee members in Sports I vote Conservative. It is of interest that, apart from the one Free Churchman already noted, there are no contacts with any church; again, however, the overwhelming majority would describe themselves as Church of England.

Sports II (Chart X, p. 83) is made up of another cricket club, the table tennis league, Post Office sports, and the Comrades' Club. Its committee men are all of a lower occupational status, and Sports II joins the lower part of the Conservative connexion. (There is even one man here from the Labour connexion.) Here are the Oddfellows, the Foresters, and the Buffaloes, the last taking the place of the Freemasons. The games played in Sports II are in part the same as those played in Sports I, but in part other games are substituted. For instance, squash has disappeared to be replaced by table tennis: the 'class' games (rugger, for example) and those requiring expensive equipment have gone.

Any new-comer to Banbury must be struck by the fact that apart from rugger (which is played by comparatively few, relies on a limited number of schools which play the game, and needs a large team) there is no sport for which one club represents the town. (There is a soccer side, but this is discounted here since it is sponsored by a large firm which uses its own name in conjunction with that of the town. The firm employs professional players who live neither in the town nor in the district. Nor is there a supporters' club which could be called a voluntary association.) In part this duplication of clubs is an effect of the lack of open spaces in the town centre, made more acute by the fact that the town's old recreation ground was sold to the aluminium factory for its sports section. But this is not the decisive factor. Banbury people do not engage in sport as an exercise in competitive athleticism but as an occasion for social intercourse: as a competitor remarked of a tennis tournament in which he was playing, 'these do's are 75 per cent. social and 25 per cent. tennis'. With this attitude dominant the 'right atmosphere' and fellow-members who are the 'right sort' are more important considerations than the standard of play. In short, social comfort decides which club you join and social comfort is promoted if the club is homogeneous from the point of view of social status. Thus we find that cricket club *A* in the Sports I group has a committee of occupational-status classes 1, 2, and 3, while cricket club *B* in Sports II has classes 3, 4, and 5. The same is true of the Chestnuts and the Borough Bowls.

The occupational-status frontier, which bisects the Conservative connexion and the sporting associations of Banbury, bisects the whole world of voluntary associations in the town. Each chart has a horizontal line across it: all the committees above the line have an occupational-status median of 1 or 2 and all below it of 4 or 5. This is particularly noticeable in the sports, hobbies, and occupational associations; and also with those types of association which are identified primarily with one class. The cultural and social service associations, for example, are identified with class 2 and mutual aid with class 4.[1] Moreover, committees with medians of classes 1 and 2 on the one hand and of class 5 on the other are more homogeneous than those in the central classes, as Table 19 makes plain. This table shows the average deviation from the median, so that committees having small deviations are more homogeneous than those having large average deviations. Committees with a median of three or four show a wide range of occupational-status classes while those with a median of 1 and 2 or of 5 are more concentrated in those classes.

TABLE 19

Range of Occupational Status in Committees of Different Median

Average deviation from median	*Committee's median*			
	1 and 2	*3 and 4*	*5*	*Total*
0–0·29	1	1	1	3
0·30–0·59	16	3	9	28
0·60–0·99	10	10	4	24
1·0 and over	2	11	3	16

The associations with a median of 3 or 4 and with a wide status range are those which lie on the status frontier in Chart XIII. Their function is common to those on both sides of the frontier: they therefore straddle it. But there is only one line which crosses the status frontier, i.e. only one man who is a committee member of a high-status committee is also a member of a low-status committee. The worlds of the status groups are as separate as the more formal worlds of politics and religion.

In sum, two main factors decide what association a man joins: his political-religious adherence and his social status. Of these social status is dominant, since two men of common adherence will join different associations if their occupational status falls on different sides of the frontier; on the other hand, given a common occupational status two men may well join the same association despite differences of religion or politics, provided there are adequate taboos on religious

[1] Comparable functional differences in the type of voluntary association between one social class and another were reported for Yankee City (op. cit.). See especially pp. 319, 320.

and political discussion. In practice in Banbury this means that while Liberals and Conservatives of similar status will join common associations, Labour is isolated because there is neither parity of status nor of outlook. The Conservative/Liberal territory contains the core of the 'local traditional system' (to adapt Brennan's phrase),[1] while Labour territory represents a major part of the non-traditional sector. It represents an invasion into the field of formal associations by status groups who traditionally are not formally organized.

[1] Brennan, Cooney, and Pollins, op. cit., chap. 3 et seq.

6

HOUSES AND NEIGHBOURS

HOUSES

ENTER Banbury by any of the half-dozen main roads and your first impression is not of an old town, but of a town built since the end of the First World War; a town, moreover, which is still growing. The houses are brick, semi-detached, and remarkably uniform. It is only as you reach the town centre that you see the old Banbury and realize from the jumble of styles of architecture and the mixture of building and roofing materials that it is indeed an old town.

Although the houses range in age from buildings just finished to those which are 400 years old, they are all essentially English in their conception and appearance. None of them, for example, is shut off by *grilles* with carefully locked gates as are many French houses; and unlike American houses, all their living rooms have doors. They do not reveal the full variety of housing patterns to be found in England; notably there are no blocks of flats as there are in large towns, and the very big houses are found only in the country outside the Borough boundaries.

Nevertheless, there is wide variety, not only in age, but in size, amenities, and siting. The range of houses reflects the social status range. The houses as buildings are ranked on a social status scale.

This scale is modified by the views of the traditionalist and the non-traditionalist; the former often tending to prefer the older, well-tried type of house in an established neighbourhood while the latter tend to prefer 'modern' houses farther out of town. If these preferences are ignored, the scale is one which at the lower end gives low marks to age because here age is associated with lack of space, sanitation, and convenience. For the same reason in the lower and middle ranges it gives high marks to modernity; but it gives high marks to age in the upper range where age is sanctified by tradition and can be had at the same time as space, sanitation, and convenience. It is a scale which before 1914 gave high marks to large size and in which size is still relevant. The worst houses are the smallest and the best the largest. But the demand for adequate sleeping and living space by those in smaller houses and the lack of domestic servants among those in large houses has led to an increasing tendency since 1918 to concentrate on the three-bedroomed house. It is a scale, furthermore, which gives low marks to council ownership and high marks to private ownership and especially to owner-occupancy, for this is associated with independence and substance. Indeed the factor of ownership has to a considerable extent superseded that of size.

Taking these three criteria, and ignoring the modifications caused by traditionalism and non-traditionalism, an attempt has been made to classify and rank the houses surveyed in Banbury on the basis of the three used in combination. The grouping is inevitably rather crude, for in practice one group shades imperceptibly into the next. The First World War has been taken as the division by age, but there were some 'modern' houses built before 1914 and some 'nineteenth-century' houses built after 1918. Ownership has been divided into private and Council (private including those rented from a private landlord, owned outright, or being bought on a mortgage). Rateable value has been used as an indication of size.[1]

The classification results in a sixfold ranking which is set out in Table 20. The geographic distribution of the ranks is shown in Chart XIV.

Houses in rank 6, 31 per cent. of the total, are generally agreed to be the worst. There are, for example, the tight-packed terraces in the narrow streets and alleys that lie behind the shops in the town centre, between it and the canal, and across the canal and railway to the east. They were mostly built in the nineteenth century and the majority are owned by private landlords. Some are older, notably in Neithrop, a hamlet which has been swallowed up by the town. Their sites are unattractive; many of them are built on land liable to flood and may

[1] Observation and evidence received showed that there are limitations to the valid use of rateable value alone as an index of the status of houses. A complete revaluation was in progress during the course of the survey, but its results would not be available in time. There was evidence that the revaluation, when it came out, would be likely not only to alter the rateable values of Banbury in relation to other local authority areas, but the relation of rateable values to each other within the town. However, rateable values are used here as an indication of size since the number of rooms of itself is inadequate because of the general trend to three-bedroomed houses. The field-workers were not in a position to take a complicated series of measurements. This has inevitably left some problems unsolved. Highly-rated houses may be divided among a number of households, or these may be counted separately for rating purposes. However, since the rateable-value groups are large, since Council houses are treated separately, and since the groups are divided by age, rateable value may reasonably be taken as a broad measure of size. But the author is aware that a status factor remains concealed within it.

TABLE 20

Houses in Banbury

Status and Characteristics of the Main Types (904 houses)

	House rank					
	6	5	4	3	2	1
Definition						
Date built . .	Pre-1914*	All dates†	Pre-1914	Post-1918	Post-1918	Pre-1914
Ownership .	Private	Council	Private	Private	Private	Private
Rateable value (£)	0–9	All R.V.s‡	10–18	10–18	19+	19+ §
Numbers per rank in sample .	279	217	129	180	63	36
Per cent. . .	31	24	14	20	7	4
Other characteristics of the groups (shown % of the number in each rank)						
% tenant occupiers . .	92	100	64	37	44	36
Number of bedrooms, % with:						
1 . .	7	2	8	2	¶	¶
2 . .	54	11	21	8	¶	¶
3 . .	31	79	44	89	83	33
4 and over .	9	8	27	¶	17	66
% with no bathroom‖ . .	94	17	71	12	14	0
% with no indoor W.C. . .	89	14	74	15	8	0
% terrace . .	91	25	78	31	9	58
% semi-detached	4	72	6	60	62	22
% detached .	2	¶	4	5	19	20
% other . .	3	3	12	4	10	0
% with no garden or one only .	70	5	47	3	8	36

* Eight houses appeared in the sample which were built after 1914 with a rateable value of £9 or under. Their characteristics were essentially similar to those of rank 6 with which they have therefore been included.

† All but fifteen of these were built after 1914 and all after 1911.

‡ The rateable value range is from £0–18 except in the case of a few large pre-1914 houses requisitioned under the emergency powers of the 1939–45 war. Seventy-seven per cent. have rateable values from £10–12.

§ Houses are only listed in this column when they are occupied by one family only and have modern conveniences. Thirty-four are excluded because they are shared by more than one household, or have no bathroom, although they are rated over £19.

‖ 'No bathroom' means that there is no separate room in which there is a fixed bath. There may be a fixed bath in another room, e.g. the kitchen. A bathroom and a W.C. combined has been counted as a separate bathroom.

¶ Indicates 'none' or 'negligible'.

have their ground-floor rooms awash after a heavy rainstorm; they are close to the railway with its ever-present noise and dirt, and to factories and warehouses. The terraces run the length of the streets and alleys. The front doors, which open straight into the room, open straight on to the street. In some there is no access except through the house to the back-yard, which may be common to several houses. The day the dustman calls is, therefore, marked by the row of dust-bins dumped outside the front doors. The houses themselves are

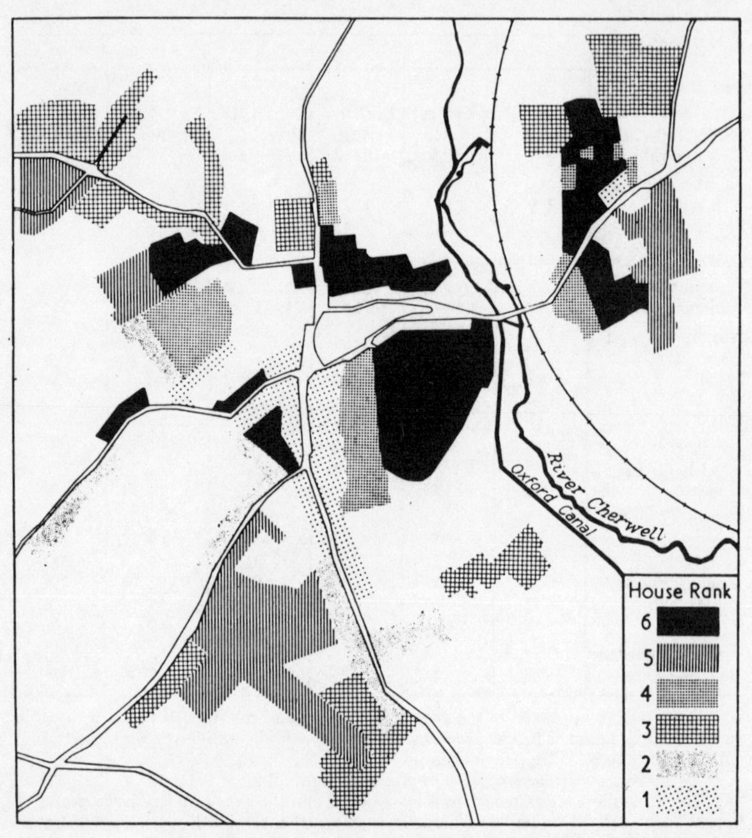

CHART XIV. Residential areas in Banbury

small: one or two rooms upstairs and down. In them family life is lived in a crowd, overcrowded in cases like that of the couple with three children who were interviewed in one such one-bedroomed house. The houses have no bathrooms and no indoor lavatories.

They include the houses that are sometimes spoken of as 'the little slum houses down by the canal', and it is in houses such as these, in rooms and divided houses as well as in some of the Council houses, that the 'roughs' (see Chapter 8, p. 153) are found. But, as Table 21 shows, as many of these houses are occupied by skilled workers as by semi-skilled and unskilled put together. This is perhaps surprising until analysis shows that of the skilled workers in these houses more than three-quarters are over forty, nearly 60 per cent. are over fifty, and 43 per cent. are over sixty (the comparable figures for the adult male population are 56 per cent., 32 per cent., and 18 per cent.); that, in contrast with the town as a whole, 46 per cent. are members of old crafts compared with 23 per cent. in new crafts; furthermore 17 per cent. are railway workers compared with 15 per cent. in all transport in the total male population. These are the older, independent, 'respectable' craftsmen whose homes are 'clean and decent' and who 'keep themselves to themselves'.

TABLE 21

Occupational Status and House Rank

Occupational status (Hall/Jones scale): Class	*Male household heads only Numbers in sample — House rank* 6	5	4	3	2	1	*Total*
1	0	0	0	5	6	3	14
2	1	0	2	5	8	8	24
3	3	10	7	18	8	12	58
4	11	14	12	18	4	3	62
5	92	72	50	62	15	4	295
6	62	60	6	33	3	1	165
7	25	24	8	6	1	2	66
Total	194	180	85	147	45	33	684
	Percentages						
1 and 2	0	0	0	7	31	33	6
3	2	6	8	12	18	36	8
4	6	8	14	12	9	9	9
5	47	40	59	42	33	12	43
6	32	33	7	22	7	3	24
7	13	13	9	4	2	6	10

Most would agree that Council houses, rank 5, which make up 24 per cent. of the total, are better than these, although by no means does everyone in rank 6 wish to move to rank 5. Relatively few skilled workers, but many semi-skilled and about 40 per cent. of the unskilled workers, live in them. They lie on the outskirts of the town to the south-west, north-west, and east.

Banbury Borough Council built one road of houses to rent just before the First World War. But most of the council houses were built between the wars or after 1945. They represent an entirely different type of architecture, as well as a revolution in ownership, from the nineteenth-century terrace cottages. Many of them are semi-detached; those that are terraced are built in groups of only four to six houses in contrast with the street-long rows of the earlier period. They all have running water and inside lavatories (except for one group which have their lavatories beside the backdoor). Except for the earliest few, they have bathrooms with fixed baths. Most of them have three bedrooms, so that privacy for parents from children and boys from girls in terms of sleeping space is possible. Some houses have one all-purpose kitchen-living room downstairs, others have two downstairs rooms. In either case the most common pattern of living is in one room; mending, radio, homework, and a worker's tea all happening at once in the same room.

Some of the larger old houses, even though they have not been modernized, rank higher than Council houses. They have been given rank 4 here and form about 14 per cent. of the total. They are given a higher rank because they are larger, because they are privately owned, and because they have not yet lost their traditional 'respectable' position. But they are an awkward group to define statistically and the frontier between them and the other old houses is blurred in practice. They have more in common with rank 6 houses than with the Council houses. Rank 4, like a number of rank 6 houses, are occupied by craftsmen, but also by a higher proportion of clerical workers (Hall/Jones class 4). These houses lie farther away from the canal and railway than those of rank 6, but still near the town centre. A typical house of this kind has a narrow entrance hall, a strip of ground some 18 inches to 3 feet wide between the front door and the pavement and sometimes a separate back garden large enough to grow a few vegetables. These houses have at least two and sometimes as many as four or five bedrooms, if you count the attics, which are frequently too damp, through bad roofing, to sleep in. Home life here is less crowded and neighbours and passers-by a little farther away. But most of them still have no bathroom, no inside lavatory, and no constant hot water. They are inconvenient for the housewife to run. A few are well maintained and have been 'modernized' by the additions of both bathroom and indoor lavatory.

Higher in status than any of these groups are the privately-owned post-1918 houses, ranks 3 and 2. They are divided into two ranks by their size, the larger houses, which are about 7 per cent. of all houses, ranking higher than the smaller, which make about 20 per cent. of the total.

The rank 3 houses are not much larger than Council houses, indeed smaller sometimes than the most modern Council houses, and they have the same sort of 'modern conveniences'. Two groups of the rank 3 houses are owned by companies and rented, mainly to manual workers. The rest are usually 'owner-occupied', sometimes owned outright but generally on a mortgage. Some of the owners are skilled workers but mostly they are clerks, school teachers, or the lower ranks of government officers. The builders and owners of these houses were at pains to show that they are 'individualists' and, furthermore, that the houses are not Council houses. So they have been careful to avoid the uniformity of the Council estate. Except in the post-1945 houses, built when economy regulations were strict, and in common with similar houses anywhere in the country, rank 3 houses are ornamented with mock-tudor beams and have different porches or different gable ends for each one. They are found as ribbon development on the roads which lead out of Banbury to the west, north-west, north, and east. They are in no way specific to Banbury.

Houses more substantial than these, the rank 2 houses, sometimes with three bedrooms and sometimes four, are found on the hilly land to the south and west, where there is a prospect of fields and woods. It is here that the more well-to-do live, the larger tradesmen, and senior officials. Their houses, again owner-occupied, are set well back from the road and have gardens covering at least half an acre. Some are semi-detached but a noticeable number stand on their own; in either case most have garages. Needless to say they have lavatories, bathrooms, and constant hot water. They give the impression of ease and comfort, for not only have their owners the money to heat as many rooms as they wish and the custom of so doing, but they carpet and furnish their rooms well too.

Lying between these houses and the town centre are the 'good old houses' of Banbury, rank 1. They have the merit of age, the added merits of large size and private ownership without the demerit of inconvenience. Forming 4 per cent. of the total, they are eighteenth- and nineteenth-century buildings, some terraced, some detached, whose gardens, even in the terraces, are separated from their neighbours by high brick walls. They are all larger than the 'substantial' inter-war houses. They are where the 'best people', bankers, wealthy tradesmen, doctors, and professional men always used to live, and where some of them still do. But increasingly as they fall empty these old houses are turned into offices, boarding-houses, or public buildings. There is some evidence that they are being displaced by rank 2 houses. Rank 1 houses were built for the way of life of earlier generations, when a middle-class housewife could command a number of servants and when the average household was two or three times its present size. There are few who have the means, inclination, or need to run such houses in Banbury today; professional men such as doctors and dentists are among the exceptions, for frequently they need to have space to work at home while living in town.

More and more the well-to-do are leaving the town and moving into houses in the neighbouring villages. Here they live in the substantial type of modern house described above, in old houses of 'character' which have been 'modernized' or in houses converted from cottages.

Also in the villages are the homes of the 'country gentry'. These may be anything from the converted cottage or farmhouse described above to the more substantial house which has always been a 'gentleman's residence'.

Finally there are the great houses of the district, built for the aristocracy of past centuries when a house might be the equivalent of a whole hamlet.[1] Traditionally such houses remained in one family, succeeding generations adding and adapting. But only four of the forty-three houses in the Banbury district large enough to be named on the one-inch ordnance survey map have been in the same family for more than two generations. In one case the family lives in one wing and derives income from putting the house and its collection on view; in another case the house is divided into flats; and in the other two cases a few rooms are lived in and the rest of the house closed. Most of the other large houses have changed hands many times within living memory, and are now owned by members of the non-traditional upper classes.[2] They bought the house to match their

[1] One such house near the district is built round a court-yard and has its own brew-house, slaughter-house, laundry, buttery, and dairy, even dungeons, as well as stables, coach-houses, and private church. It has been in the same family for at least three centuries, but has been empty for four years; the plaster is falling from the ceiling of the banqueting hall, weeds ramp over the terraces and choke the lakes, the trees in the park rot where they fall, the contents of the house have been sold up. This is an extreme but not unique example.

[2] Men who have won their wealth and their titles (where they have one) by reaching the head of some large national or international business concern. See chapter 8, p. 158.

status. Either they are retired or their work requires that they use the house at weekends, often to entertain friends from outside the Banbury district.

In these houses, where there is money to keep them up, home life is at its most spacious and provides the greatest contrast with the first houses described where home life is inevitably cramped.

This contrast, and indeed the whole range in the variety of houses, is important: to some extent the physical conditions of a house determine the kind of behaviour which is possible in the home; this in turn affects manners and attitudes. For example, the manners which demand that no man shall remain seated when a woman is standing, that children shall open doors for grown-ups and men for women, are physically impossible in the small and over-crowded kitchen-living room. There is only room for one person to go to the door at once and someone at the table is pinned against the wall so that he cannot rise without causing a general upheaval. Manners instead demand that the one comfortable seat nearest to the fire shall always be relinquished to the honoured or welcome visitor.

The function of the immediate family to pass on the ways of behaviour, manners, and attitudes of the parents to the children (which will be discussed in the following chapter) is made easier by the differentiation in housing. For one type of home life tends to be associated with a type of house and the type of house and home life with a social class or status group. Table 21, which shows the occupational status of householders against the house rank, gives some indication of how the status of a family and its house are related.

It is notable that the modern tendency is towards a narrower range of houses; the largest houses can be sold only with great difficulty, the smallest are scheduled for slum clearance. Nevertheless, a wide range remains and since the type of house varies with the social class of the occupants this range tends to harden the class distinctions. In short, differences in houses are born of the status system and the differences themselves perpetuate the distinctions between the status groups.

NEIGHBOURHOODS

This close interaction between houses and social status groups is further accentuated because houses of a similar sort tend to be built together. For this reason it was possible to draw Chart XIV, p. 94, which shows the geographic distribution of the houses in the six ranks.

Banbury has some residential areas confined to houses of a particular social status, but it is still too small to be entirely divided in this way. There are many places where houses of very different social status stand cheek by jowl. Although since 1918 estates of several hundred houses have been built, the map shows how often the six ranks are intermingled, even though it inevitably conceals some details. Half a dozen houses in rank 1 may adjoin a dozen in rank 6. This is especially true in the older part of the town near the centre where the divisions are still made between two ends or two sides of one street. But where the house stands is none the less important for that; the distinctions are clearly drawn. The place is judged by the intrinsic merit of the site and by the houses that surround it.

The worst houses are frequently found on intrinsically bad sites and the best on intrinsically good ones. Moreover, the east side of the canal and the railway is the 'wrong' side. Houses of otherwise equivalent status are likely to drop one rank if they are on the east side.

Intrinsic site value apart, the surrounding houses must be 'right'. 'The houses in Pemberton Road are not what they were since the Council houses were built at the end of the road', as the field-workers were frequently told. The Pemberton Road houses were rank 2 before the Council houses came, now they are 3. A 'good old house' ceases to be such when all other houses in the street have been divided into tenements. In one street of Regency terraces all the houses have 'gone down' in this way.

A street, a 'residential area', or a 'neighbourhood' tends to acquire the status of the majority of houses in it. But the occupants of the houses also play a part in deciding its status. Council houses, for example, are ranked among themselves. The ranking is not by size, rateable value, or site but by the purpose for which the houses were built. All the groups of Council houses which were built for slum clearance rank lower than those which were built to meet the general demand for new houses. The slum clearance houses rank according to where their original occupants came from. They took on and still tend to have the rank order of the slums of their origin. Thus Coronation Street was built to clear one of the worst slums, a series of courts, in the town. It is therefore the 'bottom' of the Council house streets. The houses built after the Second World War rank highest. This is partly because they are new, the most spacious, and best equipped of all Council houses. But it is at least as much because, two-thirds of all houses built after the war being Council houses, their occupants have been drawn from more varied social backgrounds; they include people of a higher social status than was ever the case before.

A neighbourhood in this sense, that is in terms of an area of similar houses with occupants of similar social background, may run into several hundreds of houses. But a neighbourhood in terms of the area from which neighbourhood friends are drawn and in which face-to-face groups of neighbours are found is much smaller than this.

NEIGHBOURS

The social relations between neighbours was the subject of a special study in seven selected streets ranging from 'rough' working class to middle class. A research worker lived in each street for a period of at least six weeks.[1] The findings of this study have been compressed for ease of comparison into tabular form and are set out in Tables 22 and 23. The tables and the rest of this chapter are principally concerned with neighbour relations among the women in the streets studied.

Most people have social relationships with their neighbours at three levels. The first, that involving the most immediate impact, is with next-door neighbours. All households, in the interest of a quiet life, if nothing else, have to come to some working arrangment with the people next door. The second level is the participation of housewives in small groups in the street where they live. Usually these groups, when they exist, are of one age-group and tend to be located at one point in the street. However, it is unusual for housewives to be actively involved in a group with a well-developed structure and so most of the street groups merely define the limits within which people are acceptable as partners in gossip. Within these boundaries the only substantial relationships are likely to be pairs. The third level of relationships between neighbours is the street as a whole, seen in the co-operative activity of its residents or in the pressure to conformity the street exerts upon them.

No household can ever prepare itself completely against its future problems. It will at some time need other people's help. Furthermore, people need to gratify their feelings of sociability and the small, exclusive, immediate family is seldom sufficient for this purpose. Those who are most concerned with their neighbours are those who are most tied to their homes and immediate locality; that is, old people,

[1] For further details of method, &c., see Appendix 5.

TABLE 22

Social Background to Neighbour Relations in Seven Banbury Streets

	Sonniton Street	*Tracey Avenue*	*Statham Terrace*	*Oldside Street*	*Sky View*	*Warriner Lane*	*Larkin Drive*
No. houses	75	94	23	95	90	56	50
Date	Pre-war	1930's	19th c.	19th c.	Post-war	18th c.	1930's
Type	Council	Semi-det.	Terrace	Villa	Council	Cottage	Semi-det.
Layout	Through road	Cul-de-sac	Through road	Cul-de-sac	Through road	Through road	Cul-de-sac
Class and status	Superior Respectable Ordinary Rough	Superior Respectable Ordinary	Ordinary Rough	Respectable Ordinary Rough	Superior Respectable Ordinary Rough	Ordinary Rough	Professional Lower middle class
Predominant age-group	50's	Early 40's	None	60's	30's	None	Early 40's
Young children	Very few	Many	Few	Almost none	Many	Few	Many
Average annual removals for last 10 years	1·6%	2%	1·2%	1%	1%	1·4%	2·5%
Households with relatives in Banbury	4/5	1/4	3/4	4/5	3/5	4/5	1/4
Place of origin	Mainly Banburian	North Country	Slight Banburian majority	Mainly Banburian	Slight immigrant majority	Mainly Banburian	Mainly immigrant
% who belong to Associations	15%	10%	5%	10%	10%	5%	40%
Social integration	Integrated	Each end highly integrated	Very little integrated	Integrated	Integrated but each end split by class	Integrated	Integrated but split by class
Primary groups	Only one strong group	Several groups	Only pairs	Only one strong group	Several groups	Several, split by age	Two strong groups

TABLE 23

Seven Families and Their Neighbour Relations

	Trubshaw	*Maxwell*	*Stafford*	*Beckett*	*Suddell*	*Morgan*	*Clayton*
House type	Semi-det.	Terraced cottage	Semi-det.	Terraced	Terraced	Semi-det.	Semi-det.
Class and status	Professional middle class	Ordinary working class	Ordinary working class	Respectable working class	Rough working class	Respectable working class	Respectable working class
Age	30's	Late 30's	40's	70's	30's	50's	50's
Children	One	Two	One	None	Three	Three	Two
Length of residence	6 years	8 years	5 years	40 years	6 years	18 years	26 years
Relatives in Banbury H	None	Yes	None	Dead	None	None	Yes
Relatives in Banbury W	None	None	Nearby	None	Yes	None	Yes
Place of origin H	Immigrant	Banburian	Immigrant	Banburian	Immigrant	Immigrant	Banburian
Place of origin W	Immigrant	Immigrant	Banbury district	Banburian	Banburian	Immigrant	Banburian
Membership of Associations	Yes, strong	None	None	Church	Weak, R.C.	Co-op. Guild	Church Conservative
Participation in neighbour relations							
In the street	No	Yes	Yes	No	No	No	Yes
In Primary groups	On fringe	Yes, and also pair	In centre	No	Yes	On fringe	In centre
With immediate neighbours: Mutual aid	Dependent and willing to help	Same	Independent but willing to help	Very independent	Dependent and willing to help	Very independent but willing to help	Independent but willing to help
Sociability: with neighbour 1	Indifferent	Friendly	Friendly	Acquaintance	Indifferent	Acquaintance	Friendly
with neighbour 2	Friendly	Intimate	Hostile	No neighbour (end of road)	Intimate	Acquaintance	Acquaintance

young mothers, and the lower social-status groups. In spite of the need which people have of their neighbours, they may be reluctant to get involved in case too many inroads are made on their notions of privacy and independence.

Many factors are relevant to the amount and quality of neighbouring in Banbury, but for the purposes of this study nine were taken as specially relevant: house type and layout; age; children; length of residence; place of origin; kin; social class and social status; friendships outside the street; and associational interests.

The role and indeed the definition of neighbours varies with social class. Broadly speaking, in working-class streets near neighbours are the most important source of friendship and of help. In the middle class, friendships outside the street are at least as important as those with neighbours. In the upper class neighbours are those of the same class who live within a much wider area; the area is defined to include all those who may conveniently be visited for a meal or for some activity in the intervals between meals. Those living nearby of different social class are not included among the 'neighbours'.

The traditional working-class concept of neighbouring stresses the value of open-handed friendship to neighbours. It is conceived as a warm, freely-giving, freely-demanding relationship in which interdependence rather than independence is stressed. Among the middle classes the traditional relationships between neighbours presumes them to be at a much greater social distance. They are to be acknowledged but they are less often close friends. At Christmas when sociable impulses are nearer the surface they may be invited in for a drink, but at all other times of the year the principle to be followed is 'hedge green, friendship green'. In the upper class a new-comer used to learn whom he could recognize as his neighbours by having visiting cards left at his house, a convention which is no longer observed.

It is often said that the poorest people are the most neighbourly and this is widely believed both by those who are poor and those who are not. 'I suppose it is because they live on top of each other' remarked one housewife on a post-war housing estate. A housewife in a middle-class road studied gave a more historical explanation. 'They have gone through the same hard times together and they realize that they are in the same boat.' The poor people spoke for themselves through the person of a young woman in Statham Terrace: 'Well I didn't think that I was going to like it when I first came here but now I wouldn't exchange it, the people are so friendly here. They would do anything for you.'

The wife of the weekly-wage-earner, who buys in goods as they are needed and who has neither large stocks nor resources, is more dependent than the middle-class housewife. The wage-earner's wife may need to borrow if there is some unusual demand and it is from the neighbours that she borrows. A mutual dependence develops. For example, the neighbour of Mrs. Suddell, three or four doors along in Statham Terrace, minds the children when Mr. and Mrs. Suddell go to the pictures. In return for these services, but not upon any explicit bargaining, the Taylor household borrow anything they need: when Mrs. Taylor had all her towels in the wash, her daughter borrowed a clean one to go swimming. Since it is the poor and the bad manager who borrow most frequently, to be independent of your neighbours in this sense is a mark of prestige. Mrs. Morgan in Tracey Avenue said: 'My mother taught me not to rely on other people.' On one occasion when Mrs. Morgan was out shopping, Mr. Morgan, who had just come home from work, was unable to find sugar for his tea. He borrowed a cupful from the woman next door. When his wife returned she made it plain to him that she would rather he had not done this. On the other hand, Mrs. Morgan does not mind other people borrowing from her. At least three families come to her as first port of call when they need assistance. One neighbour asks for help when the children get out of hand; the neighbour who lives on the other side calls in for small items if she runs out; another neighbour's daughter calls round when she needs help in dressmaking or wants to borrow the sewing machine. Mrs. Clayton's position in Sonniton Street is similar. When she wanted to look up a train for her son she borrowed a timetable from across the road. Normally, however, there are few occasions when she needs to borrow from her neighbours. More frequently they come to her: the daughter of a family who lives opposite is sent across for shillings for the gas; an old lady came to ask her to take a prescription to the chemist; the woman next door came to borrow salt at dinner time. It is recognized in the street that Mrs. Clayton can always be relied upon to help her neighbours.

The working-class concept of neighbouring in fact changes with status and changes also with the traditional or non-traditional attitude to life. Within the working class in Banbury there are three status groups: the 'rough', the 'ordinary', and the 'respectable'. The self-styled 'ordinary working-class' people, like the Maxwells and the Staffords, follow closest the traditional concept of neighbouring. The 'roughs,' like the Suddells, and the 'respectables,' the Claytons and the Morgans, deviate most from it.

The 'roughs', often the poorest families, would like to lean heavily upon their neighbours but they are discouraged. Their personal appearance and the state of their houses add to their unattractiveness as companions. The 'respectables', on the other hand, are not expelled, they withdraw: they are 'stand-offish'. They are bent on improving their own social positions and intimate neighbouring is a part of the life of the social class they wish to leave behind.

The middle class are far less dependent on their neighbours for borrowing, for they have greater resources. Further, they depend less on their neighbours as a group from which to pick their friends. They have friends in other parts of the town and more frequently belong to associations. Even the young mother tied to the house may talk to friends by telephone and she can 'phone the shops or the doctor in a crisis. The Trubshaws, for example, in Larkin Drive had as strong friendships with people outside as they had with their neighbours in the Drive. They also maintained friendships with people in other towns. Nevertheless, they cannot be completely independent of their neighbours. When her child had an accident Mrs. Trubshaw had to call on her neighbour for immediate help. Generally, borrowing and lending is in non-essentials: an exchange of cuttings for the garden, keeping an eye on the house when its occupants are on holiday, perhaps baby-sitting.

Larkin Drive was the street of highest class composition in which neighbour relations were studied by the direct method of a research worker living in the street. Above this level neighbours cease to be relevant in the sense of next-door neighbours. Members of the upper and upper-middle classes are able to be independent of their neighbours because their households are large enough to meet crises unaided or their resources and power great enough to employ immediate outside help.

It has been observed that the town is not closely divided into separate residential areas and that quite often people of different social status live cheek by jowl. This mixture is most noticeable in the oldest and the newest areas of the town: in Oldside Street and Sky View.

When the social class and status of the majority of residents in a street is similar, there is considerable pressure to conform to common standards. In Tracey Avenue, for example, there is strong competition in conspicuous expenditure. The principal objects sought after are television sets and also gramophones, which are extremely popular among teen-age girls. Furthermore, there is considerable chain effect when improvements to houses are made. A cemented back path was reproduced in five gardens and a new inner door more often than that. The initiator remarked: 'You can't do anything here without someone seeing it and asking if you would mind if he did the same.'

Sonniton Street, a street of early Council houses, is dominated by a one-class group connected with the Church of England and the Conservative party. The class of this group is similar to Tracey Avenue, but here the pressure to conform is to a standard of respectability rather than to conspicuous expenditure: neatly kept gardens and highly polished houses (i.e. a daily polishing) and carefully curtained windows are among the standards to be maintained. These are standards that are closely associated with those of the Banbury traditionalist of the 'respectable' working class and the lower-middle class.

Where there is a mixture of social-status groups in one street, members of one group draw together and away from others. The Suddells, for example, in the nineteenth-century terrace, have little to do with their next-door neighbours whose status is higher. They do not even know what job the man has; they do no more than pass the time of day if they happen to be at the door together. Their children, although they are the same age, only speak to each other when they pass in the common back-yard. In Sky View on the new Council estate there is a wide range of social status. As one woman said: 'Council houses are a lot better than they were—they used to be for slum people.' In this street there are teachers, lorry drivers, clerks, engine drivers, labourers, bus conductors, commercial travellers, and shop assistants; shift workers and day workers. There are two sets of childrens' play groups. The Stafford's children are well dressed and with one or two other children are easily distinguished from another group of children who live nearby and play in the same street. The Stafford's group wear school caps, ties, coloured blazers, and their socks are usually pulled up. The other group wear cloth caps with crowns buttoned to peaks, pullover shirts, socks down, and their trousers either torn or patched. In Larkin Drive there is also a wide range of social status. The professional people form a group distinct from the lower-middle-class group. The few working-class people are isolated.

The changed definition of neighbour in the upper class is the logical conclusion of this separation into status groups which occurs in all classes. The titled man, for example, who lives in a village in the district, counts as his neighbour, and he is thinking in terms of the person who lives nearest to him, the retired colonel who lives at the other end of the village. He ignores all those villagers who live in the houses in between. They are not his neighbours.

Social distance may be more easily preserved when it is helped by physical distance, as in the case of this titled man, whose house was surrounded by large and secluded grounds. The terraced cottage, in contrast, permits little privacy. Its layout encourages close social relations with the neighbours but makes it difficult for them to withdraw from each other. At the worst, if you do not like the people you have to get out.

The cases of the Maxwells and the Suddells illustrate this. The Maxwells live in Warriner Lane, a street of old terraced cottages with no front garden and a shared courtyard at the back. They are on very close terms with the people next door. After dinner each day the wives share a pot of tea and when one of them wants to be relieved of the children the other wife takes over. The children know the neighbouring mother as 'auntie'. The Suddells live in the same kind of house, but are among those already referred to who have little to do with their neighbours because of the difference in status between them. To withdraw altogether is difficult, short of moving house, and the two households are very much aware of each other: their radios can be heard clearly through the shared wall. Nevertheless, the Suddell's higher-status neighbours have withdrawn, despite the inconvenience involved. Since the Suddell's small children play on the pavement outside the house, the neighbours require their child to play in the ten-by-six-foot yard at the back. The status difference between the two households has overcome the expected friendly results of living so close together.

Latter-day developments in Council housing have favoured a much greater distance between neighbours, approaching the traditional middle-class pattern. This is sometimes unacceptable to traditionally-minded working-class people.[1] On the post-war Council housing

[1] See L. Kuper, (ed.) *Living in Towns*, 'Blueprint for Living Together' (London, The Cresset Press, 1953). Also J. Mogey, *Family and Neighbourhood* (op. cit.).

estate high brick walls were built between the walls of adjoining houses to ensure privacy. Mrs. Stafford and her next-door neighbour wished, however, to be close friends; they left a chair on each side of the wall so that they could look over and have a chat when they wanted.

In the smaller middle-class houses on the inter-war and post-war estates, the physical distance may be no greater than on the Council housing estates: nevertheless a greater social distance is often preserved.

The upper-middle and upper classes, residents in the rank 2 and rank 1 houses in Banbury, in the country cottages, and the 'gentleman's residences', like those in the large country houses, have, by the layout of the houses they have chosen, avoided close proximity with those whose property abuts their own. Often they have no next-door neighbours, for there is no door next their own.

Apart from the rifts between groups of neighbours of widely different social status, the greatest social distance was found between northerners and other residents. The immigrants in Banbury who have come from the north of England (and this accounts for many of those who came in the second half of the 1930's, see Appendix 2, *B*) tend to have a different conception of the neighbour's role from the local population, and from other immigrants. The northerner expects more sociability than the midlander is prepared to give. The northerners tend to be segregated in areas of their own which reduces the amount of provocation they might give to others by their different expectations of neighbourhood life. The older streets of the town tend to be weighted with Banburians (Table 22 shows that this tendency was reflected in the seven streets studied) and the newer streets with true immigrants. Tracey Avenue and Larkin Drive are mainly composed of immigrants. Sonniton Street, Oldside Street, and Warriner Lane are mainly composed of Banburians.

Tracey Avenue is known locally as 'Little Rochdale' because of the origin of its residents. Most of the men came from the depressed areas during the 1930's to look for work. When they found it they looked for houses for their families. Tracey Avenue was just being completed and naturally attracted them. This 'community within a community' was a much more comfortable setting for the immigrant than being surrounded by neighbours who are natives of the town.

In Sonniton Street, a street mainly of Banburians, a middle-aged woman from the north found it impossible to get into the charmed circle of 'respectable' people, even though she attended the local church and joined the local Conservative Women's Association. In the same street a Scots family lived in complete isolation from the other residents because they thought them 'unfriendly'. Their problem was undoubtedly increased because Sonniton Street is an old-established street with a defined structure. A substantial number of its residents have lived there for thirty or forty years.

Families who move into an old house in an established neighbourhood face rather different problems from those who are living on a new housing estate. The new-comer in an established neighbourhood always runs the risk of attracting other people's friends or of finding a social life which has no spare places. The first few months are critical because this is the period of exploration during which there is a chance of selecting friends and deciding at which level to engage them. It is also a testing time when the established residents are likely to make their overtures and to decide whether to become involved. It seems likely that the northerners in Sonniton Street, because of their different concept of neighbouring, failed during this critical period. At whatever point the failure comes, it may be said with a fair degree of certainty that working-class families from the north of England or from Scotland are very unlikely to settle on intimate terms as neighbours to Banburians.

No such prediction can be made for the middle class. In Larkin Drive immigrants came from many areas and all were equally acceptable. The middle-class concept of neighbouring is apparently sufficiently nearly common to north, south, and midlands.

The following chapter will describe the strength which the extended family gives to the traditional social structure of Banbury. The extended family plays a less important role in the day-to-day life of the immigrants because they have usually left their kinsfolk behind in another town. Only 29 per cent. of the immigrant householders have relatives in Banbury compared with 87 per cent. of the Banburians. The research workers thought that this difference might show itself in the relative dependence of immigrants and Banburians upon their neighbours. The young Banburian housewife spends time with her mother which leaves her with that much less time to spend with her neighbours. The help mothers give to daughters means that much less reliance upon a neighbour's goodwill. But in practice it was found that Banburians and immigrants behaved in much the same way towards their neighbours. Banburians, like immigrants, chose friends of their own age-group from among neighbours and relied on them for emergency borrowing.[1] Furthermore, in the more serious cases of need, childbirth for example, the mother will usually come to her daughter's aid even if it means a long journey.

The seven streets studied vary a great deal in the kinship ties of their residents. In Larkin Drive and Tracey Avenue, each with a high proportion of immigrants, about a quarter of the households have relatives in Banbury; whereas in Warriner Lane, Oldside Street, and Sonniton Street four out of five households have relatives in Banbury. But these relatives may not be in the same street. In Oldside Street only 11 per cent. of the houses were related by ties of kinship. A larger proportion (26 per cent.) of Tracey Avenue residents have relatives living in the same street, many of them being brothers and sisters who migrated together in search of jobs.

Even where a family has relatives in the same street they usually find it more convenient to neighbour, that is unless relatives live almost next door. It is only where relations with neighbours are poor for other reasons, differences in social status for example, that kinship plays a dominant role. Mrs. Suddell lived within five minutes' walk of her mother's house and she was round there every morning. The only neighbour with whom she was in touch was considerably older than she was and this made it difficult for them to be close friends.[2]

For the majority of working-class people, therefore, the neighbouring relationship is an important functioning day-to-day relationship which, for Banburian and immigrant alike, the extended family does not provide.

In Banbury age-groups tend to be segregated into streets and areas. There are few streets without either a child or a granny in them. But the tendency to age-grouping is so marked that walking through the town you may pass through streets where, from nearly every house, an elderly face peeps out between the aspidistra and the lace curtains; streets where you meet groups of secondary school children coming home; streets where there is a pram in nearly every garden.

This impression was confirmed by a census of the child population undertaken in 1948/9 by the Local Education Authority. The post-war housing estates are mainly occupied by young married couples with young families. Houses built towards the end of the inter-war

[1] In Ireland Mogey reports that even in an emergency you do not borrow from a neighbour who is not a relative.

[2] Mogey (op. cit.) reports for St. Ebbe's that immediate borrowing is from the kin. Statham Terrace, where Mrs. Suddell lives, lies in the 'St. Ebbe's' of Banbury.

period tend to have the younger middle-aged couples whose children are at grammar school or just starting out to work. The groups of Council houses and of private houses built earlier in the inter-war years tend to be occupied by people in their later middle age, either with grown-up children at home, or whose children have married and left home. Streets of older houses tend to be occupied almost exclusively by the elderly, or, where the older generation is dying off, by elderly people alongside a new generation of young married couples. Consequently the oldest streets of all have the most mixed age-groups.

This pattern was reflected in the seven streets studied. Warriner Lane and Statham Terrace were both well-mixed, but the other five streets, Sky View, Oldside Street, Tracey Avenue, Sonniton Street, and Larkin Drive were predominantly one age-group. Oldside Street by virtue of the high number of old people among its residents and their consequently increased mortality rate will, within the next decade, become much more mixed in age.

The implications of segregation by age are not unimportant because the need for neighbours is of a different order at different times of life. In the same way that the social life of a woman is closely bound up with the life-cycle of her family (see the following chapter) so are her relations with her neighbours closely bound up with it.

This is particularly noticeable in the working class. The young married woman with small children is tied to the house and she has very great need of company. Her ability to keep house is not yet backed by experience, so she finds herself borrowing from her neighbours more often than she would like.

The children often provide the basis for contact that the younger mother needs. Not only do they introduce their parents to each other (where this is necessary) by their uninhibited relations, but their lives provide a great part of the conversation between mothers. The degree of intimacy between the children may sometimes even set the tone for the parents' relationship.

When families were large and houses small, children were not often invited in to play, but now, especially in the housing estates, it is a common practice. The Stafford's children had regular visitors to watch the children's TV programmes.

Different methods of rearing children also influence neighbour relations; for the less controlled the children are (and the 'roughs' are the least controlled) the more chance there is that they will annoy the neighbours or fight with their children. The children of the 'respectable' take less part in the neighbourhood life than other children. They are not allowed to play in the street if the general tone is too far below theirs. Their parents restrict their choice of companions. Such strong parental control is, of course, only possible where there are small families.

As her children grow up they become less of a liability and a mother can move about more freely; she may even go back to work. This takes her physically out of the neighbourhood life and gives her new friends and interests at work. At middle age her own home ties are at their weakest; she may visit her married children or they may visit her once a week.

In Sonniton Street, where the middle-aged group predominates, the relationships formed by mothers when their children were young have lingered on. The children have left home and the housewives have a lot of time on their hands. So old friends get together to take up new interests or pursue old ones more actively. The morning coffee party in the café in the town centre, the Church, the Mothers' Union, the Co-op. Guild, all come into their own.

As she moves into old age the physical mobility of the housewife declines. She is less able to go out to work, to spend long hours shopping or to visit her children in bad weather. Her dependence upon the goodwill of her neighbours increases, but the time she can bear to stand gossiping in the street decreases.

In streets where there is a wide age-range, the young neighbours may help the aged. The old men who live in a house in Statham Terrace often ask Mrs. Suddell to bake a pie or cake for them. In return they provide her with certain services and with fruit and extra sugar. (There was still food rationing at the time of the survey.) 'I usually do little things like that for [them]. [They] do little things for me in return. I use [their] garden to hang my washing in. Whenever the dustbin is heavy and [they] come by, I ask [them] to help me carry it out.'

But when most of the people in a street are old very considerable isolation may result. In Oldside Street at the time of the survey thirteen old people lived alone. In the winter of 1950 one of them died and the neighbours knew nothing about it until a relative, who had come to clear the house through after the death, lit bonfires of rubbish in the garden. The active residents of the street meet daily as they return from shopping, but others may go for three weeks, as did

Mrs. Beckett during an illness, without seeing anyone except a tradesman. There was no one who had an obligation to call upon Mrs. Beckett at this time. She has no children and her neighbours felt no obligation towards her. Important though it is, the neighbour relation is a casual, informal one.

Although the majority of working-class women draw their friends from among their neighbours, some have a set of friends made elsewhere. The minority who go out to work not only have a second source of friends but they spend less time with the neighbours, a less satisfactory situation for those who are left in the house without companionship. At the same time the working women are more dependent on their neighbour's goodwill. Parcels have to be taken in; the dustman warned about moving extra rubbish; the children have to be invited in if their mother is late back from work. The relations between the neighbours are no longer reciprocal.

Sometimes friendships made at work are continued after marriage, although the wife stops working. Mrs. Suddell in Statham Terrace had weekly visits from such friends, so that, although she had few social contacts among her neighbours, she was never without visitors.

But working-class husbands rarely bring their work-mates home. Even when work-mates are also neighbours it by no means follows that they will spend leisure time together. If they meet at all outside work it is usually only in the pub.

Friendships formed between neighbours usually last only as long as they are living on top of each other. There are some which last after one of the friends has gone to another district of the town. One woman interviewed had broken down and cried when her neighbour (twenty-five years together) moved to a new house in a district only fifteen minutes walk away. They still continue to visit each other every couple of weeks.

This case, however, stands out as an exception to the common working-class pattern that active friendships are between people who live close together and that for them physical distance leads to social distance.

This pattern provides a marked contrast with that of the middle class. Members of the middle class rely upon friends at least as much as upon friendly neighbours for their social life: friends found either in the traditional Banbury 'sets' or through their husbands' colleagues. The Trubshaws in Larkin Drive are examples of this pattern. Mr. Trubshaw is on the staff of the aluminium factory and he and his wife exchange visits with other members of the staff. She takes the children to tea with other young wives and their families. A mutual baby-sitting arrangement with a neighbour makes it possible for them to spend evenings out together with his colleagues playing bridge or driving to the theatre in the neighbouring town.

Middle-class people in Banbury, as elsewhere, as the previous chapter showed, find more of their outlets in formal associations, whether they be sports, cultural, political, or religious. With greater economic and social resources they have less need to rely on their neighbours.

This perhaps is the single most striking finding of the study of neighbour relations in Banbury, that the quality and quantity of these relations change remarkably from one social class to another. This being so, the second important conclusion, that when they are found as neighbours people of different social status do not mix, is perhaps not surprising. A mixture of social classes in a street reduces the intensity of neighbour relations.

The neighbour is of paramount importance as a source of friendship and help in the working class. Yet the relationship is not one which involves any formal relationship or set of obligations. It may be short-lived.[1] Neighbours may be more important than kin day-by-day, but in the major crises, birth and death for example, in every observed case the kin took over.

[1] Mobility in Banbury was calculated at something under one in four over a ten-year period. Furthermore, the continuity of contact seldom extends beyond the generation because houses rarely pass to the children. Oldside Street, where a number of houses have passed through several generations, is an exception.

7

THE FAMILY

THE EXTENDED FAMILY

IN Banbury and in the neighbouring villages there are a number of unusual surnames which occur frequently; some appear in old records as far back as the seventeenth century, others even earlier.[1] Not infrequently one name is associated with a particular village, suggesting an extensive local family. Undoubtedly, in many of the villages the network of blood relations and marriage connexions takes in a large proportion of the village and has ramifications throughout the district. In one village evidence collected showed that half the inhabitants were native born: all their family trees (counted back only to grandparents) were found to be connected at least once with each other, nearly everybody belonging to one of four or five major family groups. In such circumstances it seemed possible that the extended family might be a widely recognized and a functioning group, more so, at all events, than among the mobile immigrant population.

A special study was made therefore of the extended families of fifty people of varied social backgrounds living in the town. In general the test was designed to discover how much people knew about their relatives and how much contact they had with them.[2] Particular attention was paid to a comparison of Banburians and immigrants.

Further, the field-worker who studied neighbour relations in seven selected streets in the town also paid particular attention to the role of the kin group in the daily lives of the people among whom he lived.[3]

Three general conclusions follow from these studies. The first is, as one would expect, that what there is of the extended family derives from the immediate family; it is the immediate family which is the important functioning social unit. Second, that the extended family

[1] Cf. Oxford (Mogey, op. cit., p. 77).
[2] For details of the method of study and analysis see Appendix 6.
[3] See the previous chapter on neighbour relations and also Appendix 5 for details of the method of study.

is shallow and narrow: knowledge rarely extends beyond grandparents, nor does it extend far in width. Third, the range of knowledge and contact is wide: at one extreme the informant knew almost everything about his relatives and was in frequent contact with them, while at the other extreme he knew almost nothing and there was no contact; moreover, the 'average' family constitutes a small minority. Among members of the extended families studied, there was no consistent pattern of relationships carrying with it any customary or predictable forms of behaviour. One possible exception to this statement is that the tie between parents and children tends to remain strong after the children have set up their own homes, particularly the tie between mother and daughter.

The fifty subjects of the special kinship study (twenty-five married couples) were asked questions to reveal their knowledge of members of their extended family (i.e. their relatives) and their extent of contact with them. The relatives each informant was asked about included the members of what originally were three immediate families: first, the informant's own, i.e. his parents and his brothers and sisters and their spouses; second, his father's, i.e. his father's parents, brothers, and sisters, and their spouses; third, his mother's, i.e. his mother's parents, brothers, and sisters, and their spouses. The relatives in question extended therefore through three generations in depth, from the informant to his grandparents and, in width, out to his aunts and uncles. It took no account of cousins or of his own nephews and nieces.

Chart XV (p. 118) sets out these relatives in the form of a family tree, looking at the relationships from the point of view of the informant.

The facts asked about these relatives were:

(i) their Christian names;
(ii) the surnames of men whom the women of the family had married;
(iii) their home, i.e. the last place of residence of the dead and the present place of residence of the living;
(iv) their origin, i.e. the place of their upbringing (not necessarily their place of birth);
(v) the occupations of men members of the family (both those of the blood and by marriage);
(vi) the years of their birth and death.

Replies were accepted at their face value and recorded as positive although not all were strictly accurate. Dates were often given as estimates and were accepted as such; a negative reply here therefore means that the informant was so much at sea that he could give no estimate at all. Secondly, the number of parents' brothers and sisters who died as infants must be larger than is known.

The implication of the replies received inevitably varies with the relative asked about; for example, in the case of Christian names it is more difficult to answer about grandparents than about uncles and aunts, and brothers and sisters, since grandparents are not usually

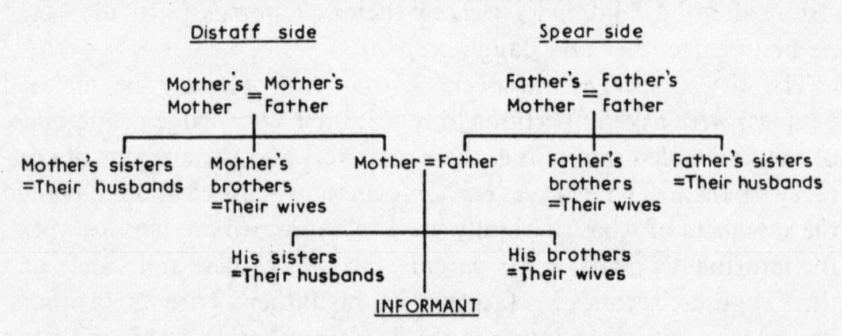

CHART XV. The Family Tree. Relatives asked about in kinship study

addressed by their Christian names, while the other relatives are. Similarly, knowledge of the last home of someone who is dead and knowledge of the present home of someone who is still alive may not be comparable facts.

The results of this part of the kinship study are set out in Table 24. This shows the percentage of relatives in each category about whom information was supplied in answer to the questions put.

The extent of contact which informants had with their relatives was measured by collecting information about whether they visited each other regularly and, if they did not, whether they communicated by post.

Three degrees of contact were used in the final analysis:

(*a*) regular visits: visits made at least once a year;

(*b*) infrequent contact: visits made less frequently than once a year and those who communicated by post but did not visit;

(*c*) no contact.

It is obviously difficult to classify visits in such a way that a comparison may be made between those who live far from their relatives

TABLE 24

*Informants' Knowledge about Certain Members of Their Extended Families (per cent.)**

	Christian name	*Sur-name*	*Maiden name*	*Home*	*Origin*	*Occupa-tion*	*Dates*
(*a*) *Own original immediate family*							
Brothers' wives	86	...	77	...	89	N.A.	58
Sisters' husbands	82	98	N.A.	...	84	96	59
Brothers	98	...	N.A.	99	...	100	95
Sisters	100	...	...	98	...	N.A.	98
Father	100	...	N.A.	100	...	100	94
Mother	100	...	94	...	...	N.A.	96
(*b*) *Maternal relatives*							
Uncles' wives	44	...	21	...	50	N.A.	26
Aunts' husbands	44	69	N.A.	...	42	67	34
Uncles	86	...	N.A.	85	...	80	89
Aunts	82	...	...	79	...	N.A.	58
Grandfather	40	...	N.A.	88	46	70	52
Grandmother	38	...	30	...	44	N.A.	40
(*c*) *Paternal relatives*							
Uncles' wives	36	...	17	...	30	N.A.	14
Aunts' husbands	28	51	N.A.	...	36	57	25
Uncles	70	...	N.A.	67	...	54	53
Aunts	64	...	...	69	...	N.A.	54
Grandfather	44	...	N.A.	80	38	66	42
Grandmother	38	...	32	...	44	N.A.	34

Note: '...' indicates that the information is known by implication since it is known for another relative with whom it is common, e.g., paternal aunt's maiden name is known since ego knows his own surname or her own maiden name. 'N.A.' means 'not applicable'.

* Certain corrections for incomplete knowledge have been made to this table. For details see Appendix 6.

and those whose relatives live in Banbury: to compare, for example, an annual visit to a relative living so far away that the fares alone cost £5 with 'popping in' to see one who lives 'just down the road'. The category (*a*), regular visits, allows these visits to count equally; the stress is on regularity rather than on frequency. A visit was defined as a call at the home of the informant by his relative, or vice-versa. Meetings 'in town', i.e. in the town centre rather than in the home, were not counted as visits. Visits occurring less frequently than annually were put with communication by post, which included Christmas cards, in category (*b*), infrequent contact. Only those, therefore, who were certainly out of all direct touch with relatives were put in category (*c*), no contact.

Table 25 shows the results of this inquiry; it shows the percentage of informants who visit at least one of their aunts and uncles, and of their brothers and sisters, and also the percentage of each of these relatives who are visited.

TABLE 25

Extent of Contact with Kin: Men and Women compared

	Visits with aunts and uncles (parents' sibs) now living			*Visits with brothers and sisters (own sibs) now living*		
	Informants			*Informants*		
	Men	*Women*	*All*	*Men*	*Women*	*All*
(*a*) *Per cent. who visit at least one such relative*						
(i) Regular visits .	44	50	48	78	91	85
(ii) Infrequent contact . . .	23	27	24	13	4	8
(iii) No contact .	33	23	28	9	5	7
(*b*) *Per cent. of such relatives who are visited*						
(i) Regular visits .	18	29	24	35	65	48
(ii) Infrequent contact . . .	11	28	20	32	18	26
(iii) No contact .	71	43	56	33	17	26

(*c*) *Per cent. of male and female relatives who are visited*

	Uncles	*Aunts*	*Brothers*	*Sisters*
(i) Regular visits	17	29	49	48
(ii) Infrequent contact . .	29	15	28	23
(iii) No contact	54	56	23	29

The evidence of Tables 24 and 25 leads to the first two of the general conclusions: the paramount importance of the immediate family and the (almost certainly consequent) shallowness and narrowness of the extended family. Knowledge of and contact with those who were members of one immediate family, now scattered, are greater than with other kin members. Broadly speaking, the farther one moves away from the original immediate family, the less the knowledge and contact. It had been found useless to ask about great-grandparents, since in a pilot study so few positive replies had been received.

Furthermore, the knowledge of grandparents is very partial. The reason most often given for not knowing the facts about grandparents was that the informant had never known them. 'She died before I was born' or 'He died when I was only a nipper' were typical explanations given. All informants showed almost 100 per cent. knowledge of their parents; yet parents apparently, despite the strong tie they have with their own parents, do not talk much to their children about them. For the majority of those surveyed, it seems, the family is a matter of the living only. Lineage is of no very great consequence, at least not farther back than three generations.

Informants knew the married names (surnames of aunts' husbands) of only one-half to two-thirds of the aunts, the home and Christian names of only two-thirds of paternal aunts and uncles, and four-fifths of maternal aunts and uncles. Since such relatives are ordinarily called by their Christian names, knowledge of an individual must be very slender if his name is not known.

Compared with this, knowledge of the informants' brothers and sisters is almost complete. Furthermore, the most striking feature of Table 25 is the number of aunts and uncles who are out of all direct contact. Just under a half of the informants paid regular visits to just under a quarter of aunts and uncles living. Just over a quarter of the informants had no contact at all with any aunt or uncle. Against this, it should be pointed out that in many cases their activities are known to each other through one member of the family with whom both are in contact; in fact a number of the families were found to have one member who acts thus as a sort of family information bureau; this member is almost always a woman.[1]

Speaking generally, therefore, the closest ties maintained in the extended family seem to be those between parents and children; ties among brothers and sisters come second; ties with aunts and uncles are of a much lower order.[2]

Not only are the ties between parents and children of greater importance than those between brothers and sisters, there is some evidence to suggest that the parents are usually vital in keeping the married children together. When the parents die the family focus goes with them.[3] The Claytons in Sonniton Street (see previous chapter) are in their fifties and neither of them have any parents alive.

[1] Also noted for Bethnal Green: M. Young and P. Willmott, *Family and Kinship in East London* (Routledge and Kegan Paul, London, 1957), pp. 61, 62.

[2] This is also in line with the Bethnal Green findings: Young and Willmott, op. cit., pp. 63 et seq.

[3] Cf. ibid., p. 59

However, they both have brothers and sisters in the town and visit one of them every fortnight. But Mrs. Clayton takes a lively interest in her neighbours and it is among them that she has most of her friends.

Knowledge about relatives by marriage, the husbands and wives of aunts and uncles and of brothers and sisters, is never so full as it is for comparable relatives of the blood. By this measure 'in-laws' are not taken fully into the family group, either on the maternal or the paternal side. Or, put another way, there is generally no functioning extended family whose concern it is to know or absorb the 'in-laws'.

But these generalizations must be seen in the light of the third finding; the very great range in the fifty cases studied in knowledge of the extended family. This was indeed the single most striking finding on reading the results. The range is shown in Table 26. Knowledge of relatives ranged from 0 to 100 per cent. The figures include, for example, five who knew nothing about any of their aunts and uncles on either the maternal or the paternal side, three knowing neither the number nor the sex of these relatives; and seven who could answer everything about all their aunts and uncles on both sides.

TABLE 26

Range of Knowledge about Relatives (per cent.)

	Informants' knowledge about:			
	Fathers' parents	*Mothers' parents*	*Paternal aunts and uncles*	*Maternal aunts and uncles*
No knowledge . . .	20	22	22	10
Complete knowledge . .	2	14	26	28

Clearly, if so wide a range can be found it is justifiable to conclude that there is neither a customary level of knowledge nor a group of relatives outside a person's own original immediate family about whom it is customary to know. This, however, is not at all the same thing as saying there is no 'ideal': most informants felt they 'ought' to know more than they did.

The size of the sample was too small to show whether these wide variations are connected with other social characteristics of the informants. Nevertheless, the evidence, when taken with evidence from other studies in the town, suggests certain connexions: first, that the extended family is of greater importance for women than for men; secondly, that it is more important for Banburians than for immigrants; thirdly, that it is more important when an economic function is connected with it.

When there is knowledge it is more likely to be held by women and more likely to be among women; and it is more likely to be among members of the distaff line. In Table 24 knowledge of the maternal side of the family is compared with that of the paternal and is almost always greater. Knowledge of maternal aunts and uncles is nearly 20 per cent. fuller. There is less difference in knowledge of grandparents, but such bias as there is shows again in favour of the maternal side. Table 25 compares the extent of contact maintained by men and women respectively. It shows a consistently higher proportion of women than men who keep up with some aunt or uncle and that more aunts than uncles are visited regularly. Similarly, relations between sisters are better maintained than between brothers. In Table 27 visits to paternal and maternal relatives are compared; the figures show that the distaff line, as well as knowing rather more about their relatives, also keep in touch rather more; two-thirds of paternal relatives but only one half of maternal relatives are out of all contact.

TABLE 27

Extent of Contact with Kin: Maternal and Paternal Relatives Compared

Per cent. of relatives whom informant visits	*Relatives*	
	Paternal	*Maternal*
(i) Regular visits . . .	23	25
(ii) Infrequent contact . .	14	26
(iii) No contact . . .	63	49

Furthermore, of 104 married men (out of a total of 838) in the schedule inquiry who did not, as is customary, head a household of their own, nearly 75 per cent. lived with their wives' parents compared with just under 20 per cent. who lived with their own parents, proportions similar to those found in Bethnal Green by Young and Willmott. In the relatively rare cases (20 per cent. of all households surveyed in the schedule inquiry) in which a household contained members other than those of the immediate family, over 70 per cent. of them were relatives of a member of the family. Three-quarters of the relatives were relatives of the wife or daughter, further evidence of the proportionately greater strength of ties on the distaff side.

It seems likely that these closer ties among the women arise partly from the position of women in English society and partly from the particular nature of the mother–daughter relationship. While customary obligations within the extended family as a whole cannot be traced there seem, from evidence collected in Banbury, to be customary obligations between mother and daughter. Apparently the old saw holds good:

> A son's a son till he gets a wife
> A daughter's a daughter all her life.[1]

For example, the field-worker observed that the mother of a girl having a baby in Banbury will come from several hundred miles away as surely as she will from two streets away, so strong is this customary obligation. The Maxwells in Warriner Lane (see previous chapter) demonstrate the closeness of the mother–daughter tie and what happens to it when the mother and daughter are separated by fifty miles. Mrs. Maxwell came from a large town in the industrial midlands during the war to work at a local factory and it was here she met her husband. She visits her own parents three or four times a year and during the long summer holidays the eldest boy goes to stay with them. In contrast, both she and her husband have little to do with her relatives by marriage, although they live within walking distance. There is no ill-feeling, but there is also no need of their company. Mrs. Maxwell has a very close friend in her next-door neighbour and the two neighbouring families spend much of their leisure time together. Mrs. Maxwell's mother stayed with her at the birth of both of her children. Similarly, a resident of Tracey Avenue has a married son living in the street, but she depends on her neighbours for petty borrowing rather than on her daughter-in-law.

The dependent position of women, dependents first of their fathers and then of their husbands, gives them an economic interest in maintaining ties within the extended family. At the extreme, if a man dies or leaves his wife she has no legal call on her husband's

[1] This relationship is repeatedly reported from urban working-class areas; see particularly Young and Willmott (op. cit.), where it forms the main theme of the study; Mogey (op. cit.), pp. 54–55 and footnote.

family nor on her own; she must rely on the affection of her family if she is to be able to 'go home to mother'.[1]

Furthermore, the work of a woman is entirely bound up with the family, and she sees herself always as part of a family unit. She has, moreover, fewer social outlets than her husband whose life is divided between home and work. While he accepts certain obligations towards his parents, it seems that he is little otherwise concerned about his relatives. He sees himself more as an independent unit responsible for maintaining his wife and home and the immediate family he has founded. She it is, therefore, who accepts responsibility for maintaining the ties between members of the extended family. (It was noted earlier that where one person keeps members of the extended family in touch with each other, that person is almost always a woman.)[2]

Table 28 compares the knowledge of their relatives held by Banburians and immigrants. In both cases the pattern of the general conclusions is followed and knowledge is greater for members of former immediate families. But the knowledge of the Banburian is a good deal fuller than that of the immigrant. Banburians, on average, also maintain more contact with their relatives than do immigrants; the figures are set out in Table 29. Since nearly 90 per cent. of the Banburians have at least one relative living in Banbury compared with less than one-third of the immigrants (according to the findings of the schedule inquiry set out in Table 30), it is clearly easier for them to maintain contact. Therefore, in Table 29 the second column under the heading 'Banburian' shows the percentages for visits with relatives living outside the district. In this column the figures are more comparable with the immigrant figures since travelling is involved in both cases. Even with this allowance Banburians come out at least as high, and generally considerably higher, than immigrants, both in the frequency of their contacts and the proportion of their relatives whom they visit.

[1] Cf. Young and Willmott (op. cit., p. 158): '. . . the wife had to cling to the family into which she was born, and in particular to her mother, as the only other means of assuring herself against isolation. . . . The extended family was her trade union, organised in the main by women and for women, its solidarity her protection against being alone.'

[2] It is probable that this close relationship among women and with the distaff side is less true where there is property to be handed on, since the daughter of a man of property is likely to marry a man who is in a position to provide for her if he dies or leaves her. The one informant in the kinship sample who came of a propertied family knew more of his father's side of the family than of his mother's and said emphatically 'when a Makepeace woman marries she ceases to be a Makepeace—it does not do to have two stags in one herd'.

TABLE 28

*A Comparison of the Knowledge Banburians and Immigrants have of their Extended Families**

	Banburian							Immigrant						
	Christian name	Surname	Maiden name	Home	Origin	Occupation	Dates	Christian name	Surname	Maiden name	Home	Origin	Occupation	Dates
(a) Own original immediate family														
Brothers' wives	91	...	93	...	95	N.A.	74	80	...	60	...	82	N.A.	43
Sisters' husbands	100	100	N.A.	...	97	98	72	64	96	N.A.	...	71	93	45
Brothers	100	...	N.A.	100	...	100	95	96	...	N.A.	98	...	100	95
Sisters	100	...	...	100	...	N.A.	100	100	...	...	96	...	N.A.	96
Father	100	...	N.A.	100	96	100	92	100	...	N.A.	100	88	100	96
Mother	100	...	100	...	96	N.A.	92	100	...	88	...	92	N.A.	100
(b) Maternal relatives														
Uncles' wives	46	...	29	...	58	N.A.	30	36	...	8	...	40	N.A.	16
Aunts' husbands	56	72	N.A.	...	52	69	41	27	66	N.A.	...	31	65	22
Uncles	84	...	N.A.	84	...	72	47	89	...	N.A.	86	...	89	75
Aunts	83	...	...	80	...	N.A.	67	80	...	...	79	...	N.A.	50
Grandfather	56	...	N.A.	96	52	76	64	24	...	N.A.	90	36	64	40
Grandmother	56	...	44	...	60	N.A.	48	20	...	16	...	28	N.A.	32
(c) Paternal relatives														
Uncles' wives	42	...	22	...	44	N.A.	20	34	...	12	...	22	N.A.	12
Aunts' husbands	29	58	N.A.	...	41	60	30	27	48	N.A.	...	27	49	12
Uncles	79	...	N.A.	73	...	63	60	64	...	N.A.	68	...	53	49
Aunts	73	...	...	76	...	N.A.	57	52	...	...	58	...	N.A.	50
Grandfather	56	...	N.A.	100	44	72	36	32	...	N.A.	72	36	60	48
Grandmother	48	...	48	...	64	N.A.	44	28	...	16	...	24	N.A.	24

* Certain corrections for incomplete knowledge have been made to this table. For details see Appendix 6.
... indicates that the information is known by implication. N.A. means 'not applicable'.

TABLE 29

Extent of Contact with Kin: Banburian and Immigrant Compared

	Banburian			
	All	Outside area	Immigrant	All informants
A. *Visits with Aunts and Uncles (Parents' Siblings) Now Living*				
(*a*) *Per cent. of informants who visit at least one such relative*				
(i) Regular visits . .	64	48	28	48
(ii) Infrequent contact .	19	33	29	24
(iii) No contact . . .	17	19	44	28
(*b*) *Per cent. of such relatives who are visited*				
(i) Regular visits . .	33	29	11	24
(ii) Infrequent contact .	24	19	14	20
(iii) No contact . . .	43	52	75	56
B. *Visits with Brothers and Sisters (Own Siblings) Now Living*				
(*a*) *Per cent. of informants who visit at least one such relative*				
(i) Regular visits . .	96	73	73	85
(ii) Infrequent contact .	4	20	14	8
(iii) No contact . . .	0	7	13	7
(*b*) *Per cent. of such relatives who are visited*				
(i) Regular visits . .	66	59	33	48
(ii) Infrequent contact .	18	22	32	26
(iii) No contact . . .	16	19	35	26

TABLE 30

Banburians and Immigrants with No Relatives Locally

Population over 21 only

	% *having no relatives in:*	
Place of origin	*Banbury*	*District*
True Banburians . . .	13·0	71·0
Secondary Banburians . .	29·0	71·0
District	41·0	40·0
True immigrants . . .	71·0	89·0

It seems likely, therefore, that at least some Banburians follow a tradition which demands a higher level of interaction among the extended family. Apparently, close relations within the kin group are more likely to be maintained among stable populations. The importance of the extended family in one form or another has been stressed for Ireland[1] and rural Wales[2] and, by Young and Willmott, for the East End of London.[3] In these cases the families concerned have been associated with the district for a number of generations. Young and Willmott stress the weakening of family ties when members move away from their home district.

But while it is true in Banbury that, on average, Banburians have higher knowledge of and closer contact with their extended families than do immigrants, by no means all Banburians follow this pattern. Some fall among those with little knowledge of or contact with their extended families. It should be pointed out that, of the 45 Bethnal Green wives interviewed by Young and Willmott, in 18 cases the close mother–daughter relationship, described as so strongly typical of Bethnal Green, did not function: 11 mothers were dead and 7 lived far from London. And one of the remaining 27 wives had broken off relations with her mother. This typical Bethnal Green pattern therefore functioned for less than 60 per cent. of the sample.

Furthermore, in Banbury a number of immigrants have full knowledge of and high contact with their relatives. It is perhaps surprising to find that over one-quarter of immigrants have relatives in the town. Four reasons are offered for this: firstly, children of immigrants, themselves classed as immigrants because they were over seven when they came to the town, are now grown-up and have parents and siblings in the town in separate households; secondly, to some extent one member of a family acts as a 'pioneer' and, if he likes the town and finds work prospects good, recommends his siblings to immigrate too[4]; thirdly, there is a small but distinct tendency for parents to retire to the town to be near their migrant children.

But a fourth reason most probably also operates which, as well as helping to explain the number of immigrant relatives in the town, must also explain the high level of knowledge of and contact with relatives recorded by a number of immigrants. It is that the amount and strength of kinship ties varies widely in different areas of the British Isles.

It will be remembered that Table 2, p. 13, which showed the

[1] C. M. Arensberg and S. T. Kimball, *Family and Community in Ireland* (Cambridge, Mass., Harvard Univ. Press, 1940). J. M. Mogey, *Rural Life in Northern Ireland* (O.U.P., 1947).

[2] A. D. Rees, *Life in a Welsh Countryside* (University of Wales Press, Cardiff, 1950).

[3] Op. cit.

[4] A similar movement is reported from Bethnal Green to Greenleigh (Young and Willmott, op. cit., pp. 100, 101).

places of origin of immigrants in order of the numbers from each came out in almost precise geographic order, most immigrants coming from the nearer areas. When, however, the places of origin of immigrants who have relatives in Banbury are listed, as they are in Table 31, the order is quite different. The most remote area, Ireland, has the second highest number of such immigrants, while the Home Counties and London, both relatively near, occupy the bottom two places. The order of the present table must be taken as an indirect comment on the relative strength of kinship ties in different parts of the country.

TABLE 31

Origin of Immigrants who have Relatives in Banbury

Place of origin	*% with relatives in Banbury*	*Order of distance from Banbury. (1 being the nearest)*
10–25 mile radius	47·5	1
N. Ireland and Eire	40·0	9
S. and SW. England	37·8	6
Industrial Midlands	30·6	2
Rest	29·5	–
Wales	26·9	7
Lancs. and Cheshire	25·3	5
Scotland	23·3	8
Yorkshire	22·2	5
Home Counties	20·9	3
London	20·7	4

Undoubtedly in some areas the extended family is recognized and functions in a way quite unlike anything found in Banbury. This was illustrated by some of the case histories, the most remarkable of which was that of a Scot, all of whose family had been connected with the herring fleet. His account suggested that a kinship system operated in association with the purchase and crewing of a boat and that cross-cousin marriages were preferred as a means of keeping the boat in the family.

In this case there were economic reasons for maintaining family ties as well as an association with a particular locality (although they no longer applied to the informant himself). These economic factors, as well as a stable population, also apply to the extended families in rural Ireland and rural Wales according to the reports previously mentioned. These economic ties are connected with inheritance and with mutual aid at the harvest, and so on.

This is in line with the third conclusion of the present study, that the extended family is more widely recognized when economic interests are involved. It has already been shown that one probable reason for women's greater interest is an economic one (pp. 124–5). Among the traditionalist tradespeople of Banbury there is also an economic incentive, that of 'keeping the business in the family'. For among this group of people, owners of shops and small businesses, family counts and lineage counts for those who have been in the town for more than a generation. There are, furthermore, numbers of connexions by blood and marriage between one family business and another. These kinship connexions are remembered (others, it seems, are conveniently forgotten). For this group of people family connexions form an essential part of the social structure. It is the group from which the town leadership used to be exclusively drawn and which still supplies many of the leaders. For these reasons one informant was able to say with some justification, 'Banbury is still run by the old families'.

In this section of the town, traditional in structure and outlook, members of a family not only derive their position from their family's position, but also from their own position in the family. Grandmother Shaw may really be 'beyond it' now, but just because she is the Shaw 'matriarch' she must be consulted on church affairs. Similarly her grandson is expected one day to run and own the Shaw's shop and is therefore given the status due to such an heir. Prestige is accorded to those families who not only have a prosperous business, but who have held it in the family for more than a generation. A leading position is therefore given to the oldest local business family which extends back 200 years.

There is, however, evidence that this traditional group is being weakened in a number of ways. First, the practices are not always maintained by people who accept different standards and prestige values. In fact nowadays, for example, old Grandmother Shaw is not always consulted about the Church bazaar and while traditionalists consider this 'very wrong' they also say that it is a 'sign of the times'. Second, traditionalist tradesmen, as Chapter 2 pointed out, are increasingly finding that it is not worthwhile to stay in business; there are fewer 'family shops' in Banbury every year. Third, anxieties about an heir to the business are increasing. The normal practice was to pass it to one or two sons, the eldest son in particular being dissuaded from taking up another profession. But with the smaller families of today there is not always a son to inherit the business. Furthermore, the son may not be open to persuasion: it is rumoured that the Shaw grandson wants to become a doctor and it is not thought likely that his father will stand in his way.

Members of the traditional upper class in the Banbury district are another group among whom economic interests and family ties are closely connected and whose recognition of the extended family is deep and wide. Their position is based largely upon their inherited social status and the inherited means to maintain it. Sir William (see Chapter 1) is an example of this group, but, like most men in it, he feels that his is the 'last generation'. His son is unlikely to want to struggle to maintain the house and grounds when his father dies. And comparatively high social status is nowadays accorded even by traditional middle-class Banbury to prominent and wealthy men without 'family connexions'.

At the other end of the scale, the 'rough' working-class rely on their families very considerably: here not means but absence of means is the reason. Reciprocity can span the years in the kin group, an arrangement which is not possible in the unstable and casual relations with neighbours, who if they are of higher status often discourage the 'roughs'.

The case of Mrs. Suddell, reported in the previous chapter (p. 111), who spent a great deal of time with her mother, is an illustration of this. Mrs. Suddell's case is like so many reported by Young and Willmott for Bethnal Green, and in Bethnal Green the proportion of unskilled workers (22 per cent.) was particularly high.

In conclusion, there is some evidence for saying that the extended family may be of greater importance for particular social groups: notably, for the stable section of the population, i.e. the Banburians; for groups where economic interests are associated with the extended family, i.e. in the traditional family business and among the traditional upper class; among the poorer sections of the working class; for women, who have economic and social reasons for maintaining relations with the kin group.

For those families which are well integrated in the wider kin group, this group is undoubtedly of considerable social importance. But the most striking evidence from Banbury is less that the extended family may be a functioning social group among some sections of the population than that there is no predictable pattern to be found. The only customary obligations which can be traced are those between parents and children and especially between mothers and daughters.

Apart from the mother–daughter relationship, even among those groups in which the extended family is likely to be of greater importance, close relations with the kin are by no means always present. And close relations may be found in families which do not fall into these special categories.

The final conclusion must be, therefore, that for the most part such ties as exist within the extended family derive less from customary obligation than from affection born in the immediate family. But the ties need not be maintained after the immediate family has broken up. If they are maintained it is because the affection is maintained. Some sense of responsibility may be added, which, if invoked in a crisis, might obtain a response. The range of behaviour shows, on the one hand, how little binding these ties may be and, on the other, how seriously they may be taken.

THE IMMEDIATE FAMILY

The structure of the extended family is thus largely determined by the structure of the immediate family and by the relations within it. Available evidence suggests that, generally speaking, the immediate family in Banbury follows the pattern for the country as a whole and has been subject to similar changes.

The statistical evidence is set out in Appendix 7 and may be summarized briefly here.

The earlier age at marriage is most marked: 62 per cent. of those born in the years 1920–5 were married before they were twenty-five years old compared with only 26 per cent. of those born before 1885. The popular ages for marriage in Banbury at the time of the survey were twenty-five to twenty-nine for men and twenty to twenty-four for women, the men marrying women three years younger than themselves. Variations about the average age for marriage correlate, as in the country as a whole, with factors which may be taken as an indication of social class. Higher occupation-status groups and higher income groups, compared with lower, and particularly salary earners compared with those who receive wages or profits and fees, tend to marry later.

Similarly, the number of children in the family has dropped, so that now the concentration is on the one- or two-child family. Here again, there is considerable range: families with no children and with twelve children were recorded. The size of the family correlates with other factors in a way known to be true of the nation as a whole, again indicating social class differences. Manual workers tend to have more children than non-manual workers (except class 6: semi-skilled). The number of families with four or more children decreases continuously from the lowest income grades upwards (except in the £1,000 plus group where figures are small). Salary earners, the group to marry notably later in life, are also the group in which fewest large families are found when an analysis by source of income is made.

It is the custom, as well as the ideal in Banbury, for every immediate family to have a house of its own. Eighty-eight per cent. of the married men recorded in the schedule inquiry were household heads. In a time of national housing shortage and, more particularly, in a town which had increased its population more rapidly than it could build houses, so high a figure shows how strong the custom is that a couple should leave their parents' home and set up on their own.

It is the younger married men who have, at the moment, no household of their own; there are more married people than household heads between the ages twenty and thirty-five, while the reverse is the case in all the higher age-groups. It is not uncommon, particularly in the poorer working-class homes, for a couple to have rooms in the house of one of their parents until the first baby is expected, when it is assumed they will find a place of their own. As was shown earlier it is usually the wife's parents' home which is chosen.

Further, the household is customarily exclusive to the couple and their children. Eighty per cent. of the households in the sample which were headed by a married man were composed only of the immediate family. This exclusiveness accounts, too, for the households headed by single people (7 per cent. of the total).

Of its nature the immediate family is a short-lived unit, which lasts only for a part of the life of its members. Although almost everyone in Banbury was at one time a member of an immediate family, at the time the sample inquiry was made only 47 per cent. of those in the town who were or had been married were members of whole families. A whole family is defined as one household composed of a man, his wife, and all their children. This is not the same thing as 'complete', which has been used to describe families who will have no more children. Families have been considered complete, following the convention, when the wife is over forty-five years old. 'Whole' families therefore may not be 'complete'.

The stages which Banbury families had reached when the sample was taken are set out in Chart XVI. Only those who are or have been married are included. The three horizontal columns divide the diagram into: first, young couples, where the wife is under forty-five

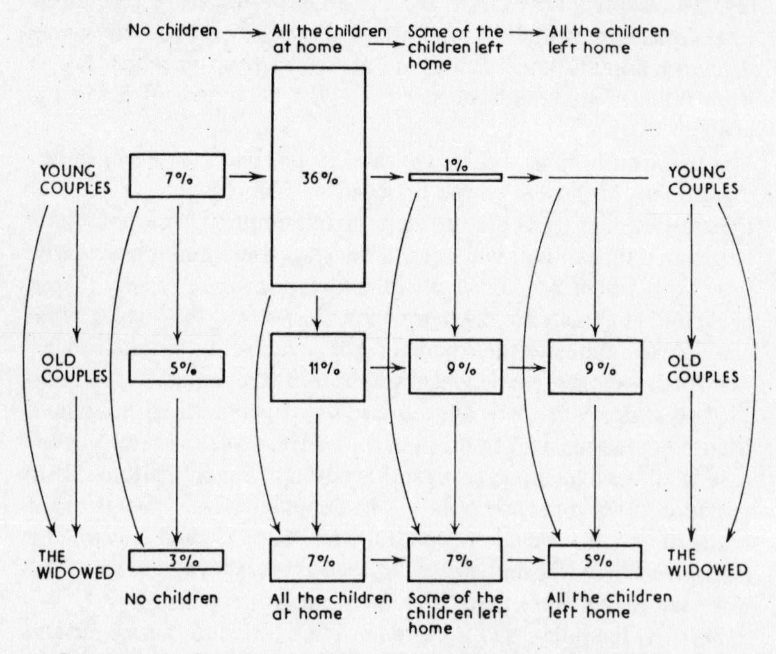

CHART XVI. Percentages of Families at each stage of the Family Cycle

and, therefore, the family cannot be considered as complete; second, old couples, where the wife is over forty-five and families have been assumed to be complete; third, the widowed, separated, and divorced. The vertical columns show the stages their families have reached, first, those with no children; second, whole families, i.e. all the children at home; third, some children have left home; fourth, all the children have left home. The arrows indicate the routes in the family cycle which may be taken. The diagram has been drawn to a scale showing the proportions in each stage, worked out as a percentage of all those who are or have been married.

While the largest single groups are those with all their children at home, nevertheless nearly half (46 per cent.) are families who have no children, whose children are already leaving home, or whose head is widowed. Old couples and widowed people, all of whose children have left home, together account for about 14 per cent. of the total.

The immediate family is tending to break up earlier and more completely nowadays in Banbury as elsewhere. Although the later school-leaving age and an increased amount of higher education means that many children are dependent on their parents for longer than they were, nevertheless, the fall in the age at marriage, the increased number of marriages, smaller families, and the tendency for unmarried daughters to leave home to work more than offset this. In 1 per cent. of the cases shown in Chart XVI the children have started to leave home before the wife is forty-five, or half-way through her adult life (in two cases all the children had left home by this time, a figure likely to be larger in fifteen to twenty years' time, when those now marrying reach their forties.)

Since most women marry and few married women work (18 per cent.), their lives follow a pattern dictated by the family cycle. The custom of 'one family, one household' means that when the family breaks up the house is emptied. Nowadays, therefore, from middle life onwards, the housewife has much less to occupy her time and attention, a period which is also being prolonged at the other end by the increased expectation of life. The implications of this situation have been discussed for America by Margaret Mead, who points the connexion between this under-employment at home and a return to work or increased activity in voluntary associations.[1] In Banbury it is women in their fifties and sixties who fill the women's organizations, but few return to work. It is only in a very few non-traditional homes that wives work because they want to: behaviour which shocks the traditionalist. She only goes to work from force of economic circumstances. The life of men, on the other hand, is less affected by these factors, being broadly divided into school life, working life, and retirement.

Margaret Mead has discussed the implications of the 'non-fit' between these two patterns, men tending to reach a 'plateau' in their working lives in later middle age when their wives start upon a new burst of activity. Attention in Banbury was not attracted to the problem in this form; the proportion of women's organizations is low compared with America and the intensity of activity seems lower

[1] M. Mead, *Male and Female* (London, Gollancz, 1950), pp. 339–41.

too. Attention was attracted rather to the under-employment of women in those years.

A wife cannot resign from her work without breaking from her husband and children, nor can she leave her husband without losing her job. Her occupation is rightly returned as 'married woman'. This is a unique status in a society otherwise based on individual contract, specialization, and separation of function.

Therefore it is not perhaps surprising that women, compared with men, tend to show group characteristics regardless of other social factors like class. Their training from childhood sets them apart from boys and together as potential wives and mothers. A concept of what is appropriate to the female runs from the nursery through education to employment. The girls are sent more often to private schools and less often have higher education. They hold less responsible posts than men when they are in paid employment (those in occupational status 1 in Banbury can be counted on the fingers of one hand) and of the more responsible posts they do hold, the more important ones, e.g. secretaries and school teachers, are associated with their traditional status, as helpmates to men or in charge of children. When they work in industry they do the cleaner, lighter jobs (see Table 3).

Work for women being looked upon as filling in time before marriage or as an unfortunate necessity in a bad or broken marriage, it is the wife-mother role that stamps women's attitudes above other sectional interests. The role of keeping the family together spills over into their attitudes in wider fields, for they have been shown in previous chapters to be more traditional on balance than men. They are more religious and more conservative in politics. Maintenance of the institution of the family apparently leads them to show more concern about maintaining established institutions generally.

FUNCTIONS OF THE FAMILY

R. M. McIver has said '. . . the family has been gradually stripped of functions irrelevant to its peculiar character as a system of more or less enduring social relationships based on the fact of sex'.[1] The State and other outside agencies nowadays help the family and undertake functions which in earlier periods or in other societies were undertaken by parents and kinsmen. Maternity and child welfare services, the health service, social security, education, and technical

[1] R. M. McIver, *Society* (Farrar & Rinehart, N.Y., 1945), p. 212.

training are obvious examples. Yet, observations in Banbury indicate that a number of important social functions remain to the family.

In some cases in Banbury the family still functions as an economic unit (not merely a consuming unit). This is the case among middle-class traditionalist tradesmen with family businesses or shops, and artisans who run small businesses on their own account. Fathers and sons or brothers work together and wives and mothers take 'phone calls and help with the office work.

Formal education may have been taken from the family, but in informal education, in teaching social assumptions, moral attitudes, and everyday behaviour its role is important although not exclusive. In addition to attitudes of this sort many other fundamental social assumptions are first learned at home; the relation of parents to children and the social role of the sexes for example.

Every father of a family has attachments to outside bodies, to religious and political institutions, for example, and interests and attitudes connected with them. So has his wife, but wide differences between husband and wife were not often found. The sample inquiry showed that husbands and wives had the same politics in 83 per cent. of known cases and the same religious denomination in 80 per cent.

These attachments are shared, at least at first, by the children. Children 'inherit' their parents' religious denomination. Their first religious teaching (or lack of it) is at home. Family prayers and church-going are, for all but a few, a thing of the past. But religion remains a family loyalty. 'Well, we were all Methodists (or whatever it may have been) at home' was a frequent way of answering the question 'What is your religion?' Similarly, political attachment is frequently looked upon as a family loyalty. In answer to a question about politics the reply often given was 'Oh, we're all Conservative (or Labour) here'. Children accept, at least at first, their parents' political attitudes. Their parents' loyalties were frequently part at least of the explanation of the behaviour of people who voted eccentrically in terms of their social class: the working-class Conservative frequently had Conservative parents and the middle-class Labour voter, Labour parents.

Parental attitudes are reflected, furthermore, in the use made of outside agencies, for example, their choice of schools. The majority of Banbury parents send their children to State or State-aided schools and they have some choice among them. Most people simply send their children to the nearest school. But some groups with a particular attitude to education base their choice on other factors: religion, tradition, and ambition being the most important. Roman Catholics send their children to the Roman Catholic State-aided school, very few Protestants do. Free Churchmen avoid, if they can, sending their children to a Church of England school, although few Anglicans make a particular point of choosing an Anglican school. Native traditionalists send their children to the school they went to themselves, and sometimes their parents before them. Some even take their children right across town to attend the same school if, for example, they have moved away from the old house by the canal. Those ambitious for their children send them to a school with a good reputation for getting 'scholarships' to the Grammar school.[1]

But perhaps the family's most important social role relates to social status. Each immediate family has its own position in society: a position which is almost entirely derived from the father, although the mother makes a material contribution to its maintenance. As an individual the father's position derives from his occupation and income, his social status, and, more broadly, from his social class. When a woman marries she takes her husband's social position. She can modify the position within rather narrow limits by the standards she maintains in the home and by what she does with the money he gives her, since both factors affect status. But it is her husband's income and class which decide the limits. In the rare cases, where her father had a widely different social status, there is some modification (especially if she inherited property) and she brings with her something of the attitudes and manners of another class; but even so her status is nearer her husband's than her father's. Most often, however, her husband has a status little different from her father. This is shown in Table 32 which plots the status of fathers (using occupational status as the index) against the status of the men their daughters marry.

Children inevitably take the social position of their parents while they are young. Family does not determine the social status its adult children will have, but it does determine the status group in which they start life. From the example and direct teaching of their parents children learn as they grow to mix with other families whose manners and attitudes are the same as their own and to recognize the barrier

[1] The evidence for these conclusions was collected principally in interviews with nearly all the head teachers of State and State-aided schools in Banbury. Head teachers of all but one of the private schools were also interviewed.

when they try to mix with people who have learned differently. This is shown clearly in Sky View, where the children of families of different status form different play groups (see the previous chapter). If, later in life, they wish to change their status (either up or down) the children must learn new accents and turns of phrase; to eat meals with different names at unaccustomed times, and new manners to use at table; subtly different kinds of clothes to wear; new attitudes, interests, and ways of spending time and money.

TABLE 32

Occupations of Women's Fathers and Husbands

Husbands' class	%* Fathers' class (Hall/Jones scale)				Nos. in sample
	1 and 2	*3 and 4*	*5*	*6 and 7*	
1 and 2	11	44	33	11	9
3 and 4	8	21	51	21	63
5	3	11	64	21	135
6 and 7	2	8	50	40	62
Numbers in sample	11	37	153	68	269

* Totals do not always add to 100 because of rounding.

Several studies, both here and in America, have shown the close association between the children's education and their family's social status.[1] Furthermore, education and training are becoming increasingly closely associated with occupational status and replacing the possession of a small amount of capital as the basis for upward social mobility. The Banbury evidence confirms the general conclusions. In Banbury the type of primary school (State, private, or preparatory) to which a child goes is determined largely by his parents' social status. Furthermore, of children who start in State elementary schools those from families of higher social status are more likely to go to grammar school than those of lower social status. This was shown by an analysis of past pupils of the grammar school according to their fathers' occupational status grading. The higher grades were over-represented and the lower, especially class 7 (Hall/Jones scale), under-represented in terms of the distribution of occupation in the whole town.

[1] See, for example, D. V. Glass (ed.), *Social Mobility in Britain* (Routledge & Kegan Paul, 1954).

The majority of children go to State or State-aided schools both because of the cost of private education and because it is, for the majority, the normal thing to do. In a working-class area the uniform of a private school marks the children out among the neighbours as 'different': 'they're a bit above themselves'.

The implications of grammar-school education, traditionally a preserve of the middle class, is clearly understood by working-class parents. This understanding is reflected, on the one hand, by the rivalry of parents over their childrens' showing in the tests to decide whether they shall go to a grammar school. On the other hand, it is reflected in parents' anxiety as to whether their grammar-school-educated children will be ashamed of them. 'Of course, if she (the daughter) passes for the Grammar we shall have to move from here', said one woman. Working-class parents know that if their children go to grammar school, they may not only become qualified for jobs which will bring them into association with the middle class, but they may learn the manners and tastes of this class as well. The ambivalence is further demonstrated by the fact that although many parents are anxious 'to get their children into the Grammar' they also let them leave or take them away at fifteen or sixteen. Relatively few of working-class origin stay to the sixth or go on to a university.

George, a traditional worker, was not bothered when his son failed to get a grammar-school place. He was in fact happier that he should continue at the same school he had been to himself and go into a 'steady' job at fifteen. Ted, the non-traditional trade unionist, on the other hand, was most anxious that his son should 'pass for the Grammar' and was delighted when he did. But Ted had more than one brush with the headmaster over his son's behaviour. (Ted was always on his son's side, convinced he was victimized for political reasons.) His son eventually left before he was sixteen.

Middle-class parents, by contrast, follow the traditional pattern, as the tradesmen Shaw and Grey did, and send their children to one of the private day-schools in the town. Some make considerable sacrifices to do so. After this their children go to the State grammar school if they can obtain a place there or to a small public or boarding school. They do not send them to State primary schools because they say they are 'rough' and they do not want their children to 'pick up an accent'. In short, they look to the private schools to teach middle-class manners and they are prepared to trust the grammar school to carry on its tradition of doing the same. There is, furthermore, no alternative in Banbury itself for parents who wish their children to have a grammar-school education, since there is no independent grammar school; the nearest is more than twenty miles away.

In the upper class and on its frontier in Banbury and district, the field-workers found no case where parents have taken advantage of free education. From the professional classes upwards, and including a few of the wealthier tradesmen, all parents send their children to a pre-preparatory school in Banbury and later away to board at a public school, spending perhaps £400–£500 per annum for ten to fourteen years on each of their children's education. Public-school education is, in fact, of so great importance as a class factor that it is used in the following chapter as a primary definition of the traditional upper class in Banbury and district.[1]

In this vital matter of education, the State, through successive Education Acts, has modified the influence of family status, particularly in the working class. The education of children according to their 'ability and aptitude', one aim of the 1944 Education Act, is based on a non-traditional principle: that people should be judged on their merits. Buying education for children at public and private schools is based on a traditional principle: that people should be judged according to their family and that family status should pass to the children. The State here plays the role of the non-traditionalist, and the fee-paying parents uphold tradition, paying as they do for a level of education that could be had free if their children merited it.

There are a few cases of middle-class parents, all non-traditionalists, who have chosen to send their children to the State primary schools. They thereby save the school fees and they give a number of additional reasons for their choice: that it is good for the children to 'mix a bit'; that their chance of a 'scholarship' is better; that the neighbouring State school is 'new and (with an implied "therefore") very good; a nice school'. But these are exceptions.

Members of the new professional classes in Banbury can send their children either to the elementary school or to a private

[1] O. Banks, *Parity and Prestige in English Secondary Education: A Study in Educational Sociology* (Routledge & Kegan Paul, 1955), chap. 16, has suggested that educational changes follow social changes, rather than that education is a determinant of social structure or an initiator of change. But as a class 'mark' used to preserve the in-group of the traditional upper class, the public school is of undoubted importance, as the following chapter suggests.

school or to the pre-prep. school which (1950) bars 'tradesmen's children'. There is no tradition in Banbury for them to follow as, for example, there is for the doctors. The doctors' children 'always' go to the exclusive pre-prep. Nevertheless, none of the new professionals, as far as the field-workers discovered, send or plan to send their children to State primary schools. They see their choice as lying between the private or the pre-prep. Their decision is an individual one, but one which is made solely between the middle-class and the upper-class patterns. For they see themselves as above the 'ordinary run' who send their children to elementary schools.

This group of people is identified as non-traditional because its members do not belong to the traditional social structure of Banbury. In many cases they do not choose to identify themselves with it. Their occupations are non-traditional, and, moreover, so are many of their attitudes, those towards work and religion for example. A number of them were themselves State-educated. Non-traditional in other respects these parents accept traditionalism in education. They wish to pass the status they have achieved on to their children. They also wish to free them from the limitations of status which they themselves started with, i.e. they wish to give their children chances for more upward mobility than they can hope for themselves. The pull of the traditional social class structure is indeed remarkably strong, for these non-traditionalists behave as the traditionalist who has 'worked his way up in business' (the traditional route for upward mobility) behaves.

To sum up therefore, the family remains particularly important in two respects: in teaching certain fundamental social and moral attitudes and in its influence upon social status.

Social change and scientific advance have been rapid in the lifetime of Banbury people. For social change to be possible older assumptions and attitudes must be rejected, that is, family teaching rejected. The new ways are more readily accepted by the young. The rapid changes have therefore tended to widen the always-existing gap between the generations. Nevertheless, the family is still the giver of many of the patterns of social behaviour and of many of the moral and social attitudes learned in childhood. These must be accepted, modified, or rejected later on. The influence of parents may be weaker than in a more stable period, but whatever position a son or daughter takes up when adult it will be coloured, even in rejection, by the practices and precepts of the parents.

Secondly, the family remains important as the first giver of social status, with the advantages or limitations this may imply. These are greater for those who remain in Banbury and live within the traditional society, for here lineage as well as personal attainment is taken into account in judging social status.

8

SOCIAL STATUS AND SOCIAL CLASS

IT is not possible to construct for Banbury and district a simple *n*-fold class system. That is to say, the total population cannot be placed in a series of horizontal groupings, members of each group being assumed to have parity with each other and able to recognize each other as social equals if they should meet. Nor is it possible to place people upon one social status scale, ranked on a basis of commonly agreed social characteristics. There is a reasonably clear-cut status system within the traditional society, linked with the traditional class system. Among non-traditionalists there are numbers of status groups based most often on occupational status, but on a variety of occupational hierarchies rather than on one single system. Prediction about the class and status position of a traditionalist may be fairly accurate; only the roughest prediction is possible for the non-traditionalist. Some very broad equivalence between traditionalists and non-traditionalists on a three-fold system can be seen at a fairly high level of abstraction.

These conclusions, which are described and justified below, were reached by participation in the life of the town at all levels and by observation of who associated socially with whom in both formal and informal groups. The study of formal associations provided a valuable guide for those in the middle ranges, but informal associations were not neglected here and assumed greater importance for those who do not take much part in formal associations. The bridge sets, sherry parties, and tea parties, the 'regulars' at pubs and hotels, and associations among neighbours, are examples of the informal groups observed.

Direct questioning about social class was almost confined to members of the adult tutorial class which was associated with the survey. Its results largely served to show that the indirect method of observation was likely to be the most satisfactory.

Elizabeth Bott[1] has shown that probably everybody has a working 'construct' of the social class system based upon their own

[1] *The Concept of Class as a Reference Group* (op. cit.), pp. 259 et seq.

experiences and aspirations, a construct which may or may not fit the facts of the social structure as seen by the sociologist. Moreover, status groups are so complex and confusing that they may be pressed into almost any conceptual framework. These two facts affect the social theorist, the field-worker, and the layman alike.

At first the adult students produced as many different class systems as there were students. This was before the subject had been treated in lectures. After the six-fold classification used by Warner had been explained to them, almost all concluded that such a system also applied to Banbury! After all, it was neat, they had all heard of upper, middle, and lower classes (although they said 'working' not 'lower') and they were prepared to accept sub-divisions they had not thought of in the large areas of society of which they had not direct knowledge. Further theoretical discussion led to further amendment of the students' concepts.

In any case, direct questioning about social class, both inside the adult class and outside it, met an initial reticence that amounted to a taboo. The reasons for this reticence are connected with the class system itself and with the changes that are taking place within it. There are certain social rules which say that the existence of status and class differences should be assumed but not spoken about. One effect of this is to make people pretend, to themselves as well as to others, that the differences do not exist or are less pervasive than is in fact the case. It is the existence of these rules which in part makes the class system workable. It is 'not done' to 'set yourself up' or 'write the other man down' although it is done every day by implication and sometimes remarkably directly. An example of this attitude came from a Colonel's wife speaking to a new-comer to a village on whom she had called. 'I think you'll like the *X*'s,' she said, 'and then there are the *Y*'s and the *Z*'s; otherwise I don't think there is anybody. But of course it's bad luck for you there are no children in the village.' (The new-comer had a young family.) Happily this startling picture of rural depopulation was contradicted by statistics which showed that the village had a population of about 500 with a normal complement of children. Yet this woman, who referred to 98 per cent. of her fellow villagers as 'nobody', as people you would not 'know', although in fact she knew a great many through the Women's Institute, saw no contradiction in saying: 'I shouldn't mind the socialists so much if they didn't bring class into everything.' Her real complaint was, of course, that the socialists, instead of taking class for granted, talk about class and, worse still, question it.

Reticence which springs from this taboo is increased because class is associated with politics, itself a taboo subject except among intimates and those of known common allegiance as Chapter 3 showed. In consequence, even those who accept the rightness of the traditional class system tend to be self-conscious about it and feel that perhaps 'it's not quite democratic'. This attitude leads to the self-justifying 'well, anyway, we're all workers nowadays'. It may even lead to a denial of obvious fact. One informant, for example, denied that one of the most exclusive clubs in town was in fact exclusive at all. 'Oh no,' she said, 'nowadays anyone can join.' The club's constitution may not formally bar anyone, but analysis showed that in practice by no means 'anyone' joined.

Given time these difficulties could be, and were, overcome among friendly informants. But, added to the reticence which springs from the social taboos, there is honest confusion about the status system in Banbury. Banbury is no longer a place where 'you know where you are' as, according to informants, it used to be. It was a society, apparently, in which the status of individuals and their families, indeed of individuals as members of their families, was clearly understood. Now a great many immigrants and the unfamiliar hierarchy of a large factory have been added. For example, the people of Banbury find it difficult to place a man such as a department head who is employed (a sign of low status) and yet has more power (a sign of high status) than many in the town who are their own masters; or again, a metallurgist, a skill previously unknown in the town, who appears to have little or no authority (low status) and yet has a university education (very high status). The confusion is increased because people of this sort are usually immigrants whose family background is unknown and many of whose associations are outside the district. Nobody knows where to put them and, in fact, they cannot be 'put' into the traditional status system of Banbury, it has no place for them. Some individuals have worked their way in, many others have not and are not concerned to do so.

To have built up a picture of the status system in Banbury from information given by townspeople about their 'sets' would have been a difficult task. Lengthy interviews would have been necessary to break down initial resistance. Added to this are the dangers of reification and the partial and confused nature of individual knowledge, for outside the traditional system the status system is fragmentary. A very great many people would therefore have had to be interviewed if all levels of the town were to be adequately covered. Such large-scale intensive interviewing was beyond the resources available.

The methods of observation and participation used have produced results which can be described but which have not been precisely measured. For the class structure revealed by the evidence collected was in many ways different from what had been expected: the impossibility, for example, of placing everybody, even broadly, in one class system had not been suspected at the outset. Statistical data, measuring objective status characteristics, was collected on the assumption of a unitary system. Consequently only partial measurement of the groups finally identified and described below is possible. The author prefers, however, to describe groups which have been seen to exist rather than to classify people on an objective characteristic, thus apparently identifying and measuring a group, although it has not been observed in operation.

Since social class, where it exists, is, by definition, an open system (as opposed to a closed caste system, for example) there are no hard and fast lines between classes. Rather there are a great many status grades which shade off imperceptibly into each other. Each status grade has observable social characteristics and associated attitudes which differentiate it from its neighbours.

For the traditional area these status grades can be validly grouped together, on the basis of certain shared characteristics, into three classes. Such a threefold system is not uncommonly used, although few studies make any clear differentiation between upper and middle classes. Indeed, most studies of social class hitherto made in this country have tended to pay little attention to the upper class. It is, after all, a numerically small group and studies involving social class have tended to be made in places where the upper class do not live. In the context of Banbury and district it was impossible to ignore the existence of upper-class people. Furthermore, in so far as this class sets the standards and the aspirations of traditional social class attitudes, if only indirectly below the level of its frontier with the middle class, it is important out of all proportion to its size.[1]

In the present study the dividing line between classes has been

[1] Although few studies make any clear differentiation between upper and middle classes R. Lewis and A. Maude, *The English Middle Classes* (Phoenix House, 1949), p. 17, differentiate between upper and upper middle.

drawn at the points where the social characteristics of the status groups show the most fundamental changes. That is to say, members of the class above have characteristics which it is difficult or impossible to acquire in an adult lifetime. But, because the system is continuous, there are in each case status groups on the frontiers between the classes, which partake of the characteristics and the values of the class above and the class below them. Therefore they cannot be allocated to one class or the other.[1]

It is easier to move up within a class than between classes, except for those who start on the frontier between classes. In practice, in terms of face-to-face relationships, belonging to a class (or moving up or down) involves being accepted in a 'set' which has a status in a wider context. The context may be different from but not unassociated with the class allocation people give themselves in relation to the country as a whole and to their political-interest class, e.g. 'middle class' or 'worker'. The techniques of acceptance or rejection are subtle. You must possess appropriate characteristics: occupation, home, residence area, income (suitably spent), manners, and attitudes. You must know or learn the language and the current private 'passwords' of the group. You must be introduced. If you fail in these particulars you will simply be 'not known'. Nothing is said or done. The barrier is one of silence. This is also true for those who are dropped for some offence against the code of their class; they may never discover what their alleged offence is and certainly have no chance of defence. They simply find that invitations cease and backs are turned at the bar. In the working class rejection may be as silent or it may be more open; open mockery, for example, of language that is too 'haw-haw'.

For social status, and to that extent social class, involves a totality of status differences: no one characteristic is an adequate index to it. The prime essentials of social class are the manner of life a man leads and the people he associates with on a basis of equality.[2] In social class home and working life meet and the roles of husband and wife

[1] This construction is different from that used by Lloyd Warner and his associates in *Jonesville* (op. cit., p. 24), where each status group has been put into a class and the class breaks do not fit the most abrupt changes in social behaviour. In *Jonesville* one of these is said to fall between the upper-middle and lower-middle groups in the middle class and the second between the upper-lower and lower-lower groups in the lower class. Not, that is to say, between the upper and middle classes and the middle and lower classes respectively.

[2] Compare T. H. Marshall: 'The essence of social class is the way a man is treated by his fellows (and, reciprocally, the way he treats them), not the qualities or the possessions which cause that treatment.' *Sociol. Rev.* 1934.

are both important: how much money he provides and how she spends it; where and what sort of house he provides and how she runs it; if he is to be acceptable to a group of people so must she be. For social status is a family rather than a purely individual matter. Factors like occupation and income are important because they determine the manner of life that is possible: size and equipment of house, furnishings, dress, hospitality, and so on, hours of work and amount of leisure time. The status carried by the occupation itself plays some determining role in social class but is not necessarily paramount.

But these factors are by no means the only ones. People may choose to live differently from the way in which their income and occupation status would lead one to expect. Cases of people who were living according to the customs, the values, and attitudes of a grade 'above' or 'below' them (in terms of their income and occupation position), and who were accepted by the grade of their choice, were found at three different social status levels. Examples were also found of people who have failed to be accepted by their 'economic' peers and who therefore had a lower status than expected.

Moreover, factors which are not purely social can come in. Attention was focused during the field-work on social rather than psychological factors, but it was noticed that personality was often the explanation for individuals who were 'misplaced' in terms of their class; individuals who, while apparently lacking certain essential social qualifications, had 'got in' to a superior group or who, with the qualifications, were nevertheless out-grouped.

For social class is judged in practice by the impression produced by the sum total of status-giving characteristics. The qualifying 'tests' for admission to a status group may be passed by those who possess most but not all of a given set of characteristics. That is why individuals are found who associate not merely in a different status group from what one might expect, judged on the basis of 'objective' characteristics alone, but even in a different class.

Table 33 shows the main outlines of the social class and status system for Banbury and district (the class system in the rural area was not observed below the level of the gentry and the large farmers). Table 34 shows the main characteristics of these groups. It should be pointed out that the tables represent a considerable abstraction in the sense that this is not the way any one person in the town thinks of it. Furthermore, the characteristics given are those possessed by

TABLE 33

Social Class and Social Status Groups

TRADITIONAL CLASS SYSTEM				NON-TRADITIONAL STATUS GROUPS	
CLASS		STATUS GROUP			*Reference to Traditional Status groups*
		RURAL	TOWN		
UPPER	1	COUNTY		1 Industrial Upper	1–3
	2	GENTRY		2 Banbury Senior Directors and Managers	2–4
	3	UPPER FRONTIER		3 Newer Professions	
MIDDLE	4		MIDDLE		
	5	LOWER FRONTIER		4 Industrial Technicians and Staffs	4–6
	6		RESPECTABLE	5 Respectable	6
WORKING	7		ORDINARY	6 Ordinary	7
	8		ROUGH	7 Rough	8

an 'ideal type' at the centre of the group. Not everyone in the group necessarily possesses all of them.

Traditional and non-traditional status groups have been separated. The former fall into a fairly clear class system which the latter do not. Equivalences are suggested between the two sides of Table 33 on the basis of known associations on terms of equality between traditionalists and non-traditionalists. It will be seen that they range fairly widely, showing both the lack of system among the non-traditionalists and the fluidity of the total situation.

In the traditional class system the three classes identified have been called upper, middle, and working. The single most important characteristic which divides the upper from the middle class is one of education. Members of the traditional upper class in the Banbury district were all educated at one of the major public schools.[1]

In contrast, a common educational background is by no means a characteristic of the Banbury middle class. Its members were not educated at public schools in the upper-class definition, although some went to minor public schools. A number were educated at private schools, others at local grammar schools, and others again received only an elementary education. Education, therefore, does not necessarily provide a distinction between the middle class and the working class, although it is true that the majority of the working class have received only an elementary education while a much higher proportion of the middle class received a secondary education. The single most important characteristic which divides the middle class from the working class is occupation. The middle class are either employed non-manual workers with some power and responsibility or are proprietors. The working class are manual workers, but not necessarily without responsibility over others.

Two status groups have been identified in the upper class: 'county'

[1] While the precise definition of a 'public school' is difficult and membership of the Headmasters' Conference certainly too broad for use here, the upper class regard about two dozen as 'good' public schools and most of the aristocracy patronize two or three of these. The Banbury and district telephone directory shows a total of 92 men and women in the district who bear titles, senior rank in the services (Colonel or over), or who live in a house called 'hall', 'park', &c., with the village name as prefix. 24 are in the last category, 39 hold senior rank in the services, 29 bear titles. 21 of the total of 92 are women. Of the 71 men, 36 are in *Who's Who*; 26 of these are shown as having been educated at one of nine major English public schools (16 at Eton); 3 at Scots or Irish public schools, and 3 privately; the remaining 4 gave no particulars. Apart from any who are members of the non-traditional upper class, an analysis of the remaining 34 who are not listed in *Who's Who* would probably give a broadly similar result. The majority passed from public school to Sandhurst, Oxford, or Cambridge. None went to a 'provincial' university.

and 'gentry'. The 'county' is headed by the few aristocrats who live in the district. The aristocracy, nationally, is drawn from nobles who have inherited their titles; it is an informal social group and one which forms the centre of the court circle; the crown is its head. For the rest, the 'county' includes retired senior officers from the services and some landed gentry (often younger sons of aristocrats or in some way related), provided that they play an active part in the affairs of the district or in one of the hunts. The 'gentry' is composed of men and women from the same sort of families and with the same sort of education as the 'county' who, either from choice, because they are retired or widowed, or from lack of means, participate in public life on a reduced scale.

The 'upper frontier' group lies between the middle and upper classes. The majority of its members had the same sort of education as the upper class; their manner of life and their attitudes are in many ways similar. But they 'work for a living' (many are in the older professions) as servants of the upper class and of other classes. Their personal associates are drawn partly from the upper class, where their educational background makes them acceptable, and partly from the middle class.

This 'upper frontier' group is perhaps nationally most often called 'upper-middle', but since in Banbury some of its members associate on terms of ease with some members of the gentry who are definitely upper class (as well as with middle-class people), this title has been avoided. Further the, rather loose, common use of 'upper-middle' also covers groups of professional and business men who do not share the upper-class characteristics so typical of the Banbury 'upper frontier'.[1]

Below the 'upper frontier' comes a status group 'middle' which is the centre of the middle class. There are a number of interest groups within it, the divisions into Anglican, Free Church, and Roman Catholic being perhaps the most important. It is the group from which the traditional political leaders in the town are drawn and also its social leaders. In Chart V, p. 40, its representatives are in that group which clusters round the Chestnuts Bowls. The tradesmen and the businessmen of the town form the backbone of this group.

[1] It is an apposite comment on occupation as an index of status that the social class of doctors (of the same medical rank) varies from one part of the country to another, from middle class to upper class, including the 'frontier' cases. It may be relevant to their status in Banbury, where they mostly fall in the upper frontier group, that there it is possible for general practitioners to live in, or almost in, the country, a characteristic piece of upper-class behaviour. Those, therefore, who appreciate the rural life are likely to self-select themselves to areas like Banbury.

The 'lower frontier' group lies between the middle class and the working class. Among its representatives are those found around the Borough Bowls (as some members of the status group above cluster round the Chestnuts). In the same way that the 'upper frontier' is divided in characteristics and associations between the upper and the middle classes, so are members of the 'lower frontier' status group divided between the middle and working classes. Its members include both manual and non-manual workers; among non-manual workers it includes both those who work on their own account and employed office workers; among manual workers it includes skilled men working on their own account and employed skilled workers. This group might be called 'lower-middle class', but equally some of its members might be called 'superior working class'; it is, in fact, a frontier group and has therefore been so named.

The working class itself is composed chiefly, but not exclusively, of manual workers (some are routine non-manual workers, for example) and does not include all manual workers. It has been divided into three status groups: 'respectable', 'ordinary', and 'rough'. This division has some relation to amount of skill and income, but the actual ranking for a family is made not on the basis of these factors alone, but on steadiness at work and excellence of house-keeping in addition. The 'rough' are identified by their failure to conform to these standards, by a failure to be 'clean and decent'; they are families where father is not regularly employed, where the house and children are not kept clean, and whose members are 'in trouble' with the police from time to time.[1]

The widest range of knowledge and social recognition between the status groups in Table 34 is two groups distant from your own (except, of course, in terms of business relationships, of master and man, or tradesman and customer, for example). Thus members of the county do not 'know' anyone below some of the doctors (the 'upper frontier' ones), neither do the gentry, the gap made by the public school 'test' is too great; the upper frontier know members of the gentry and the middle class; the middle class range from upper frontier to lower frontier; the ordinary worker from respectable to rough, and so on. Beyond these ranges the gulf is so wide that informal contacts do not take place.

[1] Compare W. Baldamus and N. Timms, 'The Problem Family. A Sociological Approach', *Brit. J. Sociol.*, Dec. 1955.

The gulf is wide because the way of life, interests, and attitudes of the three classes are so markedly different. Differences of occupational status, wealth, education, type of house, and residence area are frequently discussed in relation to social class. All these are relevant in Banbury as elsewhere and correlate with social class. They have been discussed in previous chapters. But it is the combination of such factors in association with differing sets of values and attitudes which lead to the existence of such wide social class differences and consequently to the extreme social distance that there is between one class and another.

One of the effects of the objective class characteristics in combination is that as social status increases so does scale of living: houses not only increase in size and amenities, but are found farther and farther away from the town centre. All members of the upper class live right outside Banbury Borough in the rural area of the district; the middle class live in villages which neighbour the town or on the higher land to the south and west of the Borough. The working class live either in the crowded town centre or in the council estates on the outskirts, government action having upset what would otherwise have been a neat ecological map. It is still probably true that more of the traditional working class live in the town centre, many of those in the council estates on the outskirts being non-traditional workers, but the correlation is far from perfect.[1] This geographic distance, of course, emphasizes the social distance between the classes and is commonly found in any 'class' society of this sort.[2]

But this is by no means the whole story of the relationship between social class and geography; the size of the geographic area within which relationships at the face-to-face level are maintained also increases with social status. The basis of the upper-class social circle is national, with the west end of London as its 'town centre', *The Times* as its local paper, and certain national events, e.g. Ascot, as its focal points. It is a social circle whose members may have international connexions. It is remarkable of the upper class that they have practically no contact with Banbury itself; any contact they may have is limited to acts of patronage, presidencies of Banbury associations

[1] There is some similarity between Mogey's 'status-assenting' group and my traditional group, a similarity which is discussed in Chapter 10. He found (op. cit., pp. 140 ff.) that more status-assenting lived in St. Ebbe's (near the town centre) than in Barton (the Council estate on the outskirts).

[2] Although according to Warner *et al.* the upper class in American towns live in the 'best' areas in town, unlike the English upper class who shun town life altogether, unless they still maintain a town house in the west end of London.

for example. Nor are immediate neighbours of any account in the upper class: a neighbour is a member of the same class within a radius of about thirty miles (see Chapter 6).

This wide basis for the face-to-face group is possible because members of the upper class can command the physical means of communication; they own cars and have telephones. So do many members of the middle class in Banbury and district, but they use their cars principally for business, for occasional journeys connected with the activities of their voluntary associations, and for holiday travel. If it could be measured, the proportion of their local to trunk calls would be found to be much higher than that of the upper class. For Banbury is the basis of the friendship circle in the middle class. Its members have friends outside Banbury, but are unconnected with any nationally based social group (a number of their voluntary organizations are nationally organized, however). They have some relationships with their next-door neighbours, but their social circle is principally drawn from members of their own class with like interests to themselves living in the town or nearby villages.

The geographic horizon of the working class is more restricted again. The majority form their most important friendship groups in the street where they live and often within a part only of that street. The men have friends at work, but these are rarely leisure-time associates even when they live nearby. Nor do many members of this class take an active part in voluntary associations. The pub they go to is at the end of the street or just round the corner.

In another sense, also, a wider area of communication is possible for those of higher status, for command of language increases with social class. In the upper class not only is the command of written and spoken English high, but the common manner of speech given by the public schools is a class mark, and one which it is difficult (some say impossible) to acquire in adulthood.[1] Middle-class command of language is reasonably good, but some solecisms are common and the accent of place of origin may usually be detected, for here speech is less standardized than in the upper class. Working-class command of language is less great, grammar tends to be inaccurate, and the accent and idiom of place of origin marked; vocabulary is more limited and less ability to deal with abstract ideas is shown. When members of the traditional working class belong to

[1] Now known as 'U' following Ross: 'U and Non-U. An Essay in Sociological Linguistics', *Encounter*, Nov. 1955.

voluntary associations, they commonly excuse themselves from office on such grounds as 'I'm not handy with my pen'.[1]

The factor which nowadays does not correlate steadily with class in Banbury, as elsewhere in England, is income and/or wealth, although the lowest incomes tend to be found at the bottom and the most wealth at the top. The way in which income is obtained does still vary reasonably consistently with class in the traditional system.[2] Independent means and profits and fees in the upper class, profits and fees or salary and sometimes independent means in the middle class 'and wages in the working class. Nowadays in Banbury a number of middle-class people are wealthier than some of the gentry (whose 'independent means' produce for them in some cases less than the wage of a skilled manual worker). Some workers, furthermore, earn more than some members of the middle class.

Although this is the case, it does not lead the possessors of these relatively high incomes to adopt the manner of life of the class above. Wealthy middle-class people in Banbury do not have nannies or send their children to major public schools; it would be out of class pattern and they do not wish, apparently, to attempt to change their class. Rather they live up to the highest standards set for the Banbury middle class. Similarly, the better-off workers do not adopt the middle-class pattern, they live more lavishly on the working-class scale: they eat well, drink and smoke more, have TV sets, and new outfits for the wife and children for every public holiday. But they do not move from the rent-controlled or Council house and buy an owner-occupied house on a mortgage (which would be uneconomic for them but necessary if they wished to move into the middle class), nor do they join voluntary associations which are essentially middle class, nor send their children to private schools.

The evidence from Banbury is that the goals of the classes are different and that although income may not correlate with class, the way that income is spent does correlate with it; a choice is made on the basis of the values set by the class. Those who wish to raise their status aspire to the standards of a 'set' in the status group immediately above them, not to those of the class above them. Similarly, those whose means are reduced do not in consequence adopt the life

[1] Mogey (op. cit., pp. 61, 154) has noted the limited communication possible for language reasons among the subjects of his Oxford survey.

[2] It will be remembered that Lloyd Warner uses 'source of income' as one of his main indices to social class. W. Lloyd Warner, M. Meeker, K. Eells, *Social Class in America: A Manual for the Measurement of Social Status* (Chicago, 1949).

of the class below, but live on a smaller scale within the values of the class to which they were brought up.

An attitude which is common to people in all classes within the traditional system is acceptance of loyalty to established institutions. Loyalty to the crown in the person of the monarch as a symbol of national unity is one example. Hence the importance to the traditional system of the aristocracy, leaders of the upper class, numerically few though they are. Traditionalists in Banbury and district accord status to the upper class by asking them to patronize their associations, although it is doubtful how clear they may be about distinctions between traditional and non-traditional members of the upper class, except for those few aristocratic families who have had associations with Banbury and district for many centuries. Loyalty to established institutions is also connected with conservatism in politics, or with anti-socialism. The working-class Conservative was explained in terms of traditionalism in Chapter 3. A connexion between traditionalism and active religious adherence was also suggested (Chapter 4).

A loyalty to the traditional class system, or to its values, is also common to people who remain within it. Although touching the cap or curtseying to the squire and his lady have passed out of custom within living memory in Banbury district, all agree that 'There'll always be classes, stands to reason' and stress the importance of 'breeding', i.e. the inherited basis of social class. The ideals of the gentleman and 'gentlemanly' and 'ladylike' behaviour are found in all classes, although the interpretations of each differ from one class to another. Furthermore, the right to lead of those in a higher class, or in a higher status group within a class, is accepted. It is a right to lead, or a duty to follow, which is given by social position, a position which pervades many aspects of life. Traditionally, members of the upper class have positions of directorial power and responsibility and assume and are granted leadership roles at the national level outside the purely economic field. The middle class in the town have power and responsibility over others or at least freedom from masters. In the life of the town they assume leadership roles outside the economic field (but do not aspire to leadership, economic or other, at national level). The traditional working class (fewer of whom are found nowadays) work for masters and follow where they lead.

The traditional class system is therefore in many senses a total system: status in one field giving status in another.[1] It rests upon the principle of social inheritance, children of families in each class being differently trained both formally and informally to fit their status.[2]

But the number of people in Banbury and district who do not fit the traditional system is increasing. They include those who have positions they have not inherited, those who have moved up by new routes (State-aided education for example), those who have high status in one sphere and low in another. There are persons with considerable power, authority, and wealth whose family backgrounds the gentry 'don't know'. There are occupations that cannot be placed and there are ways of life and attitudes alien to the traditional class system.

People with these characteristics are non-traditionalists.[3] They do not have a class system of their own. It is typical of non-traditionalism in Banbury that it is not a unity: the only factor which non-traditionalists have in common is non-conformity in some respect to the traditions of Banbury. Non-traditionalists of whatever status in Banbury are essentially without class in the traditional sense because they have not inherited an established position in an established system. Many of them are immigrants.[4]

No recently ennobled working-class peers live in Banbury district, but there are those who have recently risen in rank, although from less lowly origins. They fail to fit into the traditional upper class not only because of family background and schooling, but also because their attitudes and interests differ from those of the traditionalist. Not only may the wealth of these non-traditionalists frequently be greater than that of the traditional aristocracy, but their power in terms of industry and possibly also of government may be greater. Furthermore, their area of communication is often wider; their social circle international. This is true, for example, of directors and senior managers of the aluminium factory as well as of other industrialists who live in the district but who are otherwise unconnected with

[1] Although, of course, it cannot be completely so in what is in many ways a rational-legal society in the Weberian sense (Max Weber, *Theory of Social and Economic Organization*).

[2] Compare Young and Willmott, op. cit., who described the difficulties encountered by Bethnal Green children sent to grammar schools against the local class practice.

[3] There is some parallel here with Mogey's 'status dissenters' which is more fully discussed in Chapter 10, pp. 180–1 (J. Mogey, op. cit.).

[4] Lloyd Warner places high-status immigrants in the lower-upper class because they lack family. No such simple solution is possible in Banbury.

Banbury. Initially their power and their range of communications were derived solely from industry. They were not inherited. Looked at from the outside, in terms, for example, of their horizon, some of these people 'ought' to have a higher status than members of the traditional upper class, but so strict are the rules of the traditional class system that although traditional upper-class people may associate with them, in traditional upper-class eyes their status is lower. Nevertheless, outside the traditional upper class their status is higher in the sense that their names are more widely known among lower classes than the names of representatives of the most ancient families in the district. For the non-traditionalists are accorded popular status on the merit basis of their achievements and their contributions to national prestige. With whom they associate outside their business circle depends upon their interests and attitudes, their personality and the manner of life they adopt, and is to that extent unpredictable. Those who send their sons to public schools ensure for them an entry into the traditional system.

Similarly, members of the newer professions are not associates of members of the older professions. They are graduates, but they are of middle- or working-class origin and were educated at grammar schools and provincial universities. There is, in particular, a gap between the doctors and the graduate teachers in State schools, a gap which is resented by some of the latter. In terms of intellectual attainment members of the newer professions rank higher than non-graduate members of the gentry, who certainly do not 'know' them. They have neither the qualification of family nor school to commend them. Furthermore, non-traditionalists of this kind frequently find that their intellectual interests are not shared by members of the traditional middle class in Banbury. The differences of education and occupation, and indeed of goals and aspirations, are great. They are not anxious, therefore, to identify themselves with this class.

In contrast with traditionalists, in the upper and middle classes, the non-traditionalist is, or has been, concerned with increasing his economic status rather than with maintaining family prestige and tradition. He values individual effort above such things, an effort directed to status seen in economic terms. Furthermore, since this is so and since non-traditionalists are involved in change they tend to value established institutions less highly, or they do not value them merely because they are established. For their lives are concerned with the new rather than with maintaining the old. The non-traditionalist is not necessarily disloyal or rebellious: his older loyalties are passive, the circumstances of his life do not call them out.

The division between the traditional and the non-traditional worker is of a different order. The non-traditional worker rejects as such the traditional class system and is in consequence a Labour voter (although this may not be his only or his overt reason); he may even be an active local politician—his traditional counterpart is not. In this he shows a degree of activity in formal associations uncommon to his class and particularly to the traditionalist in it who 'leaves things like that to those who know about them' (i.e. the middle and upper classes).

Here is found the denial of the totality of the traditional class system: the situation in which the worker (lowest class) is Mayor of the town (first citizen). Here political status and social class are separated where the traditional system joins them together; leadership is no longer left in the hands of the middle class of the Borough. Genuine embarrassment was felt by the traditional middle class in the town (and by traditionalists of lower status) when their town was represented by a worker as Mayor: 'I don't know how he'll manage.'

Nevertheless, traditionalists and non-traditionalists are not utterly opposed in their ideas, nor are they unaffected by each other. Non-traditionalists in the middle and upper classes are found in Banbury and district who accept some of the traditional values and feel that 'these people (the traditionalists) have got something'. In that case they may try to 'get into' the traditional class system, that is, they try to become acceptable to a 'set' within it. How far they succeed, and at what level, depends on the extent to which they are prepared and able to adopt the way of life and acquire the manners and attitudes of the 'set'. It is easier in the middle than in the upper class, for in the middle class occupation and wealth 'rightly' spent are relatively more important.

Many fail or do not try to integrate themselves with the traditional system, possibly because the level at which they could get in does not interest them and higher levels are closed to them. An example is the provincial graduate who feels himself 'above' the Banbury middle class and yet has no entrance to the upper class. Nevertheless such non-traditionalists try to give their children the 'chances they didn't have'. (This is, of course, also true of the upwardly mobile within the traditional class system itself.) Those who have enough wealth and power send their children to traditional public schools. Those whose equivalence is rather with the traditional middle class send their children to local private schools followed by the county grammar school. So that even though they themselves may have rejected one of the essentials of the traditional system, social inheritance, they accept it for their children.

Similarly, the non-traditional worker accepts many of the traditional class values. Non-traditionalists, like traditionalists, are ranked in terms of occupation, of respectability, and so on. The non-traditionalist has rejected (as impracticable or immoral, or both) individual upward mobility; he has replaced this value by class loyalty and he is concerned with improving the status of his class as a whole. Or, if he does not go so far as to deny the value of individual upward mobility for his children, and many non-traditionalist workers do not, he at least denies the principle of inheritance when he demands equal opportunity for his children with those of other classes. He uses the resources provided by the welfare State to give his child a chance of being upwardly mobile—in contrast to the upwardly mobile traditionalist worker who sends his child, not to the State elementary school, but to a small fee-paying school where stress is laid upon deportment and (middle-class) manners. In rejecting the rightness of the traditional class system and consequently denying the right of the middle class to lead, the non-traditional worker becomes involved in a certain amount of dualism.

This was particularly noticeable, for example, in the attitude to the few middle-class members of the Labour Party. They were accorded no right to lead, nor did working-class members cry off from office on the grounds of being unhandy with their pens. But the (traditional) 'superiority' of the middle-class members was felt (they were, after all, handier with their pens, sometimes they were usefully wealthier); they were voted to office but regarded when there with some suspicion. They were people who had been brought up to a different way of life, who spoke a different language, had different associates, and might they not really be 'on the other side'? Significantly the suspicion was greatest of one who was a member of the traditional middle class, except that he had walked out of the system by rejecting its value premisses and had, for the most part, dropped or been dropped by his old associates. But he and his family were known and it was felt that he really 'belonged' on the 'other side', although he was undoubtedly loyal and useful to the party of his choice. No such suspicion necessarily attached to those who came from lower down in the traditional status scale, unless, as in fact happened in one case, they were shown to have retained enough of their traditional loyalties to affect their loyalty to the Labour Party. Nor did so great a suspicion attach to non-traditionalist middle-class members. In some cases they could claim humbler origins, which helped, and in any case they had not been brought up as part of the traditional network of the town's Conservative leadership, for it happens, not surprisingly, that they were also immigrants.

The traditional class system is under pressure from a changing economic and educational system and from the effects of 'welfare' legislation. It is increasingly difficult to pass high status on to children, both because of increased taxation and high death duties. The gentry in particular feel that they are to be the last generation; that their sons will not be able to maintain the standard of life to which they brought them up and, moreover, will probably not feel it worthwhile to try.[1]

Members of the gentry are still returned unopposed at County Council elections in many parts of the Banbury district, but in the town the right of the middle class to unquestioned and exclusive political leadership is successfully challenged. The number of workers who accept the principle that low economic status must imply all-round low status is decreasing, if the high average age of manual Conservative voters may be taken as an index.[2] People of low, but not the lowest, social status now hold positions of the highest status in local politics. Even in the rural areas (those, it must be admitted, nearest to Banbury) social leadership by the gentry, although still usual, is no longer automatic. 'Do you know, it's an extraordinary thing: the chairman of our Women's Institute is a village woman [i.e. not a lady, not a member of the gentry]', said a traditionalist member of the Institute. The traditional principle that class confers an equivalent status in all spheres of life is apparently being undermined in town and country.

Within the town the local traditional status system, under the leadership of the higher status groups in the middle class, rests upon

[1] At the beginning of his article in *Encounter* (op. cit.) Ross remarked that the only remaining distinctive characteristic of the upper class is their speech. If this is so, and there is something to be said for that point of view, it may well account for the interest in 'U' speech which his article called forth and for its jealous guarding by its possessors. It also suggests that the traditional upper class nowadays is functionless in that it is not the sole possessor of the rights to rule on estates, in industry, or in government. It may be a recognition of this sort that causes so many of the gentry to be depressed about the future of their class.

[2] See page 47.

a stable and a reasonably isolated society in which people expect to spend their lives (even if they were initially immigrants). They see their social goals in terms of this society and see them in relation to every aspect of their lives. Lineage, charitable work, local government service and public works generally, and club and pub associations are important as well as wealth and occupation.[1] For it is a close-knit society in which family, business, and social life are interwoven.

But for an increasing number of people in the middle class Banbury no longer contains their goals. These are set by the hierarchy of industry or the civil service. For such non-traditionalists, social status is not a matter of their total showing in the eyes of the town, but of their individual showing at work and socially in the eyes of their business associates, not all of whom are in Banbury and who for the most part are not involved in the town's close-knit social structure. It is unlikely, therefore, that these non-traditionalists will become fully assimilated into the local traditional system as it has existed in the past.

Nevertheless, in Banbury and district, the traditional system has considerable strength. The advantages of being brought up to your position and of 'knowing where you are' are considerable. Members of the traditional upper and middle classes, despite the changes that are taking place, have a personal sense of security of position that is not felt by non-traditionalists, who have to make their own positions and maintain their status on merit alone. From this follows the desire of the traditionalist to maintain his family position and so to train his children that they will also maintain it. The division into public, private, and State schools, and the status popularly accorded to them in that order, supports such desires. Non-traditionalists who accept these principles and send their children to the school traditionally appropriate to their class are turning their children into traditionalists by the second generation. There are a few middle-class non-traditionalists in Banbury who send their children to State schools throughout their educational careers, but they are as few in number as the middle-class socialists. The traditional principle of inherited class position is thus accepted by the majority of middle-class non-traditionalists. Doubtless the traditional system and its values will continually and subtly change as it has done historically. The pressure

[1] Compare with the 'local system' in Brennan *et al.* (op. cit.) and the discussion of the comparison in Chapter 10. Also with the 'neighbourhood-centred' St. Ebbe's (Mogey, op. cit.).

of the needs of modern industry and government, increasingly felt in Banbury, ensure that although the principle of social inheritance is accepted, the non-traditional merit basis of judging and selecting leaders cannot be ignored.

It is significant also that those workers who have become leaders in trade unions and local government in Banbury have thereby increased their social status within the working class. Some of them must in fact be placed at least on the frontiers of the middle class although they still call themselves members of the working class. This is in a sense an inversion of the traditional class situation. There, higher class meant higher political status; here higher political status increases social status, although it may not alter social class. It is significant, too, that some of these working-class leaders were men who tried, and failed, in the 1930's to be upwardly mobile in a more traditional sense, although not in Banbury. They had started to work on their own account or as small masters, but on failing came to Banbury to find work. Perhaps it is permissible to look upon their new positions as an alternative route up a newly developed non-traditional status scale.

In sum, it is a time of change in the class patterns of Banbury and one in which it is not possible to construct a class system into which everyone may be fitted, nor one in which any simple index of social class may be suggested. That is to say, no one factor such as occupation makes it possible to predict where an individual precisely falls. That social class exists is undeniable; indeed, it is probably the single most profound division in Banbury and district today. Its importance lies in the still very great differences in the manner of life, attitudes, and beliefs of the three classes: differences so great that any intimacy between members of each is difficult, if not impossible. And it is these differences which are the essence of social class distinctions.

9

SUMMARY AND CONCLUSIONS

WHEN the study of the impact of the introduction of the aluminium factory on Banbury was first planned, attention was focused on the distinction between Banburians and immigrants. It seemed likely that there were important tensions between these two groups, even that this division might be the key to the social structure of the town.

There was superficial evidence to suggest this. Immigrants of as much as fifteen or even thirty years' standing, and even those holding public office, when asked for advice or information about the town would point out that they were not Banburians. Thus they suggested the existence of a strong in-group to which, because they were immigrant, they were not admitted. Banburians, on the other hand, commented on 'all those foreigners' who had so altered the town that you no longer 'knew where you were'. 'Before the factory came', a phrase so often repeated by the Banburians, had the air of 'before the flood', with the implication that it was the immigrants who had flooded the town. But, although attention was focused from the beginning on the possibility of tension between Banburian and immigrant, in fact little further evidence of such tensions came to light.

Tensions at the level of individual assimilation to the town were found: the case, for example, of the north country woman who, although she took steps to join all the organizations that her Banburian neighbours belonged to and was assiduous in her attendance, had still not been accepted by them fifteen years later. No reason could be found for this rejection except her north country origin; no difference of status, politics, or religion existed, nor was she in any way unacceptable personally. Hers was an extreme case. Although other examples of a similar kind were found, the subjects usually being north country people, in most cases the evidence related to the early years of their immigration, a phase now passed: 'I thought I should never settle down here.' These cases, when added together, pointed to a major difference in ways and attitudes of life between the north country and the south, or at all events, Banbury, making for difficulties of assimilation rather than to a hostility between Banburians and immigrants as such.

Other than in these individual case histories, the only overt tension observed between Banburian and immigrant was in the case of housing. Frustrations about housing led to accusations by Banburians of favouritism on the part of the Borough Council towards immigrants and vice versa. There were letters in the local papers and debates in the Council chamber. Division was not on a party political basis. Many comments were made to interviewers on the subject: 'Look at those Geordies, they've only been here three years and they've got one of those new pre-fabs and our Molly was born here and has had her name down for twelve years for a house and still she hasn't got one. Not fair I reckon.' Immigrants complained that it was unfair to consider whether a man had been born in the town or how long he had lived there when making Council house allocations. Was it not enough that he was living and working in the town and was in need of a house? 'We've been here since before the war and we're still in part of one of those old houses with nowhere proper for the kiddies to sleep, boys and girls all crowded up together, they are, and those people down the road were no worse off nor us yet they've got a new house; just because he was born here and his father before him. It ain't right: I've worked here steady ever since I come.'

Houses were in fact allocated on a points system, so many points for the number of children, present accommodation, length of service in the forces and residence in the town, and so on, with special consideration for serious ill health, and for old people for whom special houses were built. There were, however, so few houses to go round that any housing committee would have found it difficult not only to do justice, but to appear to be just in its selection. So many genuine cases had to be refused for the time being.

The deviation in the proportion of Banburian to immigrant tenants in the Council houses as shown in the schedule inquiry is slightly in the Banburian favour. But the deviation is unlikely to be significant.[1] The proportion of Banburians is a reasonable one to find if Banburians and immigrants have approximately the same housing needs. But this is a difficult matter to assess. Rather more immigrants than Banburians are found in badly overcrowded conditions, in rooms

[1] Thirty-nine per cent. of heads of households in Council houses are true Banburian while 35 per cent. of all household heads are Banburians. Since a number of immigrants have Banburian wives, the proportion of households in which one of the couple is a Banburian is, of course, higher.

and divided houses. But more Banburians than immigrants are found in the old 'slum houses', some of which are also overcrowded. The figures at least indicate that the Council cannot have been seriously unfair either to Banburian or immigrant. Nevertheless, frustrations were expressed in Banburian/immigrant terms.

However, when the quietness and secretness of the English techniques of social rejection are remembered, the fact that a rift between Banburians and immigrants was publicly mentioned only in this one case was not sufficient evidence that tensions did not exist. On the other hand, there was plenty of evidence of interaction between Banburians and immigrants. They were found as friends, belonging to the same clubs, drinking together in the same pubs, and marrying each other.

In these circumstances, particularly inter-marriage, it was clear that tensions between Banburians and immigrants could not be of a high order. Nevertheless, some comparable division existed. When a man said, apologetically, 'Well, I'm not really a Banburian, you know', and when Banburians inveighed against 'those foreigners', they were stating a commonly accepted belief in an opposition between Banburians and immigrants and one which was shared by both groups. If there was no direct opposition between the groups then this belief must be the expression of some other existing social fact, some other set of tensions. It was from this contradiction, popular belief in a distinction between Banburians and immigrants and in practice co-operation without distinction among them, which led to the emergence of the concept of traditionalism opposed by non-traditionalism.

One report, which the field-workers originally attempted to interpret as a possible indication of tension between Banburians and immigrants, is an example of the initial pointers to this concept. It is the case of the Banburian tradesman who said he would refuse to serve any of his customers seen entering a new chain store (see Chapter 2, p. 30). That he should make such a pronouncement, with whatever hope of being able to fulfil it, indicated that he believed in the existence of a group with considerable local loyalty and, moreover, solidarity. It is significant that he should attempt to call upon this loyalty rather than rely upon the quality of his goods and services.

Evidence accumulated to show that there was just such an established group, a group bound together by common history and tradition, with a recognized social structure and having certain common values. This shopkeeper was one of a number of local proprietors who owned long-established factories or shops in the town, concerns which in some cases had passed through several generations of the same family. Many of them had ties of kinship, by blood or marriage, with each other, and more had grown up together in the town. Connexions of this sort were strengthened by a further set of ties, for many concerned themselves with running the affairs of the town, in church or chapel, on public bodies, and in social and sporting activities. A man on one committee was likely to be on at least one other and possibly also a rank-and-file member of yet other associations.

So many cross-threads in personal relationships meant that each was seen as a whole man. His family life was connected with his business life and these again with his religious, political, and social lives. To a considerable extent he met the same people in every case, or at least the amount of overlapping was sufficient for his behaviour in one field to become rapidly known in another.

Great value was placed on the importance of maintaining these personal relationships. The successful man was the one who had a sound business, was affluent but not too rich, who gave sufficiently freely of his time and money in the service of the town. The pressure to conform to group standards and to avoid eccentric behaviour was considerable. To maintain your business as a 'sound going concern' was more important than expanding it and possibly making a lot more money. A 'progressive' business man made enough changes to keep up with the times, to keep his business going with adequate returns, but had no desire to be ahead of the times. For economic success would not by itself bring social acceptance.

Conformity, stability, conservation of established institutions and values; these were the key-notes of the society that has been defined as traditional. But within that society analysis showed certain important divisions. The groups which clustered about certain formal associations indicated divisions in the social structure. These groups were associated with cultural differences in so far as each tended to lay greatest stress upon a different traditional value.

So there were within the traditional society the Anglican/Conservative group whose members showed a wide range of social and sporting interests, for whom conviviality and enjoyment of life were important. In contrast was the Free Church/Liberal group, very little concerned with sport, having quieter social activities, and much more concerned with cultural pursuits. The two groups held in common the value of service to the town and its people, shown in their joint activity in associations such as Rotary.

These middle-class members of traditional Banbury were followed and supported by the traditional working class. The traditional workers, in many cases also of families long established in the town, had their own networks of informal personal relations. In some cases members of the family had 'always' worked for such-and-such traditional concern. If they were church-goers they often went to a church of the same denomination as their employer, for his acceptance of the inter-locking of all sides of his life led him to employ members of his denomination in preference to others. The traditional workers shared the middle-class attitudes about the value and the rightness of 'things as they always have been'. They were not inclined to trade unions or Labour politics, accepting their position and the right of the middle class to lead. They avoided 'meddling in what doesn't concern them'. Consequently they voted Conservative or Liberal and did not themselves attempt to stand for the Council or to run formal associations. They provided the rank-and-file support in business and social life which made it possible for traditional Banbury to carry on. Their support might sometimes be merely negative, an acquiescence with the established order, 'not bothering' about things. But they did not rebel or agitate for change.

Since the traditional society is based on a long-standing network of relationships between families and friends who have lived and worked together for many years, it is not surprising to have found that many traditionalists were Banburians. But the traditional society was not exclusively composed of those born and bred in the town. It had absorbed a number of immigrants, people who came to take up traditional occupations and who were prepared to behave according to the traditional standards and to accept the traditional values. But based as it was on a series of face-to-face relationships this society could only accept a limited number of newcomers at a time. Similarly it could adapt itself to small and gradual technical and social changes. Before the 1930's the town had been able to go on relatively undisturbed, compared that is to the changes which had taken place in other parts of the country.

For this reason, the arrival of the aluminium factory represented an abrupt change. Not only did the factory itself initiate much of the change, but it also became the dramatic symbol of the opposition between old and new. For the new industry was in almost every way in direct opposition to the traditional pattern of Banbury life. Tradition and change ceased to be a matter of a traditional system slowly accepting changes which had filtered through from outside, and became an active opposition within the town itself.

Non-traditionalism, which had begun to emerge before the days of the aluminium factory, was reinforced and extended. There had been since 1919, for example, a small Labour Party supported by Banburians who had rejected the traditional system, at least in some important respects. With the arrival of the aluminium factory this small group was reinforced by numbers of immigrant workers, so that today the active strength of the Labour Party comes principally from immigrants. Many of these came from industrial areas where they had been brought up to Labour and trade-union ideas. They did not accept the traditional status system of Banbury and could not understand the acquiescence of the traditional workers in it, saying they were 'like sheep'. The social isolation of these active trade-union and Labour leaders was shown in Chapter 3. Standing right outside the closely interlocking traditional structure, they met its members only on local government or other statutory bodies.

Middle-class immigrants in industry also stood outside the traditional status system. They were concerned with getting promotion in their occupations, a possibility which was controlled by their showing at work and was not affected by their relationships in the town. Local social acceptance was not a major goal. Their network of relationships in the town was narrower than that of their traditional counterparts, but they had business, social, and kin connexions scattered over a wider area.

To some extent the wider range of social interests brought in by the immigrants had its reflection in the life of the town. But what appear to be non-traditional developments may merely be the result of increased numbers, quantitative rather than qualitative changes. A larger population may mean that there are enough like-minded people to form this or that club, a dramatic society for example, so that a formal group appears which was not previously identifiable, and informally a new 'set' appears. Such interests may have had their scattered representatives in the smaller traditional society and may not be essentially non-traditional. Nevertheless, although it was not always easy, it was usually possible in practice to identify those groups which were not opposed to traditionalism and those which were non-traditional, for the last have values and attitudes in opposition to traditionalism. The case of the Business and Professional Women's Club when compared with the older Townswomen's Guild was an example of an identifiably non-traditional association (see Chapter 5).

In sum, it was with the arrival of the immigrants that Banbury felt the full force of non-traditionalism. One important key to the social structure and culture of the town therefore is the opposition of non-traditionalism to traditionalism, an opposition which contains within it some of the problems of immigrant assimilation. This is the key rather than a simple opposition of Banburian to immigrant.

But Banbury cannot be explained in these terms alone. Another important key is social class and social status. These are at least as important a source of social division and therefore of social tension. Social class divides traditional and non-traditional alike, although, as the last chapter showed, the attitude of each group to these horizontal divisions and their impact on each is different. Each class has ways of life and values and attitudes so dissimilar that interaction between them, except in formal ways, is almost impossible, nor is it sought.

Middle-class rarely meet working-class Banburians. They go to different pubs or different parts of the same pub; while one group plays squash the other plays table tennis; there are separate bowls, tennis, and cricket clubs for each status group; different kinds of houses in different areas; different types of work, hours of work, and methods of payment; rules of behaviour, of what is 'right and proper' are sufficiently different for middle-class and working-class people not to be comfortable together in informal social circumstances. A similar wide gap exists between the upper class who live outside the town and rarely come into it for social purposes and the middle-class people who live there. The geographic horizons of the three classes show the range of their interests. By and large, the worker lives his life in his home, the nearby street, and its pub just round the corner. The middle class have friends scattered throughout the town and belong to associations based on the town. The upper class, little concerned with the town except for minor shopping, extend their range of interests and friends to cover the country and even go beyond its frontiers.

Broadly speaking, differences of this kind apply to both traditionalists and non-traditionalists. But non-traditionalists do not belong to such a highly structured class and status system as do the traditionalists. Nor are they so town-centred. This is true not only of the non-traditional middle class, whose horizons have been widened by training, work, and other out-of-town connexions, it is also true of the non-traditional worker compared with his traditional brother. The active trade unionist, for example, looks beyond the town to the regional and national centres of his union. He may travel about to attend its meetings. He is proud to be a member of the working class, but aspires to political leadership in the town and in his manner of life has adopted some middle-class habits. He simply does not fit the traditional social status pattern.

But the gulf between the non-traditional worker and the Conservative middle-class non-traditionalist is wider than the gulf between members of the traditional middle and working classes. It is formed by different daily habits and widely different political attitudes.

Among the traditional Banbury population and among immigrants who have become integrated with it, a set of social class criteria can be applied that is relevant neither for the unintegrated immigrant nor for the non-traditionalist. The traditional social system is one in which there is a high degree of interaction between all the component parts: occupation, family, formal associations, and informal groups. Social position for any individual member is the result of a combination of all these factors. A great many factors are, therefore, taken into account in according status. Cauter and Downham remark[1] that family in the sense of lineage 'almost certainly . . . carries some weight in the upper levels of the social scale, but outside this limited section of the population its influence is hard to trace'. The research workers in Banbury found, however, that not only is it counted by the traditional upper class but it carries some weight among Banburians of two or more generations residence if they belong to the traditional system. It cannot count in the same way for immigrants who do not know each other's background. Furthermore, the upwardly mobile and the non-traditionalist wish that it should not count. For them occupation status or wealth or a combination of these are relevant criteria.

Since social status is accorded on different criteria for different sections of the population, it was not possible to construct a status grading based on one factor and intended to have application to all members of the population.[2]

[1] *The Communication of Ideas* (op. cit.).

[2] The difficulties of constructing a valid occupational status scale to cover the

In sum, therefore, the town is bisected two ways: it is cut down the middle by the line which divides traditional from non-traditional; and it is cut across the middle by the line which divides the middle class from the working class. Outside the town in the district are two further groups, the traditional upper class and the non-traditional upper class.

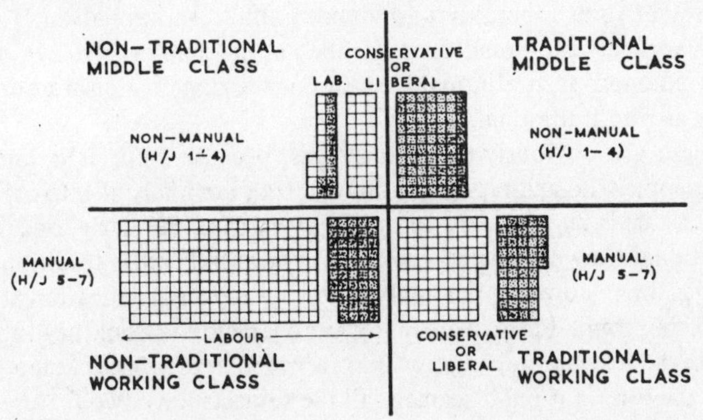

Each square represents one male household head recorded in the sample.

CHART XVII. Summary Social Structure

Chart XVII shows the four groups in the town: it shows also a, necessarily crude, attempt to measure the size of these groups. Class has been measured by occupation: all those falling above the horizontal line are in Hall/Jones classes 1–4 and have been called middle class: all those below are in classes 5–7 and have been called working class. Occupation, as has been shown, is an inadequate class index, but here it is applied to male household heads only and is therefore a little more consistent than when applied to a total population.

Traditionalism and non-traditionalism have been measured by the subjects' voting behaviour or by the firm in which they work. To vote Labour in Banbury is non-traditional in any class, therefore all Labour voters have been placed on the left of the diagram. To vote

country as a whole, difficulties which are recognized by Professor Glass and his colleagues in *Social Mobility in Britain* (op. cit.), are considerable. Even in one locality occupational status grading as a measure of social status is likely only to be valid for those whose principal status criterion is occupation: that is for those in higher status occupations who are geographically mobile and whose frame of reference is a national industry or profession rather than a locality. That is to say, except in the broadest terms, it is only likely to be valid for sections of the middle class and of non-traditionalists.

Conservative or Liberal in the working class is a sign of traditionalism, therefore all Conservative or Liberal working-class voters have been placed on the right of the diagram. Voting Conservative or Liberal is, however, not a test of position in relation to traditionalism for the middle class. While voting Labour in the middle class is certainly a sign of non-traditionalism, most middle-class people vote Conservative or Liberal but are divided about traditionalism. Those who work in traditional firms, defined as in Chapter 2 (p. 21), have been counted as traditional and those working in non-traditional firms as non-traditional.

These are obviously rough measures, because while it is known that people who exhibit one traditional trait are likely also to exhibit others, this is by no means certain in every case. Similarly, one non-traditional trait may be an eccentricity in an otherwise traditionally minded man. However, this analysis does give a rough indication of the size of the groups. Each square represents one male household head about whom the relevant information was recorded in the schedule inquiry.

In the top right-hand segment all the subjects have two features in common, i.e. they work in traditional industry and vote Conservative or Liberal. In the traditional working class, the bottom right-hand segment, those working in traditional industry are shown separately from those in non-traditional industry. The latter, judged by their voting behaviour, are traditionalists but they are more open to non-traditional influences than those who still work for traditional firms. They are, for example, more likely to come under trade-union influence.

The non-traditional working class, the bottom left-hand segment, have also been divided according to their industry. The majority work in non-traditional industry, but something like a fifth are employed by traditional firms, despite which they vote Labour. Taking the working class as a whole, i.e. all those below the horizontal line, about half of those in traditional firms are traditional in that they vote Conservative compared with less than a third of those working in non-traditional firms.

The non-traditional middle class, the top left-hand segment, is the most mixed bag. The largest single group is made up of those who vote Conservative or Liberal but who work in non-traditional industry. This segment also includes those who vote Labour and who work in non-traditional industry and those who vote Labour and work in traditional firms.

Social divisions of the greatest importance apparently occur when more than one source of disagreement or of social distance is involved. Formerly it was the coincidence of religious and political differences which led to a major cleavage. The ways of life of the Anglican/Conservative and the Free Church/Liberal were opposed in almost everything from use of leisure to government. Today, with the influence of religion weakened and of economic divisions strengthened, the most profound cleavage is found at the point where the three factors of traditionalism and non-traditionalism, social class, and politics come together. This is the point where the maximum social distance and also social tension between groups are found. It is greatest between the non-traditional Labour working class and the traditional Conservative middle class. That is to say between the bottom left and top right segments of the diagram. For here the difference of social class, which results in distance between middle and working classes for both traditionalists and non-traditionalists, is joined by the opposition of non-traditionalism to traditionalism and repeated in the disagreement between Labour and Conservative. The opposition is one, therefore, which touches upon almost every aspect of life. But in view of the wide disparities of belief and attitude, of ways of life and behaviour, what is perhaps most surprising is the absence of overt tensions, particularly in group terms, which may be observed in the town. It is partly the result of social and political techniques common to the English way of life, of avoiding known tensions or of running them off into formal channels. The technique of silence to show disapproval avoids direct expressions of tension and the machinery of government is a technique for formalizing tensions and turning them to constructive purpose.

The fact that the two groups most widely separated in ideas, beliefs, and behaviour are also so widely separated socially that in practice they rarely meet face-to-face also reduces the possibility of head-on collisions. Paradoxically, although the effect of the status system in keeping potentially opposed groups apart helps to prevent open clashes, the fact that individuals from the opposed groups do meet also plays its part. Because the social structure is complex there are some links between every part of it. While the non-traditional Labour working class may be seen as in profound opposition to the traditional Conservative middle class, this is a considerable abstraction. Members of these two groups are found who have features in common. For example, a traditionalist tradesman, a Conservative voter, is the fellow chapel deacon of an active Labour Party worker and trade unionist. Such examples are rare and isolated, but the two groups are tied to each other through many others, although the ties are indirect. The Conservative supporters are not drawn solely from the traditionalist middle class. They are joined by the non-traditionalist middle class and the traditionalist working class. Both of these last have something in common with the non-traditionalist working class. Some members of the non-traditionalist middle and working classes have non-traditional industry in common, although here, of course, the relationship which is most clearly seen is the opposition of 'the two sides of industry'. The traditionalist and non-traditionalist working class have their class in common. For both there are common problems, common interests, and common differences from non-workers. The existence of these cross-threads, by dividing the forces, reduces the amount of tension between the traditional middle class and the non-traditional working class. The many and complicated ties of opposition and co-operation that run through Banbury society modify the full force of any one set of oppositions. This is the point which was made by Max Gluckman in his broadcast talk on Feuding Societies.[1]

Not only, of course, do individuals have attachments with many groups inside Banbury, but many of them, particularly in the middle class and above, have attachments outside the town. They are, therefore, less concerned about their rejection by or lack of integration with the town than they would be if their lives were entirely centred within it. The immigrant non-traditionalist of the middle class, for example, who is not assimilated into traditional town society is little concerned by this, except perhaps to express disapproval of the town's standards, complaining, for example, of the shops and the absence of a theatre. His reaction is not violently hostile, or, if it is, he moves to a job elsewhere. His focus of interest in terms of his goals and aspirations lies outside the town, in the wider society, national or even international, provided by his profession or industry. For the most part he can make adequate social arrangements with colleagues similarly placed, with whose attitudes and ways of behaviour he has more in common than with those of the traditionalists.

These three factors, the complexity and overlapping of ties within

[1] M. Gluckman, *Custom and Conflict in Africa* (Glencoe, Ill.: The Free Press, 1956).

the town, the ties with groups outside the town, and the lack of strong shown tensions among the disparate groups, indicate that Banbury cannot be considered as a community. Michael Young has suggested that one necessary factor for the development of a community is shared history.[1] This certainly does not apply to the total population of Banbury. The number of new-comers who do not share its history for more than fifteen years is so high that it makes it obviously impossible for the condition to be fulfilled. Furthermore, given that Banbury is in a country in which people are constantly moving about to follow jobs, it is unlikely ever to be true of the total population of the town.

It is even doubtful whether there is a sense of community among all of those who were born and brought up in the town. For those who are still part of the traditional small-town society, who own, manage, or work in its traditionalist shops and smaller factories, who provide the traditional services, who belong to the close-knit and long-standing groups in clubs and pubs and who accept the traditional standards, there is certainly some sense of community, some feeling of belonging. This is expressed through loyalty to the town and its established institutions. Groups of immigrants who shared together the experiences of coming to the town and settling down there and especially those who live as neighbours have a sense of belonging to a group which is akin to a sense of community. But these are groups within the town and not the town itself.

It is possible that with continued prosperity and stability, new sets of traditions may emerge and the town may be found later to have a greater unity; the opposition of Labour and Conservative, for example, will become traditional, most probably entirely replacing the opposition of Conservative to Liberal. However, although in ways such as these the town may develop greater cohesion, it will never become a community in any full sense both because of its complexity and because it is so closely integrated with the wider English society. Change is loosening the ties of the in-turning traditional society and reducing the intensity of local relationships. In compensation, the variety of life outside the town boundaries is being brought closer, a wider range of interests and of relationships becoming possible.

[1] *The Listener*, 23 Sept. 1954.

10

EPILOGUE

It is likely that the form taken by the traditional social structure in Banbury is in many ways peculiar to the town. But a reading of other local studies suggests that the general concept of a traditional social structure is a useful one for analysis, particularly of social change, and for an appreciation of problems relating to social change.

A comparison with south-west Wales is particularly striking. In their study of this area Brennan and his associates[1] isolate a social structure which they call the 'local system'. In many ways this system is essentially similar to the local traditional system in Banbury. It is found in an area which, like Banbury, had been stable, if not stagnant. The system is characterized by the close overlapping of leadership in formal associations; by the accordance of status on a totality of factors, public service and family position being at least as important as occupation; by the high value which is placed on the maintenance of established institutions and, associated with this, the relatively low value placed on enterprise and 'getting on' in the material sense.

Stripped to its bones in this way Brennan's local system sounds remarkably like traditional Banbury. But in fact the local system of south-west Wales is the traditional system of Banbury seen through the looking glass. The close overlapping of leadership occurs not among middle-class anti-socialists, but is an overlapping of leadership in the trade unions and nonconformist chapels. The established institutions which must be maintained are not those concerned with the Anglican Church and the Conservative party, but with the chapel, the Labour Party, and the Welsh Sunday.

In fact, south-west Wales is non-traditional in Banbury terms. Immigrants to Banbury from this area who have brought with them the values of Brennan's 'local system' are among the outstanding representatives of working-class non-traditionalism in Banbury. As one woman interviewed in Banbury said: 'We're Labour voters, what else would we be coming from South Wales?'

But despite differences at this level certain fundamental social

[1] Brennan, Cooney, and Pollins, op. cit.

values are essentially similar, and in south-west Wales, as in Banbury, these values are being challenged. In both places a stable and shrinking society has been infused with new life, new industries, and personnel, although it is true that in the Welsh case immigration is more confined to the higher occupation grades. But the results of these changes are similar. In both places the ties of custom are loosening and values associated with 'getting on' and with technological and economic enterprise challenge the sanctity of tradition and of established institutions.

Other studies suggest a similar clash between traditional and non-traditional values. G. Duncan Mitchell[1] analysed an area in South Devon using Weber's concepts of rational-legal and traditional legitimacy. He showed that there social status is a total status based on traditional sanctions and that the patriarchal family is important. Until recently this society was led by the squire and the parson with an authority based 'on a belief in the sanctity of traditions'.[2] In contrast, the parish councils represent authority based on rational-legal legitimacy, on a belief 'in the legality of laws, rules and directions issued by the person in authority together with a belief in his right to be elevated to that position'. Although the squirearchy has largely disappeared, a number of parish councils do not function well nor have their full complement of councillors. In Mitchell's view this is because these south Devonians, despite a legal right to stand for election, have no belief in their social right to do so: '. . . quite suitable people would regard it as a joke if it were suggested they should sit on the council'.[3] A similar reluctance to accept office is typical of the traditional working-class Banburian.

These traditional values have survived in South Devon, despite the loss of traditional leaders, because of the comparative isolation of the area and the lack of economic change. Mitchell is concerned with the attempt to impose institutions based on other values, that is, the parish councils with their rational-legal legitimacy, upon a society whose values spring from traditional legitimacy.

Similarly traditional values have survived in Banbury because it was relatively isolated and stable. There, too, social status tends to be a total status, leadership and authority in one field implying leadership and authority in another. But in Banbury the situation is

[1] G. Duncan Mitchell, 'The Parish Council and the Rural Community', *Public Administration*, Winter 1951.

[2] Op. cit., p. 395.

[3] Ibid., p. 395.

less that people have been expected to use institutions they do not believe in, than that institutions based on non-traditional values, and the personnel to run them, have been brought into the town. The opposition of values in Banbury is, nevertheless, similar to the opposition in South Devon. Traditional society in Banbury could in fact be considered as traditional in the Weberian sense, although obviously only partially so since it exists in a state which rests upon the principles of rational-legal legitimacy. Furthermore, it has long since absorbed the idea of municipal democracy. But even here traditional Banburians modify the rational-legal principle since in practice the right of leadership is left to the middle class. The presence nowadays of working-class Borough councillors is one of the changes wrought by non-traditionalism. For non-traditional institutions in Banbury have principles in common with those of rational-legal legitimacy: status is accorded on merit, in a particular sphere of activity, as technicians or workers or candidates for office, rather than upon a total social status.

Again there is some parallel to be found between Mogey's division of the working class in Barton and St. Ebbe's into status-assenting and status-dissenting and the Banbury division into traditional and non-traditional. The status-assenting section accept 'habits, standards, word usage, and values which are typical of the area and the streets, they talk little about problems of class conflict, trade unions, work, or any other general topic'.[1] In these ways they are reminiscent of the traditional Banbury workers who prefer to 'leave things like that to those who know about them'. Acceptance of things as they are and of their lot in life is the key-note in both cases. In contrast to the status-assenting, Mogey defines the status-dissenting who 'speak about the working class . . . show signs of aspiration to move higher in the world . . .' and 'are very conscious of the distinction between themselves, that is the "respectable" or the "nice" group, and the others . . .'.[1]

This group shows certain similarities with sections of the Banbury non-traditional working class. The two groups have a negative property in common, for both are characterized by attitudes of rejection. Mogey reports that trade-union leaders and activists are drawn from the status-dissenting group in Barton and St. Ebbe's. They are drawn from the non-traditional working class in Banbury. But Mogey's status-dissenters are unlike the Banbury non-traditionalists

[1] Mogey, op. cit., p. 140.

in one important respect. Banbury non-traditionalists, like Oxford status-dissenters, reject the validity of a given social order, but not all non-traditionalists in Banbury consequently 'set themselves up' as the 'nice' people. The Oxford status-dissenters are apparently the same people as those who count themselves 'respectable' or 'nice'. Those who reject the traditional order in Banbury are here defined as non-traditional. To this extent they are 'dissenters', but they do not all fall into a 'respectable' status group. Non-traditionalists may be 'respectable', 'ordinary', or 'rough'. Furthermore, in the traditional working class there are similar divisions. The traditional 'respectable' or 'superior' people have standards connected with decency, cleanliness, and thrift rather than the upward drive and somewhat ostentatious expenditure more commonly found among non-traditional respectable groups. But despite these differences both status-dissenters and non-traditionalists are on the side of change and are in marked contrast to the status-assenters and the traditionalists, both of whom are characterized by attitudes of acceptance.

The status-assenters, furthermore, like the traditionalists, are concerned with persons rather than with abstractions and with the network of relations within and between small groups. Judgements are made from personal knowledge and not from abstract concepts. In this the status-assenters of Oxford and the traditionalists of Banbury have a good deal in common with the people of Bethnal Green described by Young and Willmott.

Of the long-standing community of Bethnal Green, where relationships are based on a network of kin and friends, they say that 'status, in so far as it is determined by job and income and education, is more or less irrelevant to a person's worth. He is judged instead, if he is judged at all, more in the round, as a person with the normal mixture of all kinds of qualities, some good, some bad, many indefinable. He is more of a life-portrait than a figure on a scale.' Bethnal Green people also are less concerned with 'getting on' than are those in the new housing estate at Greenleigh where relationships are 'window-to-window, not face-to-face'.[1]

In all these cases a traditional society can be identified, or at least a group of people who base their lives upon traditional values. Traditional societies apparently have a social structure in which some form of the family is important, and where social status tends to be a total status. They have a value system which upholds customary ways

[1] Op. cit., pp. 134, 135.

of behaving; which reveres established institutions, whether they be of the political right or left, the church or chapel, or not specially connected with either; which values the stability of things as they are rather than the doubtful advantages of 'getting on'.

It seems likely that, even in so closely integrated and highly industrialized a country as this is, and given enough time, stability, and continuity, the outlines of such a traditional society are likely to develop in any area. That is to say, any group of people living together in the same place over a period of two or three generations without major upheavals will develop a customary way of life connected with and upheld by a network of face-to-face relations in which kin plays its part. The society may be informal and little structured or it may be more formal and connected with such institutions as the church and state.

Change presents a challenge to such societies. People move about and lose touch with their family and childhood friends. Their work relationships are altered. Values are changed, questioning and rejection replace the traditional attitude of acceptance.

Traditional society offers security: life follows well-trodden paths with well-known friends. But it can be cramping; there is little approval for eccentric or rebellious behaviour. Outside the traditional framework there is little security, friends must be made and new ways of living worked out. The road may be lonely. But there is freedom to move about, to choose friends, or withdraw, to follow custom or to adopt newer ideas and values.

Is it then an almost hopeless choice that must be made between a secure and friendly but cramped traditional life and a more free but insecure and possibly lonely non-traditional life? So it might seem at any one moment of time, but in practice the choice is not quite so hopeless and impossible. For the traditional and the non-traditional constantly interact. Few non-traditionalists have rejected every traditional value and traditionalists are not entirely closed to new ideas. Traditional society is capable of absorbing some new customs. What is non-traditional today may well be traditional tomorrow and this new tradition itself open to the challenge of fresh change.

APPENDIX 1

THE SCHEDULE INQUIRY

Purpose

The purpose of the inquiry by schedule was to collect: (*a*) certain data about the structure of the population—no census had been taken for nineteen years, years in which the population of the town had increased from 13,000-odd to about 19,000; (*b*) other information which was needed for this study about family structure, housing, origin of inhabitants, their education, occupation, and income, and their religious and political adherence.

Size and selection of the sample

The sample was selected by marking every fifth address on the electoral register and information was collected about all the inhabitants of each address marked. Houses, rather than individuals, were selected since information was wanted about houses, households, and families as well as about individuals. Ideally, a sample of households was wanted, but there was no means of knowing how many households there might be at one address.

In fact, since more than one household share a house in a number of cases, the size of the sample was increased to this extent, for every household was interviewed which lived at any of the selected addresses. Where more than one family lived in the same house, they were said to be a separate household if a separate larder, table, and accounts were kept. Such 'double households' were separately marked. There were eighty-five 'double households' out of a total of 1,015 households.

Information was collected not only about all households at the selected addresses, but about all individuals living in the house. Unlike the census practice, temporary residents (e.g. visitors) were not counted. Lodgers and friends ordinarily resident at the address were included. A limited amount of information was collected about children living away from home. Generally speaking one member of the household answered for the others, a possible source of some inaccuracy.

No substitutes were taken, neither where a house was empty nor where response to the inquiry was refused.

It seems unlikely that the method of marking every fifth address has of itself led to bias. Houses are rarely built in groups of five (regular terraces on the newer estates, for example, are in groups of even numbers such as four or six houses), so that end, middle, or corner houses are unlikely to be unduly repeated. Moreover, even small streets and culs-de-sac rarely have fewer than nine houses, so that each of them is likely to be represented. It was assumed that if the sample was random of houses, it would also be a random sample of the population.

Institutions, however, were not included in the sample: the principal omissions were two hospitals (one the general hospital and the other the old 'workhouse', which now served the aged and certain maternity cases)

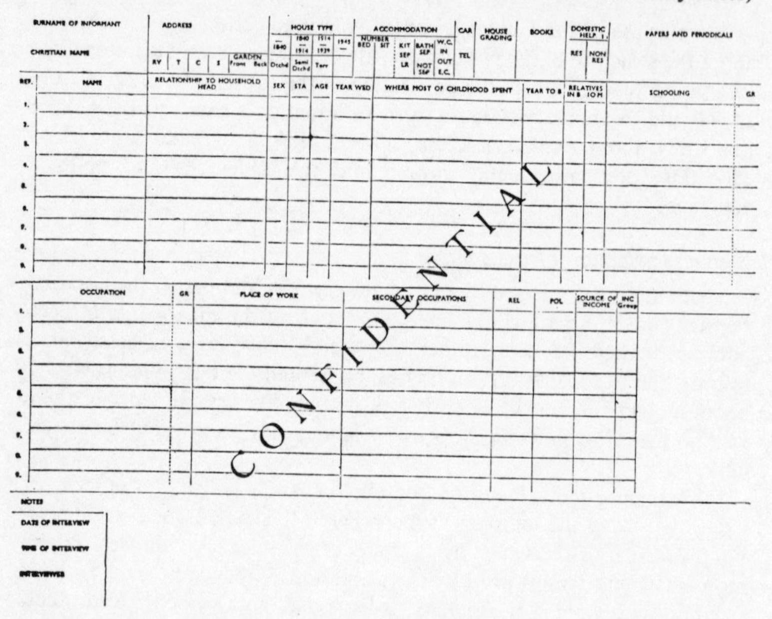

SURNAME OF INFORMANT
CHRISTIAN NAME
ADDRESS
RV | T | C | S | GARDEN Front Back
HOUSE TYPE: —1840 | 1840—1914 | 1914—1939 | 1945— ; Dtchd | Semi Dtchd | Terr
ACCOMMODATION: NUMBER BED | SIT ; KIT SEP LR ; BATH SEP NOT SEP ; W.C. IN OUT E.C.
CAR ; TEL
HOUSE GRADING
BOOKS
DOMESTIC HELP: RES | NON RES
PAPERS AND PERIODICALS

REF. | NAME | RELATIONSHIP TO HOUSEHOLD HEAD | SEX | STA | AGE | YEAR WED | WHERE MOST OF CHILDHOOD SPENT | YEAR TO B | RELATIVES IN B | IOM | SCHOOLING | GR
1.–9.

CONFIDENTIAL

OCCUPATION | GR | PLACE OF WORK | SECONDARY OCCUPATIONS | REL | POL | SOURCE OF INCOME | INC Group
1.–9.

NOTES
DATE OF INTERVIEW
TIME OF INTERVIEW
INTERVIEWER

CHART XVIII. The Schedule Form.

and the hotels. The probable effects of this are to under-represent the aged, single, and widowed; groups who live in institutions disproportionately to their numbers in the total population. The temporarily sick, except that they may be older than average, are likely to be drawn from all sections of the population, patients nowadays being sent to hospital on the basis of diagnosis rather than home circumstances.

1,015 schedules were completed covering 3,387 individuals of all ages and both sexes. Eighty-three schedules were returned 'refused' or 'house empty' (which included caravans and barges that had moved off). The completed schedules therefore represent an actual sample of 18·5 per cent. of all houses. Not all schedules have complete information on all subjects about everyone in the house: the total sample for each particular subject is given in the text.

Method of collection of information

Data was filled in on the schedule form (which see, p. 184) by the interviewers, who were issued with a set of instructions and also briefed verbally. Income was not asked for precisely: the respondent was handed a card with the income groups marked on it and asked to indicate into which group he fell. This method proved successful with a number who would otherwise have been embarrassed (some said as much). Others gave precise income and asked the interviewer to interpolate for them. The refusal rate on incomes remained fairly high however. Ninety-three out of 1,015 household heads refused their income groups. Interviewers were told to ask a come-back question on attendance at church 'Which church do you go to?' to aid assessment of genuine attendance. But the method failed to produce accurate results (see Chapter 4, p. 57). Interviewers were free to vary the order of the questioning, leaving until last those most likely to produce a refusal, for if great objection is taken to a question early in the interview the whole form is refused. In practice most left income and politics to the end.

The interviewers were the research workers and students, most of them from Oxford and most of them training for social work.

Almost all the respondents were interviewed in a three-week period in July 1950.

TABLE 35

Checks on the validity of the sample

Male: female ratio	*Per cent.*	
	Sample 1950	*Census 1951**
Male . . .	48·9	48·8
Female . . .	51·1	51·2

	1 *Sample*	2† *Estimated pop.*	3* *Census pop.*	4 *Difference* (2–3)	5 %
Male . .	1,657	8,957	9,228	−271	−2·9
Female . .	1,730	9,351	9,689	−338	−3·5
Total . .	3,387	18,308	18,917	−609	−3·2

* Census of Great Britain, 1951. One per cent. sample tables (London, 1952).

† Estimate made on size of sample (18·5 per cent.) by number in sample, e.g. $\frac{1657 \times 100}{18 \cdot 5}$.

APPENDIX 2

BANBURIANS AND IMMIGRANTS

A. Definitions

In the first instance people living in the town were asked for their definitions of these terms, since if common local definitions existed they were the obvious ones to use. But while most people were firm in their assertions that there was a real and important difference between Banburians and immigrants, it was difficult to find any consensus about the definitions.

Was it only those who had been born and bred in the town who were Banburians? There was some evidence for this. One of the first explanations about the town made to me was 'I have been here for thirty years but I'm still not a Banburian'. This was said by a man of about fifty who had given considerable public service. Against this, many people agreed that long residence was a qualification which made a man at least 'practically a Banburian'. But, when further questioned about how long was needed, hardly two replies were found to be the same. Estimates varied from fifteen to fifty years. In effect it depended on the individual, upon his age, his occupation, his politics, his attitude to life, and his readiness to conform to and accept the ways of the town. Closer acquaintance with Banbury revealed also that the definition 'born and bred' was not as simple as it appeared. The status of third generation Banburians, particularly among the leading families, was generally higher than those of first or even second generation.

Among the immigrants who had not yet qualified as being 'practically Banburian' by reason of long residence, there were distinctions too. People from the surrounding villages were already Banburians in a sense before they came to live within the Borough boundaries. They had known the town from childhood, knew and were known to the tradesmen, possibly had relatives there, and had the manners and accents of the county. Furthermore, for years people from the villages had come to live in Banbury to work or on marriage.

Among the people who came from farther afield, from Birmingham or London, Lancashire, Scotland, or Wales, there were distinctions again. When a Banburian thinks of an immigrant he is generally thinking of a factory worker from an industrial town distant in its way of life as well as geographically. He does not think of people like parsons, ministers, and doctors, although these have rarely been Banburians. Such men are accepted because of their positions and on their merits. They are few in number, not like the hundreds of factory workers who seem to swamp the shops and the streets.

Some rather more precise definitions than these had to be made if the origins of the inhabitants were to be analysed statistically. The following four categories were decided on:

1. *Born Banburian.* Those born and bred in Banbury. This category ignored the differences caused by the number of generations a family had lived in the town and ignored any period of absence that an individual might have had.

2. *Secondary Banburians.* Those who came to Banbury before they were seven years old. This definition was used in preference to a length of residence qualification in terms of years: first, because a main difficulty in deciding on the number of years is clearly that twenty years for a man of thirty is entirely different from the same period for a man of seventy or eighty; second, because if most of a man's childhood was spent in Banbury he has friends there and has grown up into the ways of the town. Seven years old is an arbitrary but reasonable age to take with these considerations in mind.

3. *District Born.* Those who were born and bred in the district. (The district is defined in Chapter 1, p. 2.)

4. *True Immigrants.* Those who came to Banbury after the age of seven. For some purposes, for example where place of upbringing is likely to have an effect, groups 2 and 3, small in themselves, have been counted with group 1 as Banburian; for other purposes they have been counted with group 4 as immigrants, for example when discussing age at arrival in the town. For many purposes contrasts have been shown between Born Banburians (1) and True Immigrants (4), ignoring groups 2 and 3 which are open to influences from both groups 1 and 4. Since children take their position and attitude in life largely from their parents, these definitions have been applied in the main only to those over twenty-one.

B. Origins of the True Immigrant Population

Table 2, p. 13, shows that, broadly speaking, the areas farthest away from Banbury have produced fewest immigrants. This generalization obscures two facts. First, that while it is true of all immigrants and of women, 16 per cent. of whom come from within the ten to twenty-five mile radius, it is less true of the men. Of male immigrants, slightly more come from the Industrial Midlands (Birmingham, the Black Country, and the Potteries) than from the nearer area; more come from Lancashire, Cheshire, and Yorkshire than from Greater London. But it is interesting that even here geography has played some part. In 1935, when the first rush of immigrants took place, there was greater unemployment in the mines and factories of South Wales and the Clyde than there was in the Midland factories, but it is from the Midlands that the majority of industrial immigrants have come.

Second, the pattern of immigration has altered over time. Before 1915 about half of all the immigrants came from the area within ten and twenty-five miles of Banbury, i.e. not more than fifteen miles outside the Banbury district itself (see Table 36). From the First World War to 1930 this pro-

TABLE 36

Place of Origin and Date of Arrival of True Immigrants

Place of origin	*Date of arrival: five-yearly periods in twentieth century*											
	Pre-1900	*1900–4*	*1905–9*	*1910–14*	*1915–19*	*1920–4*	*1925–9*	*1930–4*	*1935–9*	*1940–4*	*1945–9*	*Total*
10–25 mile radius	13	12	7	15	7	8	6	14	28	10	14	134
Industrial Midlands	3	3	4	7	2	9	8	19	35	22	15	127
Lancs., Ches., and Yorks.	..	1	..	..	..	..	6	4	61	12	27	111
London and Home Counties	3	1	2	3	16	12	11	18	37	51	34	188
South-west and south	4	2	2	3	4	7	4	12	20	5	16	79
Wales and Mon.	..	1	..	1	1	1	1	6	22	15	17	65
North-east	..	..	..	..	1	..	1	1	30	8	8	49
N. Ireland and Eire	2	..	..	..	..	1	..	1	15	11	14	44
Scotland	..	1	..	..	..	..	..	..	13	5	10	29
Other (including overseas)	1	..	1	4	4	4	3	4	21	15	27	84
Total	26	21	16	33	35	42	40	79	282	154	182	910

portion fell to between one-fifth and one-quarter of the total; London and the Home Counties and also the Industrial Midlands and South and South-west England provided an increasing number of immigrants. After 1930, and particularly in the period 1935–9, the pattern changed. The neighbouring area provided only 10 per cent. of the immigrants in 1935–9, who now came from farther afield, from areas like Lancashire, Cheshire, and Yorkshire, Wales and Monmouthshire, North-east England, Northern Ireland and Eire, and Scotland, which had provided hardly any at all in earlier periods. Only 18 out of 213 immigrants in the sample had come from these remoter areas before 1930. In the years 1930–9 they provided 153 out of 361 immigrants, i.e. 42 per cent. of the total. During the war years, although people came in from all over the British Isles, London and the Home Counties provided by far the largest group (one-third of the total). This was no doubt connected with evacuation, for Banbury as well as having expanding industry was a reception area. Since the war the immigration from the neighbouring area has fallen to 7·7 per cent. of the total although the actual numbers coming in have not altered greatly. The remoter areas provided nearly 42 per cent. of the total. One-third of this number have come from Lancashire, Cheshire, and Yorkshire; the percentage coming from north-east England has fallen from 10·6 per cent. in 1935–9 to 4·4 per cent. in 1945–9, although the proportions from Scotland and Wales have both increased. Since the war it has not been true that most people have come from the nearer places, although the largest single group has still come from London and the Home Counties. It is interesting to speculate whether the immigration from the Lancashire and Yorkshire area is accounted for by relatives and friends of the original immigrants joining them. There are some indications that this may be the case.

The conclusion drawn here from studying the places people have immigrated from is similar to that of others, that it takes a major upset for people to move very great distances.[1] It was not until after 1935, when jobs were scarce in the special areas and when the Ministry of Labour and voluntary agencies organized large-scale transfers to Banbury, that more than a handful of people immigrated from farther afield than London or Birmingham. It will be interesting to see what the future pattern is; the period 1945–9 cannot be taken as any sure indication of this because it includes the immediate post-war period of resettlement. The indications in the period are contradictory, some of the remoter areas still provide a higher proportion of immigrants than before 1935 while others are tending to return to their earlier position. It may be that the upheavals of the last twenty years and improvements in communications have given people (when they are prepared to move) rather wider horizons.

[1] A. Redford, *Labour Migration in England, 1800–1850* (Manchester, University Press, 1926), p. 164, concludes that 'The preponderance of short-distance movement by stages . . . appears to be a permanent feature of labour migration' and refers to Marshall's *Money, Credit and Commerce* (1923), pp. 7–8, where a similar view is expressed. M. P. Newton and J. R. Jeffrey, *Internal Migration* (Studies on Medical and Population Subjects, No. 5, Gen. Reg. Office) (London, H.M.S.O., 1951), p. 27, say: 'This falling-off with distance of the power of inhabited areas to attract migrants is perhaps the most significant result of this part of the analysis.'

APPENDIX 3

GRADING OF OCCUPATIONS IN BANBURY

IT would be possible to find objections to any classification which attempted to place on one scale all occupations in England and Wales. The task itself makes this inevitable, since it involves equating occupations from diverse geographic areas and dissimilar industries. For purposes of this study it was felt that there were fewer objections to be raised to the scale developed by Hall and Jones than to that of the Registrar-General. Therefore, except for purposes of national comparison, the former has been used. It has a finer grading, sevenfold as opposed to fivefold, and the basis of the compilation has been fully explained. Its limitations may, therefore, be the more readily appreciated.[1]

The purpose of the Hall/Jones scale was to grade occupations by the status that is popularly accorded to them and a number of empirical inquiries were undertaken to discover what this popular assessment was.[2] It is difficult to disentangle status and skill: our assessment of the amount of skill involved in any particular occupation will be affected by the status we attach to it and vice-versa. In practice the scale which has resulted from the inquiries of Hall and Jones is based upon a combination of the amount of skill and the degree of responsibility involved in an occupation.

The scale which they give is as follows:

Class 1. Professional and Higher Administrative, which includes all occupations calling for highly specialized experience and frequently the possession of a degree or comparable professional qualification which implies a long period of education or training; e.g. architect, surgeon, bank manager, planter.

Class 2. Managerial and Executive, which includes persons responsible for initiating and/or implementing policy; e.g. secretary of a small business employing ten to ninety-nine hands, headmaster (elementary school), personnel manager.

Class 3. Inspectional, Supervisory, and other Non-Manual Higher Grade, which includes persons who have no such responsibility for policy (as have class 2) but who have some degree of authority over others; e.g. farm bailiff, police inspector, assistant teacher (elementary school).

[1] J. Hall and D. Caradog Jones, 'The Social Grading of Occupations', *Brit. J. Sociol.* i. 1 (1950). See also C. A. Moser and J. R. Hall, 'The Social Grading of Occupations', chap. ii, *Social Mobility in Britain*, ed. D. V. Glass (Routledge & Kegan Paul, 1954).

[2] The method used to obtain this popular assessment has been criticized: for example, Elizabeth Bott (op. cit.) doubts the existence of one popularly agreed occupational status scale.

Class 4. Inspectional, Supervisory, and other Non-Manual Lower Grade, which includes, for example, insurance agent (industrial), costing clerk, relieving officer.

Class 5. Skilled Manual and Routine Grades of Non-Manual, which includes, for example, a carpenter, compositor, routine clerk, and shop assistant (drapery store).

Class 6. Semi-skilled Manual, which includes, for example, assistants in a butcher's or fishmonger's shop, an assembler, or a sheet metal worker.

Class 7. Unskilled Manual, which includes, for example, a builder's labourer, a canteen assistant, a porter.

Classes 1 and 2 are roughly equivalent to the Registrar-General's Class I, and 3 and 4 to his Class II: Classes 5, 6, and 7 to his Classes III, IV, and V respectively.

Hall and Jones drew up this scale to apply to the whole of the country and do not claim that it will necessarily apply in detail to every part of it. Detailed deviations were noticed in Banbury. Also, it is not satisfactory for people working on their own account, or with a few employees, since for such people the quality of their business rather than its size is often the deciding factor. This is just another example of the difficulty of achieving an objective measure of occupational status. Furthermore, although the divisions in the non-manual section are finer than those of the Registrar-General, the Hall/Jones Class 1 still covers far too wide a range of occupational status.[1]

However, apart from collecting material to amplify the scale in relation to the aluminium industry, which was done by consulting members of that industry, no attempt was made to modify the scale. The Banbury survey was not in a position to undertake a large-scale inquiry into occupational status alone. The scale was therefore applied as it stands with the additions mentioned.

In the present study occupational status ranking has been used strictly as such. It has been used from time to time to give an indication of social status, but it must be stressed that in the opinion of the author it does not measure social status. This is particularly true for those people who belong to the traditional system in Banbury. For them many other factors beside their occupational status are involved in their social status ranking (see Chapter 8).

[1] Barbara Wootton has made the same point. 'Social Prestige and Social Class', *Brit. J. Sociol.* v. 4, 373 (1954): 'Certainly, any classification which treats "company director" as a single category must miss vital aspects of our social structure through its inability to distinguish real industrial tycoons from small taxi-cab proprietors.'

APPENDIX 4

THE VOLUNTARY ASSOCIATION CHARTS

CHARTS IV to XIII in the text showing the connexions between voluntary associations were constructed as follows: initially one chart was made which showed all known connexions among the committees of religious and political bodies and other voluntary associations and between them and local and central government bodies (i.e. the Borough Council, the Grammar School Governors, the Hospital Management Committee, advisory bodies attached to Ministries). In the construction of this chart each committee was given a place and whenever a member was found to sit on two committees a line was drawn connecting them; if four members of committee *A* also sat on committee *B* four lines were drawn.

Certain committees were grouped from the outset, notably political parties and churches. For example, the Church of England was given one place on the chart instead of having separate positions for each of the five Anglican churches. Similarly, the men's and women's sections of each political party were grouped to give one position for each political party.

The chart was then started by placing each of the political parties as far from each other as possible. This was done because no man joins more than one political party at a time and because, as previous analysis had shown, politics are a most important basis both for grouping and for division. It is, of course, also true that churches might have been placed in these key positions, but in practice political differences are more acutely felt. If voluntary associations provided any general network of relationships for the town as a whole, connexions would show between these cornerstone positions.

The next step, therefore, was to place those associations which provide a meeting place for people of different parties in such a way that they formed a frontier behind which associations having contact with only one party could be placed. In this way the territories of each party would be shown and also the frontiers which they share.

This analysis showed certain distinct clusters in which there was close interlocking of committees. These clusters and their connexions with others are shown in Charts IV–XII and Chart XIII summarizes the structure. The lines connecting groups of associations in these charts indicate the total number of times that committees in group *A* share members with committees in group *B*. Thus in Chart XIII, the three lines from Sports II to the Anglican/Conservative/Bowling connexion represent two men from Cricket Club II and one man from the Comrades' Club. Two of these men are on the committee of the British Legion and one on the committee of Borough Bowls.

It is important to remember that the charts show only connexions between committee members. A member of committee *A* who is a rank-and-file member of association *B* does not register on the charts. It does of course often happen that there are connexions of this kind just as there are between rank-and-file members. However, since the lists of committee members were available to us and since most of the religious and political affiliations of committee members were known to the field-worker it was possible to check how far these undisclosed connexions invalidated the concept of a territory. In the descriptive analysis of the charts which appears in the text this has been taken into account.

APPENDIX 5

NEIGHBOUR RELATIONS AT THE FACE-TO-FACE LEVEL

The method

At the inception of this study a decision had to be made as to how far the statistical method could be applied. In the first district a research worker stayed with a family for about a month. She visited a number of houses with a copy of the electoral register and asked householders if they would give information on people in that area, not for the purpose of finding out about other people, but rather to correlate the householder's degree of knowledge with the intensity of neighbourhood feeling. This presented certain difficulties. The number of interviews of this kind (they took several hours) were too small to be of any significance statistically. Furthermore, even if they had been significant, those people who knew 'everybody's business' were not necessarily those who were most well integrated locally.

It was then decided, with the arrival of Cyril Smith, to continue the policy of going to live in different areas of the town, and by interviewing (with the focused-interview technique) about half a dozen people in each street to build up a picture of the groups in these streets, to assess the relative amount of isolation in each, and to gather other general material on neighbour relations. Several streets were covered in this way and a period of at least six weeks was spent in each. The social background of the inhabitants was recorded to aid in the interpretation of behaviour.

The questionnaire method would have lessened the chance of being 'captured', as Dr. Jacques has put it,[1] by one of the groups in the street. It is almost impossible to avoid forming personal relations with a host and it is extremely difficult to avoid being unduly influenced by his recommendations as to whom it would be useful or 'nice' to see.

The questionnaire method was rejected for a number of reasons. Statistical treatment was not warranted because the groupings dealt with were never more than a hundred and the number of variables always large. Furthermore, an extensive knowledge of the field is needed before a questionnaire can be usefully conceived. Little work of this kind had been undertaken at that time in sociology or anthropology. The value of the questions asked would therefore have been reduced.

[1] E. Jacques, *The Changing Culture of a Factory* (Tavistock Publications, Ltd., 1951).

In every case the purpose of the study was explained as an attempt to find out what having neighbours meant to people these days; it was explained that this was of scientific and not personal interest to the field-worker and that information given was confidential. Generally this was sufficient explanation, but the practical value of the inquiry was always questioned.

APPENDIX 6

NOTES ON THE KINSHIP STUDY

1. *The sample and its selection*

The kinship study was designed and the material collected and analysed by Charles Kimber. He selected fifty informants from the 1,000-odd who had already been interviewed in the schedule inquiry. His main concern was to balance men with women and Banburian with immigrant informants. The informants were selected from those who had responded most willingly to the previous schedule.

The informants were all married except one, and in order to keep the factors of age and status balanced between the sexes both partners of a married couple were used wherever feasible. Such a group is not, of course, a statistically valid cross-section of the community, but it can fairly be regarded as reasonably representative of married people in the working- and lower-frontier classes.

The ages of the informants were:

20–29	*30–39*	*40–49*	*50–59*	*60–69*	*70–79*
3	14	15	10	5	3

Four were salaried, 2 salaried with commission, 18 wage-earners, and 26 were housewives.

2. *Corrections made to Tables 24 and 28*

The percentages in Tables 24 and 28 were calculated after the original figures had been adjusted. Allowance was made for three informants who could give only the total number of a parent's siblings but were ignorant of their sex and for five informants who did not even know the number of a parent's siblings.

The method of adjustment was as follows: where an informant said: 'My father had five more brothers and sisters but I don't know anything about them', these sexless relatives have been allocated to males and females in the ratio of known male and female relatives of this category. 'Don't know' has been given as an answer to all the questions about each of these five relatives. Where an informant said: 'I don't know anything about my father's brothers and sisters' he has been credited with the average number of known relatives in each category. 'Don't know' has again been given as the answer to all questions about these hypothetical relatives.

The effect of these adjustments has been to raise the total of fathers' brothers from 104 which were directly accounted for to 116; of fathers' sisters from 108 directly accounted for to 125; of mothers' brothers from 73 to 79; and of mothers' sisters from 109 to 116.

Adjustments also had to be made to the figures for spouses of parents' siblings. There were four sets of figures: (i) parents' siblings known to have married, (ii) parents' siblings known not to have married, (iii) known parents' siblings of unknown marital status, (iv) unknown parents' siblings (see previous paragraph). The adjustments were made as follows: (iii) and (iv) were added together to obtain a total of parents' siblings of unknown marital status. From this total a proportion was deducted representing parents' siblings of unknown marital status who might be unmarried: the proportion deducted was in the ratio of (ii) to (i). The resulting total, which represented the number of parents' siblings assumed to be married, was added to the number of parents' siblings known to be married, i.e. (i). The effect of these adjustments has been to raise the total of fathers' brothers' wives from 69 directly accounted for to 100; of fathers' sisters' husbands from 79 to 107; of mothers' brothers' wives from 51 to 62; of mothers' sisters' husbands from 100 to 110.

APPENDIX 7

POPULATION STRUCTURE, MARRIAGE, AND THE FAMILY IN BANBURY

Age and sex composition

The population changes which Banbury has seen in the present century, first emigration and later immigration, could well have produced an age and sex structure untypical of England and Wales as a whole.

The age structure does show some interesting features, as Chart XIX shows. When comparing it with the national structure it must be remembered that the Banbury population shown in the chart covers only those people who were living in the town in 1950 in private houses. Young men serving in H.M. Forces, children or husbands working and living away from home, and all those people in institutions, hospitals, old peoples' homes, boarding-houses, and hotels are not included. These people are included in the national figures. The effects of the omissions are likely to be that the conscript age-group of men (mainly 18–20 years) will be reduced and also that the older age-groups will be reduced both because of the omission of the old peoples' homes and because the elderly tend to be sick and in hospital rather more often than the young.

The relative smallness of the 15–19 and 20–24 age-groups cannot, however, entirely be explained by the call-up; this age-group is relatively small among the women too. Men and women who in 1950 were 15–24 years old would have been between less than 1 year and 15 years old in 1935–9 when the main immigration took place. An analysis of the age of immigrants (including in this case children of all ages) in five-yearly periods shows that people with children under 3 do not move much, nor with children between 9 and 18, or that in this case they tend to leave the children behind; they are rather more mobile with children of 4–8 years old. In the ten five-yearly periods investigated (from 1900 to 1950) the age-group 25–29 is the one in which most people have immigrated. It is the peak age-group in five out of the ten cases. In three other cases, all before 1930, 30–34 years was the peak. The number of immigrants older than 35 falls sharply with a slight rise about the retiring age. This pattern of the age at which immigration is likely to take place is remarkably consistent for all the ten periods, and applies to the most important period 1935–9. Part of the shortage of people in the 15–24 age-group today in Banbury can therefore be explained by the fact that in the 1935–9 period couples with young children and with older children were under-represented. It is also likely that the young people who came in had fewer children than their Banburian counterparts. They came in many cases after a period of economic insecurity and had to make new homes in a new town; often the men lived in lodgings for some months or even years before their wives could join them, and hardly were they settled when the war broke out. All this is likely to mean that they had fewer children than they might otherwise have had. These children who did not immigrate or were not born would be in the

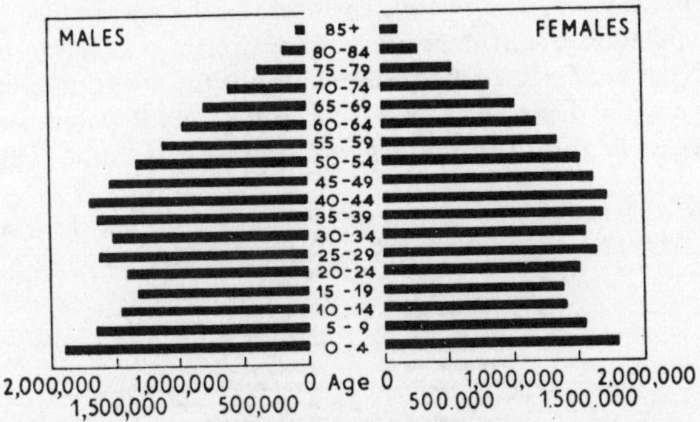

England and Wales, 1951.
Source: Census of Great Britain, pt. 1, one per cent. sample

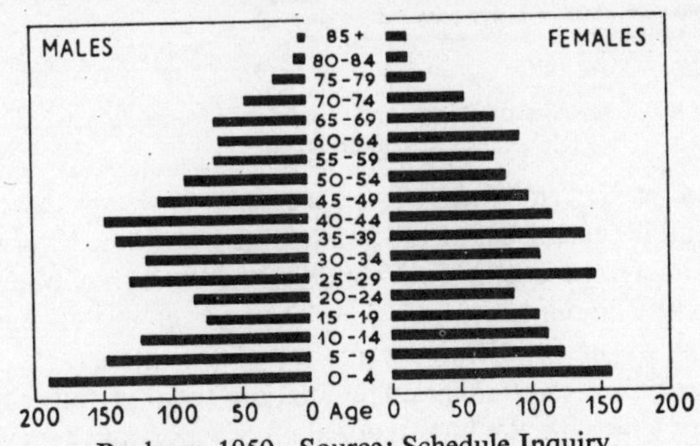

Banbury, 1950. Source: Schedule Inquiry.

CHART XIX. Population by Age and Sex.

Note: The Census was taken about 9 months after our sample.

age-group 15–24 and it is doubtless along these lines that the relative smallness of this group must be explained.

Examination of the age structure of immigrants compared with that of Banburians tends to strengthen this hypothesis. Chart XX shows this comparison. All children of immigrants who are born after they arrive in Banbury are 'born and bred in Banbury' and therefore are shown on the left-hand side of the chart. Only those children who were born to immigrants before they arrived appear themselves as immigrants on the right-hand side: hence the largeness of the young Banburian age-groups. The chart shows that among the immigrants the age-groups 15–19 and 20–24 are small, confirming that it is largely the immigrant behaviour which explains the smallness of this group in the total population. The immigrant age-groups 35–39 and 40–44 are particularly large: the bulk of these people will have arrived between 1935 and 1939 when their ages would have ranged from 20 to 35. The relative smallness of the age-groups 55–64 in the total population as seen in the chart can be explained largely by the Banburian population. From 1920 to 1925, when the town was suffering a net loss of population, this group would have been 25–40; it would be reasonable to suggest that it was from these groups that emigration took place.

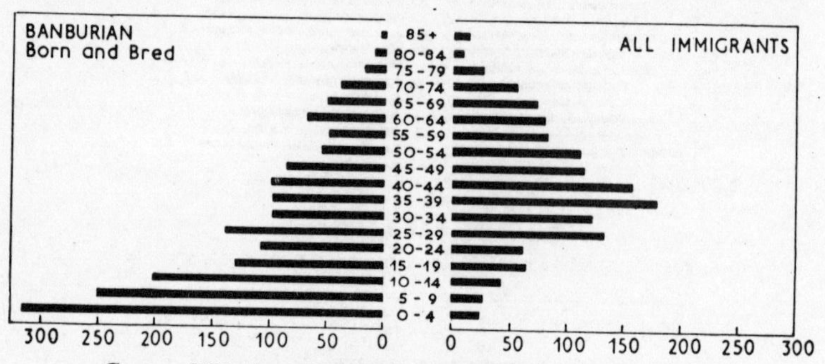

CHART XX. Age of Banburians and Immigrants compared.
Source: Schedule Inquiry.

Because the earlier emigration from the town has depleted the older age-groups and because most of the immigrants who came before the war are now middle-aged and had fewer children, the Banburian population is younger than the immigrant population. The average age of Banburians over 20 is 40·9 years and of all immigrants and of true immigrants over 20 is 45·6 years. The bulk of the immigrant population, however, falls between 40 and 60, ages of which the Banburian population is short and ages which are important in economic and public affairs. In the next generation, other things being equal, children of Banburians will preponderate in this age-group.

The over-all sex-ratio is not unusual: 48·9 per cent. of the Banbury population is male compared with 48·0 per cent. in England and Wales. The age distribution of the sexes is slightly erratic, but perhaps not more than might be expected since Banbury is such a small sample of England and Wales.

Marriage rates

The general marital structure shows no marked peculiarities when compared with England and Wales, either in the proportions married (Table 37) or in their age-groups (Table 38).

TABLE 37

Marital State

%

Marital State	Banbury Schedule Inquiry 1950		England and Wales Census 1951	
	Males	*Females*	*Males*	*Females*
Single	44·4	39·2	43·7	40·5
Married	50·8	49·1	52·4	48·8
Widowed and divorced	4·8	11·7	3·9	10·7

TABLE 38

Marital State by Age

%

Age	Banbury 1950			England and Wales 1951		
	Single	*Married*	*Widowed Divorced*	*Single*	*Married*	*Widowed Divorced*
Under 20	73·7	0·3	0	67·2	0·3	0
20–39	16·9	44·1	9·1	20·1	39·3	5·4
40–59	5·7	40·4	23·0	7·9	43·4	23·7
60 and over	3·8	15·2	67·9	4·8	17·0	70·9

About half the population of all ages is married. Slightly more men are married than women in proportion to their numbers (51 per cent. men; 49 per cent. women). But when those who have been married are added to those now married, it is found that women outnumber men (55·6 per cent. men are or have been married against 60·8 per cent. women). Although women outnumber men in the sample population (1,730 women to 1,657 men), more men are single than women (732 single men, 677 single women). As would be expected from the greater longevity of women, there are more widows than widowers (176 widows, 67 widowers). Twice as many women as men were recorded in the sample as divorced or separated (26 : 12). Only 0·9 per cent. of the men are recorded as having married more than once, against 1·6 per cent. of the women.

The highest proportion of the population is married between the ages of 30 and 50. Relatively few marry before they are twenty and the proportion remaining married declines after 50, and especially after 60, because of the death of one partner.

The proportion of the population recorded as married or having been married in the age-groups 15–54 is consistently higher than that estimated for Great Britain as a whole, but the distribution by age is not dissimilar (see Table 39). This over-all deviation may be of some significance but may have a purely mechanical explanation. The Banbury schedule inquiry ignored those people living in institutions and away on National Service. Interviewers may have failed to take complete account of all 'others in household', especially lodgers, and also some children may have been overlooked. A relatively high proportion of people in all these groups are likely to be single.

TABLE 39

Proportion of the Population Married

	Banbury 1950			*England and Wales 1951**
Age-group	*Numbers in sample*	*Numbers who are or have been married*	*% married*	*% married*
15/19	175	5	2·9	2·6
20/24	171	65	38·0	36·6
25/29	277	212	76·5	71·9
30/34	224	194	86·6	83·6
35/44	538	479	89·0	87·3
45/54	376	341	90·7	87·8

* Census, 1 per cent. sample tables.

Age at marriage

In Banbury, as in Great Britain, the age at which couples marry has fallen recently. Precise comparison is not possible because in Banbury data is available only for those alive, while for Great Britain the Census figures provide a decennial record of those who were or had been married. In Table 40 an attempt at the comparison has been made. It will be seen that the pattern of changes in the age at marriage is roughly consistent with Great Britain as a whole, but is more exaggerated. It shows again the high proportion recorded as married and shows especially a much higher proportion of young people marrying in the immediate post-war period. Failure to remember or state accurately present age and age at marriage must be borne in mind when considering Banbury figures, especially for the older members of the population (some people claimed to have been married before they were 10 years old!). The greatest deviation is among the younger people, however, where one might reasonably expect greater accuracy since less effort of memory is involved.

It is known for the country as a whole that the higher income and occupation groups tend to marry later. Chapter 2 showed that these groups are under-represented in Banbury. This would lead one to expect a rather higher rate of early marriages in Banbury. Geographic areas are also known to show different patterns in age at marriage. Irish and Scottish couples, for example, tend to marry later and are included in the national figures. Since the marriage rate in Banbury is high it is reasonable to suppose that the rate of young marriages will also be high. The increase in the number of marriages in the country as a whole has been brought about by fall in the age at marriage. Neither of these factors is inconsistent with a prosperous town in which the middle and lower income and occupation groups predominate.

TABLE 40

Proportion of the Population of Different Generations Married under 25 Years of Age

	Banbury			*Great Britain**		
Age	*Born*	*Age 24 in period*	*% married under 25*	*Born*	*Age 20–24*	*% married under 25*
65+	pre-1885	pre-1909	26	1876–81	1901	22
60–64	1885–90	1909–14	28	1886–91	1911	19
55–59	1890–5	1914–19	29			
50–54	1895–1900	1919–24	36	1896–1901	1921	22
45–49	1900–5	1924–9	33			
40–44	1905–10	1929–34	28	1906–11	1931	20
35–39	1910–15	1934–9	34			
30–34	1915–20	1939–44	48	1914–19	1939	25
25–29	1920–5	1944–9	62	1922–7	1947	32

* Royal Commission on Population, Table XIII, p. 22.

Table 41 correlates ages at marriage with their present age for all those who are or have been married, and compares men with women. Despite the increase in the numbers marrying under 25, the ages 25–29 are the most popular for men to marry except in the age-group now 25–29, where the series is incomplete because not all will have yet reached 29 years old. For women, however, the age of marriage is younger and the ages 20–24 are rather more popular than 25–29. Furthermore, proportionately more women than men marry before they are 20 years old. The number of marriages declines rapidly after the age of 25 for women and 30 for men. Few of either sex marry after they are 40.

Relative ages of husband and wife

Banbury men marry, on the average, women who are about three years younger than themselves, but this is by no means an invariable rule. Table 42 shows both that there is a considerable scatter about this mean and that

TABLE 41

Age at Marriage of Present Age-Groups: Men and Women compared

Numbers in sample

Age	Age at marriage								All once married	All
	15–19	20–24	25–29	30–34	35–39	40–44	45–49	50–		
					Men					
15–19	0								0	71
20–24	4	16							20	83
25–29	8	58	18						84	129
30–34	4	35	49	10					98	116
35–39	0	37	55	19	3				114	138
40–44	1	32	54	28	3	2			120	145
45–49	1	21	38	11	13	7	3		94	105
50–54	1	24	32	6	6	2	2	1	74	87
55–59	0	11	20	10	2	1	3	0	47	63
60–64	2	8	23	8	4	2	3	2	52	60
65–	3	29	31	18	4	6	3	4	98	134
All ages	24	271	320	110	35	20	14	7	801	1,131
					Women					
15–19	5								5	104
20–24	14	31							45	88
25–29	26	80	19						125	149
30–34	7	61	21	3					92	108
35–39	9	49	51	5	2				116	139
40–44	2	37	38	13	5	2			97	116
45–49	8	37	24	12	6	1	1		89	100
50–54	7	30	25	6	2	1	0	0	71	84
55–59	5	24	19	7	1	3	1	0	60	74
60–64	6	28	28	5	0	3	1	1	72	95
65–	16	36	38	20	5	4	0	3	122	184
All ages	105	413	263	71	21	14	3	4	894	1,241

wide variations exist. Wives 20 years older and 30 years younger than their husbands are recorded.

Age at marriage and economic status

The numbers of people marrying for the first time under the age of 25 has been examined in relation to occupational status, income group, and source of income. The results are shown in Table 43. Both the higher occupational status groups and the higher income groups marry later than the lower. This is in line with findings for the country as a whole, but in neither case are the differences striking nor the series continuous. One non-manual class (4) has more than the expected number of people marrying under 25 and is more marked in this respect than any of the manual classes. This may be explained by the relatively high proportion of women in class 4, many of whom are daughters of manual workers. Class 3 also contains a high proportion of women, but of a higher educational background and often of non-manual parents. Class 5, a manual class, has fewer than expected marrying under 25. The nature of occupations here, most of which involve an apprenticeship before skill and status is reached, and

TABLE 42

*Relative Ages of Husband and Wife**

Age of husband: Age-group	Age of wife: 15–19	20–24	25–29	30–34	35–39	40–44	45–49	50–54	55–59	60–64	65–69	70–74	75–79	80–84
15–19														
20–24	2	5	1											
25–29		9	42	7		1								
30–34		2	34	24	4			1						
35–39			12	30	45	11	1							
40–44		1	1	9	46	44	11		1					
45–49				2	7	30	39	8	1					
50–54				1	2	6	26	34	8	1	1	1		
55–59					1	3	6	9	17	7	1			
60–64								7	12	17	4			
65–69								1	5	16	20	3	3	
70–74								1	2	2	6	5	2	1
75–79										1	1	3	3	
80–84											1		1	

* This table refers only to couples where the husband is the household head. Younger married couples are therefore likely to be under-represented.

with it 'adequate' earnings for marriage, may perhaps account for this. The total differences in this part of the table (that relating to occupational status) are only of possible significance (Chi square test gives P equals approx. 0·500) and perhaps little should be concluded from them. In the case of income groups, it is only in the lowest group (under £250) that more than the expected number of people married under 25 years old. (The total differences are significant: P equals 0·025 on the Chi square test.) The third part of the table, Source of Income, shows that it is those who earn a salary rather than either those who earn profits and fees or wages who marry later in life (the total differences are significant: P equals 0·250), although under the heading of profits and fees will be included some whose incomes are £750 and over, a group which has been shown to marry late.

TABLE 43

Influence of Occupation and Income upon Age at Marriage

Occupational status class	*Numbers marrying under 25*	*Expected Number**
1	4	7
2	7	11
3	34	35
4	44	35
5	144	146
6	93	93
7	36	35
Income group		
Under £250 . .	190	162
£250–499 . .	248	265
£500–749 . .	10	18
£750+ . . .	9	12
Source of income		
Profits and fees .	41	37
Salary . . .	33	40
Wages . . .	328	325

* This column shows the number of people in each group that you would expect to marry under 25 years old if the factors of occupation, income group, and source of income had no effect upon age at marriage.

Age at marriage of Banburians and immigrants

An examination (Table 44) of the relative ages at marriage of Banburians and immigrants shows that a significant number of Banburians marry younger than immigrants. This finding may relate to a number of others.

TABLE 44

Comparison of the Numbers of Banburians and Immigrants marrying under 25 Years of Age

	Numbers married under 25 years	*All married*	*Number expected to marry under 25 years**
True Banburians . .	318	612	290
True Immigrants . .	346	789	374
Total . . .	664	1,401	664

* These figures show the number of Banburians and immigrants respectively whom one would have expected to have married under 25 years if their origin had not affected their age at marriage. It is based on the ratio of all married Banburians to immigrants (612:789). The Chi square test gives P equals 0·029.

Immigrants exceed Banburians in the higher occupation and income groups and also, and most markedly, among salary earners. These groups were shown to marry later. It is likely, therefore, that the differences shown in Table 44 are the result of immigrant salary earners in the higher occupational and income groups marrying later. The opposite proposition that these groups marry later because of their immigrant content must not be overlooked. But since national indications are that the higher status income and occupational groups marry later the first proposition is suggested as the most likely. The fact of immigration may, of course, of itself lead to some further postponement of marriage among groups who already marry later than average. The group looked at nationally is one which is peculiarly liable to migration.

Intermarriage between Banburians and immigrants

The extent to which Banburians and immigrants intermarry is one measure of the amount of distance between these two groups. Part A of Table 45 sets out the origins of husbands and wives. They are classified as true Banburians (i.e. born and bred in Banbury), secondary Banburians (came to Banbury before they were 7 years old), those born and bred in the district, and true immigrants (i.e. came to Banbury after they were 7 years old). Part B of the table groups all local born and those who came in early childhood and opposes them to immigrants on a percentage basis.

Of the local born people, who form about 54 per cent. of the total population over 21 years old, about two-thirds are married to local people. A similar number of immigrants are married to each other. Despite this fairly high rate of 'endogamous' marriages[1] it is clear that there is intermarriage between Banburian and immigrant. Furthermore, just over 50 of the existing marriages were contracted before the large-scale immigration of 1935 onwards. It is probably true to say nevertheless that the chances are in favour of choosing a partner of similar origins. It must be remembered, however, that where immigrants are married to immigrants they may come from widely separated areas. Similarly Banburians who are married to immigrants may be married to people who immigrated to the town before marriage or to people from away who only migrated to Banbury on their marriage.

Matrilocal or patrilocal residence?

There appears to be no particular trend towards patrilocal or matrilocal residence as between Banbury and elsewhere.[2] Thirty-five per cent. of

[1] The total differences in the first part of the table (*A*) are significant beyond 0·005 (Chi square test).

[2] As distinct from the tendency shown inside Banbury for young couples to live with the wife's parents (p. 123).

TABLE 45

Intermarriage between Banburians and Immigrants

Part A.

Origin of Husband	*Origin of Wife*				
	True Ban.	*Sec'y Ban.*	*District*	*Immigrant*	*All origins*
True Ban. .	119	9	33	82	243
Sec'y Ban.	12	0	5	9	26
District	21	2	18	29	70
Immigrant	82	3	18	229	332
All origins	234	14	74	349	671

*Expected Distribution of Intermarriage**

True Ban. .	85	5	27	126
Sec'y Ban.	9	0	3	14
District	24	1	8	36
Immigrant	116	7	37	173

* i.e. the distribution expected if place of origin had no effect on the choice of marriage partner. The expected distribution is calculated on the basis of the observed distribution of husbands and wives of all origins.

Part B.

Origin of Husband	*Origin of Wife*					
	Numbers in sample			%		
	Local	*Immig.*	*All*	*Local*	*Immig.*	*All*
Local	219	120	339	64·6	35·4	100·0
Immigrant	103	229	332	31·0	69·0	100·0
All	322	349	671	—	—	—

	%	
Local	68·0	34·4
Immigrant	32·0	65·6
All	100·0	100·0

local husbands have immigrant wives while 32 per cent. of local wives have immigrant husbands. Similarly, 31 per cent. of immigrant husbands have local wives and 34 per cent. of immigrant wives have local husbands. These figures might suggest a slight tendency for wives to move to their husbands' locality. The kinship study showed a similar pattern. Forty-five per cent. of all men recorded in the family histories had remained in their hometown and 38 per cent. of all women. 'Hometown' in these cases is not necessarily Banbury, for the family histories of people now living in Banbury included their widely scattered relatives. But the most striking feature remains the absence of any marked matrilocal or patrilocal tendency in either study.

The size of the family

The size of families in Banbury, as elsewhere, ranges from the childless couple to large families (a round dozen was the largest recorded). The concentration, however, is round the one- and two-child family. Table 46 shows the number of children per family where the wife is under 45, is over 45, and for the widowed, the last two columns therefore representing completed families.

TABLE 46

Size of the Family

	Banbury: numbers in sample				
Number of children	*Wife under 45*	*Wife over 45*	*Widowed*	*All parents*	
0	62	46	30	138	
1	130	92	44	266	
2	124	75	48	247	
3	45	39	29	113	
4 plus	34	54	46	134	
All sizes	395	306	197	898	
		%			*Great Britain**
0	16	15	15	15	17
1	33	30	22	30	25
2	31	24	25	27	25
3	11	13	15	13	14
4 plus	9	18	23	15	20

* From Table XVII of the report of the Royal Commission on Population for marriages of 1925. This column is probably best compared with the second Banbury column.

The average number of children per family is 1·84 (1·69 for young couples, 2·15 for old couples, 2·47 for widows and widowers).[1]

[1] If the method of taking the schedule has led to any error here it is likely to be in the direction of a failure to count all children, especially those living away from home at the time, and therefore to a possible slight underestimate in family size. A number of infants who died at birth are also likely to have been overlooked.

Family size and economic status

It has been established that in England and Wales as a whole non-manual workers tend to have fewer children than manual workers. This is also true of Banbury, but analysed on the Hall/Jones scale the index is not a continuous one, as Table 47 shows. There is a significant exception for class 6 (semi-skilled), who have fewer children than 'expected'.

TABLE 47

Occupational Status and the Number of Children per Family

Hall/Jones class	*Household heads*		*Expected number with 4 or more children**
	4 or more children	*All with children*	
1 and 2	2	35	6
3 and 4	13	116	19
5	43	256	41
6	22	158	25
7	20	62	10
All classes	100	627	—

* The number you would expect to have 4 or more children in each occupation group if occupational status did not affect the size of the family.

TABLE 48

Income and the Number of Children per Family

	Male household heads		*Expected number with 4 or more children**
	4 or more children	*All with children*	
(A) *Income groups*			
Under £250	31	104	17
£250–£499	61	444	73
£500–£999	6	48	8
£1,000 plus	1	9	1
All incomes	99	605	—
(B) *Source of income*			
Profits and fees	10	56	8
Salary	4	61	8
Wages	66	453	64
All sources	80	570	—

* The number you would expect to have 4 or more children in each group if size and source of income did not affect the size of the family. The differences are of some significance: P is approximately 0·150 (Chi square test).

Ranking by income (Table 48) shows that the proportion of families with four or more children decreases continuously from the lowest income upwards. In the £1,000 plus group the figures are small and may not be reliable.

An analysis by source of income shows that it is those who receive salaries rather than profits and fees or wages who have the fewest large families. It was this group of the three, also, which was found to marry latest in life.

Religious persuasion and the size of the family

The Royal Commission on Population showed that although the size of the Roman Catholic family has declined during the present century, it has done so at a slower rate than that of other denominations. In Banbury significant differences were found: Roman Catholics had proportionately more large families than any Protestant group. The figures are given in

TABLE 49

Religious Persuasion and the Size of the Family

Denomination	*Household heads*		Expected number with 4 or more children*
	4 or more children	*All with children*	
Church of England	87	528	94‡
Roman Catholic	20	70	12‡
Free Churches	23	154	28‡
No denomination†	8	20	4‡
All	138	772	—
All denominations:			
Church attenders	70	450	80§
Non-attenders	68	322	58§
Non-Catholics			
Church attenders	53	394	66‖
Non-attenders	65	308	52‖

* The number with 4 or more children that you would expect to find in each denomination if religious adherence had no effect upon the size of the family.

† 'No denomination' indicates those people who said they were agnostic or atheist or who did not attend church and gave no denomination.

‡ Differences highly significant: *P* equals 0·010 (Chi square test).

§ Differences of considerable significance: *P* equals 0·025 (Chi square test).

‖ Differences of high significance: *P* equals 0·013 (Chi square test).

Table 49. It should be remembered, however, that the income and occupational range of the Roman Catholic church in Banbury is much more complete than that of any of the Protestant denominations or of all of them taken together (see Chapter 4). The Roman Catholic congregation ranges from some of the highest status families in the district to a 'rascally lot of poachers' as one priest described them.

Except that those who precisely called themselves agnostic or atheist or who owned no denomination have the fewest large families of all the groups, there is no evidence to suggest that it is among the secularized part of the population that family limitation propaganda has been most successful. On the contrary, those who claim to attend church regularly have fewer large families than those who admit they do not attend regularly. This is true of all denominations taken together and of non-Catholics taken separately. Indeed, in the second case the difference is more marked than in the first. The explanation is probably that those who attend church regularly, or who claim to do so, tend to be found only rarely in the lowest income and occupational status groups where most large families are found.

Banburian and immigrant family size

While slightly more Banburians in the sample tended to have larger families than immigrants, little significance may be attached to the figures. It appears that the family-building habits of these two groups are substantially similar, with the particular immigrant exception mentioned earlier (p. 199). This is perhaps what one would expect, since, although Banburians predominate in the lower income and occupational status groups, the significant factor is that immigrants markedly predominate in the higher groups. One would therefore expect immigrants to have proportionately more small families than Banburians. The number of one-child families does, in fact, show a significant bias to immigrants. Immigrants are under-represented rather than otherwise in the age-groups from which young couples are drawn. Therefore it is likely that immigrants do tend to have more one-child or small families than Banburians.

BIBLIOGRAPHY

Banbury

BEESLEY, A., *History of Banbury* (Banbury, 1840).
MEDICAL OFFICER OF HEALTH FOR BANBURY, *Annual Reports*.
POTTS, W., *Banbury Through One Hundred Years* (Banbury, 1942).

Surveys of Localities

ARENSBERG, C. M., and KIMBALL, S. T., *Family and Community in Ireland* (Cambridge, Mass., Harvard Univ. Press, 1940).
BOOTH, C., and others, *Life of the People in London* (Macmillan, 1902, 17 vols.).
BOWLEY, A. L., and BURNETT-HURST, A. R., *Livelihood and Poverty* (G. Bell & Sons, 1915).
BRENNAN, T., COONEY, E., POLLINS, H., *Social Change in South-west Wales* (Watts, 1954).
CAUTER, T., and DOWNHAM, J. S., *The Communication of Ideas* (Chatto & Windus, 1954).
DENNIS, N., HENRIQUES, F., and SLAUGHTER, C., *Coal is our Life* (London, Eyre & Spottiswoode, 1956).
GLAISYER, J., BRENNAN, T., RITCHIE, W., &c., *County Town: Civic Survey for the Planning of Worcester* (John Murray, 1946).
KUPER, L. (ed.), *Living in Towns* (London, The Cresset Press, 1953).
LYND, R. S. and H. M., *Middletown* (New York, 1929).
MITCHELL, G. DUNCAN, 'The Parish Council and the Rural Community' (*Pub. Admin.*, Winter, 1951).
MOGEY, J. M., *Rural Life in Northern Ireland* (O.U.P., 1947).
—— *Family and Neighbourhood* (O.U.P., 1956).
REES, A. D., *Life in a Welsh Countryside* (Cardiff, Univ. of Wales Press, 1950).
ROWNTREE, B. SEEBOHM, *A Study of Town Life* (Macmillan, 1901).
—— and LAVERS, G. R., *English Life and Leisure: A Social Study* (Longmans Green, 1951).
WARNER, W. LLOYD, *Democracy in Jonesville* (Harper & Bros., New York, 1949).
—— and LUNT, P. S., *The Social Life of a Modern Community* (Yankee City Series) (New Haven, Yale University Press, 1941).
YOUNG, M., and WILLMOTT, P., *Family and Kinship in East London* (London, Routledge & Kegan Paul, 1957).

Population

Census Reports (1821–1951) (London, H.M.S.O.).
MAKOVER, H., MARSCHAK, J., and ROBINSON, H. W., 'Studies in the Mobility of Labour', *Ox. Econ. Papers*, i. 83, 1939.

NEWTON, M. P., and JEFFREY, J. R., *Internal Migration* (Studies on Medical and Population Subjects. No. 5. Gen. Reg. Office) (London, H.M.S.O., 1951).

REDFORD, A., *Labour Migration in England, 1800–1850* (Manchester, University Press, 1926).

Royal Commission on Population. *Report*, Cmd. 7695 (London: H.M.S.O., 1949).

Industry and Occupation

Classification of Occupations, 1950 (General Register Office) (London, H.M.S.O.).

HALL, J., and CARADOG JONES, D., 'The Social Grading of Occupations', *Brit. J. Sociol.* i. 1 (1950).

Religion

BIRNBAUM, N., 'Religion in America', *The Listener*, 24 May 1956.

HIGHET, J., 'Scottish Religious Adherence', *Brit. J. Sociol.* iv. 2 (1954).

—— *The Official Year Book of the Church of England* (1954).

—— *Methodist Directory* (1950).

—— *Who's Who in the Free Churches* (1951).

Social Class

BALDAMUS, W., and TIMMS, N., 'The Problem Family. A Sociological Approach', *Brit. J. Sociol.* Dec. 1955.

BANKS, O., *Parity and Prestige in English Secondary Education: a Study in Educational Sociology.* (Routledge & Kegan Paul, 1955).

BENNEY, M., and GEISS, P., 'Social Class and Politics in Greenwich', *Brit. J. Sociol.* i. 4 (1950).

BONHAM, J., 'The Middle Class Elector', *Brit. J. Sociol.* iii. 3 (1950).

BOTT, ELIZABETH, 'The Concept of Class as a Reference Group', *Human Relations*, vii. 3 (1954).

GLASS, D. V. (ed.), *Social Mobility in Britain* (Routledge & Kegan Paul, 1954).

LEWIS, R., and MAUDE, A., *The English Middle Classes* (Phoenix House, 1949).

ROSS, A. S. C.,, 'U and Non-U, An Essay in Sociological Linguistics', *Encounter*, Nov. 1955.

WARNER, W. LLOYD, MEEKER, M., and EELLS, K., *Social Class in America: A Manual for the Measurement of Social Status* (Chicago, 1949).

WOOTTON, BARBARA, 'Social Prestige and Social Class', *Brit. J. Sociol.* v. 4 (1954).

General

GLUCKMAN, MAX, *Custom and Conflict in Africa* (Glencoe, Ill., The Free Press, 1956).

JACQUES, E., *The Changing Culture of a Factory* (Tavistock Publications, Ltd., 1951).

McIver, R. M., *Society* (Farrer and Rinehart, New York, 1945).
Mead, M., *Male and Female* (London, Gollancz, 1950).
Weber, Max, *Theory of Social and Economic Organization*, ed. Talcott Parsons (Glencoe, Ill., The Free Press, 1947).
Wootton, Barbara, *Testament for Social Science* (London, Allen & Unwin, 1950).

INDEX

(I am greatly indebted to Dr. Betty Powell for her help in the compilation of this index.)

PRINTED IN GREAT BRITAIN
AT THE UNIVERSITY PRESS, OXFORD
BY VIVIAN RIDLER
PRINTER TO THE UNIVERSITY